'Dunn & Dusted'

by Paul Dunn

Paul. Dunn.

First Published 2005
by
Paul S. Dunn

Second Edition 2007

Further copies of the book can be obtained from:
Paul Dunn
New Leys Farm
Helmsley, York
YO62 5LU
Telephone: 01439 798239

ISBN 0-9551022-0-0

Designed and Printed by

HPE Print
Thornton Road Industrial Estate,
Pickering, North Yorkshire, YO18 7JB
(01751) 473578

DUNCOMBE PARK

The Dunn family have farmed land on the Helmsley Estate for three generations and although I have known Paul for many years, it wasn't until hearing his address at his father's funeral that I fully realised what a natural communicator he is. I don't think it's inappropriate to say that Willie's funeral was a really joyous occasion; Helmsley's Methodist Chapel was packed to the rafters and the service, led with characteristic warmth by the Rev. Susan Greenwood, was a wonderful celebration of a long life, well-lived. Paul's tribute was humorous, robust and poignant - he carried the whole congregation with him.

Three of his themes on that day - faith, family and farming are the cornerstones of his life and indeed of this book. Paul writes as he speaks - a no-nonsense Yorkshire approach with a good eye for the detail of a situation. As a vivid account of a rural way of life that is vanishing fast, and as a meticulous record of the unpredictable Northern weather, it is an interesting social document in its own right. But overall, we have here the testimony of a real countryman whose life has been inextricably linked to the land and to the seasons.

Polly Feversham.

Acknowledgements

There are many people who have contributed to the writing of this book which I have done in stages over a period of 4 years from 2000 - 2004, (so the information was relevant at the time but is not necessarily current.) I would like to acknowledge their help. Those people who have given me information and those who have let me print their photographs - to you I give a big thank you. The goodness and kindness of my friends is also greatly appreciated.

I want to thank especially Glenis Hobbs and Rosamund Dyson who have taken my original long manuscript and have put it on a word processor. Thanks are also expressed to Jean Miller who typed the final copy.

Thanks are also expressed to Lady Feversham, Jim Wilkinson, Ron Abbot and James Stephenson, for writing a foreword and reviews.

I want also to say a special thank you to my brother, Nicholas, for encouraging me to write this book and for giving me time off from farm work to get it done.

A big thank you also goes to my family. To Dorothy, my wife and to my children, Miriam and Philip. They have all tolerated me whilst I have been writing this book. We have had our heated arguments about it! But we have also had some good laughs, quite often at my expense!

Financially, the writing of this book has been a big step of faith and I could not have had it printed without the help from my many sponsors. I thank you for your encouragement. A proportion of profits from this book will be given to charities, the main one Cancer Research.

In conclusion, I want to acknowledge my gratitude to family and friends and, above all, to God. I can state, as St. Paul did, that by the Grace of God I am what I am.

Let me close my acknowledgements with the words of the hymn, which says:

'Tis Jesus, the first and the last
Whose spirit shall guide us safe home.
We'll praise Him for all that is past
And trust Him for all that's to come.

Paul Dunn
October 2005

Sponsors

Mr. & Mrs. R. Abbott

ACT Ltd., Farm Supplies

Acorn Auctions, General Dealers

E. & A.R. Agar, Undertakers

ARGRAIN Farm Merchants

J & K Agriservices Ltd, Dairy Engineers

J. Ashbridge, Farmer

A. Atkinson. Livestock Dealer

Ample Bosom, Ladies Lingerie

Chas. Atkinson, Tyres.

H. Atkinson, Fellmonger

Ayrton's Quad Bikes

Bainbridge Engineering, Agricultural Engineers

Russ Bainbridge.Agricultural Contractor

J.C. Bannister, Seed Merchant

BATA Farm Supplies

P.R. Barnett, Lime Spreading Contractor

Breck House Engineering, Agricultural Contractor

Blades, Electricians

Boulton & Cooper, Auctioneers

A.R. Bulmer, Haulage & Sheep Breeder

Breck House Enterprises, Sheep Scanners

Bondgate Dental Practice

Sir R. Beckett, Barrister

C. Brewer, Agricultural Seeds

Bentley Bros. Farmers

A. Brown, Painter and Decorator

E.B. Bradshaw & Sons, Agricultural Merchants

B.H. Refrigeration

Ray Chapman Motors

Craven Cattle Markets

Chapman Bodycraft, Motor Engineers

Chris Clubley, Auctioneer

M. Chipchase, Joiner

N.D. Crummack, Machinery Dealer

Cundalls, Auctioneers

J.E. Clifford & Sons, Agricultural Contractors

Claridges, Stationers

Darlington Farmers Mart

Charles Douglas, Land Rovers

Denemex, Ear Tags

S. Dean, Gardener

Dee, Atkinson & Harrison, Auctioneers

P.D. & S.J. Dennis, Auctioneers

S. Dodsworth, Livestock Haulage

Duncombe Sawmills

D.M. Eddon, Builder

Eiger International, Graphic Design

Edgemoor Veterinary Surgeons

Envirostar Ltd.. Farm Cleaning

W. Eves & Co., Fuel Merchants

Easthill Farm Accommodation

Fawcett Agriculture, Agricultural Contractors

R. Farrington, Land Rovers

M. Fenby, Building Supplies

D. Frost, Machinery Dealer

Forster, Stott & Co., Accountants

Lloyd Fraser, Haulage

W Foster, Machinery Dealer

D Gamble, Builder

Richard Green, Semex, A I Company

J Garbutt, Farmer

A E Glaves, Sheep Breeder

Goldsborough Finance Co.

Genus Breeding, AI Company

E & S Gott, Furniture Restorer

Howells & Hudson, Veterinary Surgeons

A Hall Farms Ltd.

G H Hewitt, Builder

HSBC Banking

A Hoggarth & Sons. Haulage

Hurrell & Mclean, Seeds

Harrison Hire & Sales, Pressure Washers

Hadrian Farm Supplies, Dairy Engineers

Holstein Friesian Society

Helmsley Estate, Landowners

G Inchboard, Freeze Brander

G Ibbotson & Son, Haulage

Viscount Ingleby, Landowner

Robin Jessop, Auctioneer

J V T Homes, Builders

T A Johnson, Cattle Breeding

C W G & M Kent, Cars and Repairs

N R Kermack, Veterinary Surgeon
Lindsey AI, Cattle Breeding
Leyburn Auction Mart
E Leng & Son, Farm Buildings
Macmin Ltd., Animal Minerals
R Machin. Sheep Buyer
J T Medd & Son, Farmers and Contractors
Metcalfe Farms, Agricultural Contractors
Ian Mosey, Feed Merchant
Norton & Brooksbank, Auctioneers
Newsquest, Newspapers
New Life Baptist Church
J B W Needham, Pictures
North Yorkshire Law, Solicitors
Nicholsons, Butchers
North York Moors National Park
Northallerton Auctions
B Otterburn, Agricultural Engineer
J K Otterburn, Livestock Dealer
Perns, Butchers
G Pooleman. Motor Engineer
Ian Potter Associates, Quota Sales
Provima Ltd., Molasses
Reagarth Farm Administration, Farm Accounts
M H Richardson, Cattle Breeder
J W & P Roe, Agricultural Contractors
G Richards, Auctioneer
C H Render, Motor Dealer
A Richardson, Haulage
Ripon Farm Services, Land Rover
Richardson & Smith, Auctioneers
Reed & Longstaff, Farm Minerals
Ryedale Garages

Ryeburn Ice Cream
Semen World, Cattle Breeding
E L Sherwin, Auctioneer
P Snowball, Electrician
S C & P W Smith, Farmers
P Silk, Furniture Restorer
P & D Swift, Agricultural Contractor
Theakstons, Agricultural Engineers
Tennants, Auctioneers
P Thompson, Tool Hire
Toft Lodge Veterinary Centre
N J Thomlinson, Farm Sprays
Tithebarn Ltd. Farm Minerals
B Thompson, Butcher
Thomas's Bakers
G Todd & R A Hicks, Insurance Agents
Thirsk Auction Mart
Tomlinson Antiques
Topcliffe Crane & Recovery
U.A.P. Spray Merchant
Vet Law Ltd,, Animal Solicitor
H Waines & Son, Coal Merchants
Watts & Associates, Auctioneers
Welburn Manor Farms
M Walton, Auctioneer
S Wood, Cattle Clipper
Webster Trailers - Livestock Trailers
M H Walker, Haulage
D J Wilson, Sheep Clipper
Wharfedale Farmers Auction Mart
Wytherstone Gardens
York Auction Centre
R Yates & Sons, Farm Supplies

Reviews

Three words sum up country life in North Yorkshire 'Grit, Grace & Gumption'.
Ron Abbott

It's a real trip down memory lane, but so well recorded as to become a reference to North Yorkshire life.
James Stephenson

This book is better than 'The Archers'
Jim Wilkinson

This book is more than a diary of a North Yorkshire farmer. It is a fascinating chronicle of life in all its diversity for a family living and working the land as tenant farmers between 1950 and 2000. How is it that a Yorkshire man in exile for all of that time is invited to write an introduction? Paul is a man unafraid to travel around. As one of a student team from Cliff College he came to stay at our house in Melton Mowbray, part of his summer missions. We got on so well together as good friends, sharing our love of North Yorkshire and stories of friends we both knew. Sometimes our talk lasted long into the night around our kitchen table. One dream spawned an event which continues to this day - summer camps for mainly Methodist families who want to see the church revived. After I became a tutor at Cliff College our paths continued to cross. It was here that Paul's future was clearly mapped out for him. So, as with so many of his friends, we are always welcome in each other's homes.

So this is not only a book about the Dunn family- Many people cross their paths, and many get a mention. What characters there are. As you read you feel that you can grasp what makes this part of the world tick. There is amazing energy. There is humour. There is co-operation. There is success, and failure, but a determination to defeat adversity however it comes. But the book has much to say about farming in this part of the world. Balancing stock-rearing and arable farming to keep the farm profitable, (even the prices are given) taking on new ideas, adapting to new technology - it's all here.

And the weather - you sometimes get the feeling that weather conditions rule a farmer's daily activities on the North Yorkshire Moors. It's a case of working with the elements. Paul describes it all with meticulous detail.

Here's what researchers call a primary source of information for social historians whose interest is rural England. Three words for me sum up country life in North Yorkshire: Grit, Grace and Gumption.

Ron Abbott - former tutor at Cliff College.
Curbar,
Hope Valley,
Derbyshire,
S32 3YD

As a fellow auctioneer and sexagenarian, I am flattered to be asked to review Paul's memoirs and have no hesitation in recommending them to everyone connected with northern rural life. Although hard to believe of a pulpit preacher, Paul claims to have been "a shy timid lad" and we follow his fascinating, unique life story in which we find so many experiences in common. My first "professional" contact with Paul was probably in 1970 when I sold his Friesian cow for £107 in York Market; and the book tracks dairy prices, amongst others, through to 1991 when I dispatched nine of the Dunn's herd to a seasonal top of £780, and finally with an escalation in demand to peak in 1993 by Paul steeling himself to pay nearly £1500 for a newly-calven heifer. Paul's passion for quality livestock led him into contact with a vast range of people with similar inclinations in our industry, including my old friend Richard Machin whom he first met in 1958, driving an ancient open top wagon, and twenty years later Sir Ben Gill, President of the NFU. At this time in 1999 - 2000 Paul embarked on a second career, in television, which, although not leading to Hollywood, did result in the unflinching documentary series, controversially titled "The Dying Breed".

Paul pulled no punches in his portrayal of farming and farmers in dire trouble, and very much in need of public support.

To his credit, the tide did turn and British produce has enjoyed a mini-comeback with consumers packing into Farmers' Markets, and even into the giant Superstores when we are given a fair crack of the whip.

But enough of my ramblings - you must read the book yourself if only to get the weather forecasts! It's a real trip down memory lane, but so well recorded as to become a reference work on North Yorkshire life.

James Stephenson - Auctioneer.
York Auction Centre.
Murton,
York

These poignant pages written by Paul Dunn reflect an era of the last sixty years of farming and personal history. He has kept a personal journal for many years, which has enabled him to remember with clarity many of the vagaries of the weather scene which most of us recollect only when we are reminded of them. This book is better than "The Archers" programme ('an every day story of country folk') because it is the life story of someone that we have known personally down several decades. Paul unfolds the hard parts and the easier parts year by year of his journey, from being a farmer's son and single, and part of a well known family in Ryedale, to becoming a farmer himself and also a family man. His observations take us on a time-walk from minimal machinery to almost automation, from growing maximum crop yields to an era of being paid subsidies for weeds to flourish - set aside! (Not a nice word in farming circles). Subsequently it appears the farmer is to be paid for minimal output. Paul has witnessed also the days gone by of healthy times of friendship on threshing days, to one man and his machine.

As he writes, he causes us also to follow the path of his spiritual journey. Born and brought up in a Christian home, he has been surrounded by loving parents and has been blessed and challenged as he sought and found the Saviour and Lord for himself, whom he and his own family now endeavour to serve.

Whether his stance is on the farm, in the pulpit or in the pew, Paul's story will challenge us to be overcomers in every area of our lives. Every Blessing in every way, Paul and Family.

Jim Wilkinson - farmer and friend in the Vale of York,
Hollybush Farm,
Newsham,
Thirsk
Y07 4DH

Contents

Chapter 1

My Background

When I started to write my memoirs, I was reminded of a quotation I read some years ago:

"When I was a child I laughed and wept, time crept.
  When as a youth 1 thought and talked, time walked.
  When I became a full grown man, time ran."

Time does fly doesn't it? And here I am in January 2000 putting pen to paper. Where does one begin? I once heard the late Tot Smith (a country character from Malton way) give his life story. He asked a mate for his advice on this and he said:

"There's only one place to begin. Begin at the beginning."

I think it would be fitting to write a bit about my background and my parents. Had it not been for them I wouldn't be here!

They say that opposites attract one another. In some ways my parents were opposites. Dad was outward going, while Mother was more shy and reserved. They would be termed today as an extrovert and an introvert.

Both Dad and Mother were born in Farndale, a dale on the North Yorkshire Moors, famous for its miles of daffodils. Dad was born at High End and Mother at Low End. Reading between the lines, there was a little bit of rivalry between the High and Low "Enders", whether it was farming, school, sport or Chapel! Dad, known to many as WH or Willie spent his first twenty-four years there. Then with his parents, brother and sister, he moved to Abbott Hagg Farm, Helmsley, and eventually to New Leys when he and Mother got married.

Dad was well known in the sheep farming circles, as sheep were his greatest interest. He liked to show them and started in 1953, which we continued until 1983. More about that later. He was a past Chairman and President of the Teeswater Sheep Breeders' Association and was on the committee of the Great Yorkshire Show for a while. He was a committee member of our local Ryedale Show and felt it a great honour when he was made President in 1987.

He was also an auctioneer and I think that if things could have worked out he would have liked to do this rather than farming. He liked people and was well

1

liked and respected by them.

Dad was a committed Christian and heavily involved in the life of the Methodist Church, being a Sunday school teacher, and a local preacher for over seventy years. He was one of the founder members of the Newgate Bank Top open-air service and along with others he was instrumental in fund raising and the building of the new Sunday school at Rievaulx.

Mother's name was Mary Wass. She was born at Horn End, known locally as 'Hon End', and lived there until she was married. The Wasses were a well-known Dales farming family, whose speciality was heavy horses. It was an acknowledged fact that Grandad Wass was a boy to work and he expected everyone else to be the same. In fact one of his former workmen termed him a slave driver. I think Mother inherited her characteristic for work from him. One person described Mother as not having an idle bone in her body. She often reminded us of this if we were shirking our duty. A very thrifty kind of person, she was always gathering sticks in her apron. A good cook too, she specialised in rabbit pies and stews, and the brawn, sausages, scrappings and bacon which came from our home-fed and home slaughtered pigs. She was famous for her ginger biscuits and an expert at making fruit cakes. She won many prizes at local shows,not only for baking. Her hooky and clipped mats were one of her specialities and won prizes at the shows.

Mother was given to hospitality and it didn't matter whether it was a traveller or wagon driver, she always felt they had to have the chance of a cup of tea and food. Like Dad she was a committed Christian and practiced the gift of hospitality to preachers and friends. I can remember the great baking days for the Sunday School Anniversary and Newgate teas. They were really out of this world.

I think when Dad moved to Abbott Hagg, he had a soft spot in his heart for Mother and, as the saying goes, "Absence makes the heart grow fonder". Eventually they started courting, which meant a journey for Dad of eighteen miles, either by horseback or cycle. Well, it all materialised and they got married and moved to New Leys in 1939. In those days it was the custom to have a ploughing day, when neighbours and friends would come and help the new farmer. Dad often says he wished he had a photograph of the day, as there were twenty-six pairs of horses pulling single furrow ploughs. It was one of the last horse ploughing days in the district.

I have often said there is something about real Dales people. They are friendly, hospitable and tell stories about the old characters and imitate the way they spoke. People tell me that I am carrying on the tradition. There is nothing

I like better, especially if the audience is responsive, than to take the floor and tell a good tale, imitating a character of a past generation.

I have become a fan of the Irish folk singer, Daniel O'Donnell, and one of his songs called 'Our House Is A Home" sums up what our home was like in those early years:

"There's always a fire in the kitchen,
There's always a kettle on the boil.
There's no fancy carpets or telephone,
But the one thing our house is a home.

A stranger is always welcome, be it
Any time of night or day,
So don't ever feel sad or lonesome,
Just call in as you pass this way.

It's seen many happy and sad times,
But it still remains through it all.
The times may have changed all round about you
There's still a word of welcome in the hall".

Written by Maurice Soye
Published by New Moon Music
Words reproduced by kind permission of New Moon Music

W.H. Dunn: Author's Father

Author's Mother Mary Wass on her 21st Birthday

New Leys as it was when Dad and Mam moved. Note: The rough cart track

The lorry that moved Grandad from Farndale to Abbot Hagg.

Grandad Wass setting off to go to market

One of Grandad Wass's prize horses held by my Uncle Harry who farmed at Fadmoor

Mam making Hookey rug 1957-59

Grandad Dunn (right) Garb Atkinson (in front) Stan Pennock (behind) and Atkinson boys

Dunn Family Grandma and Grandad in front. Back left to right Uncle Albert, Dad Aunty Lizzie, taken 1950's

The Wass family photo taken 1938, shorty before all five were married within four months of each other. Left to right: Tamar, Fred, John, Harry and Mary (Author's mother)

Chapter 2
My Brothers And Sister

There is an old saying, "God gives us our relations, but lets us choose our friends." Well I am thankful for both family and friends. We have to learn to appreciate people, whether friends or relatives, for what they are, rather than for what we would like them to be.

Over the years I have learnt to appreciate my two brothers and sister and I think it would be fitting to tell you a bit about them, as they will be mentioned at other stages in my memoirs.

Christopher is the eldest. He worked at home full and part-time until he married Hazel. Then he took Breck House, Bransdale in 1963. He was always an enterprising fellow, buying and selling bags, supplying some farmers with drive belts and stacksheets. Over the years Christopher and Hazel worked hard at building up the farm, now run by Christopher's younger son, Timothy, who has become quite famous for his Swaledale and Mule sheep. Timothy has also developed a successful sheep scanning business, which scans over 110,000 sheep per year. Christopher, along with his elder son, Simon, started an Agricultural Contracting business, which is again very successful. Most of our work is done by this contracting business and is now run just by Simon. Christopher was always noted to be a good singer and now sings with the York Philharmonic Choir. He is very involved in the life of the Chapel, being a Sunday school teacher, organist, circuit steward and local preacher. I mustn't forget his daughter, Joanna, who is a schoolteacher and heavily involved in Easter People.

Judith, my sister, is the youngest. I remember Mother being in bed at New Leys when she was born. In those days several nuns lived in Rievaulx and they used to visit people if they had a new baby. I remember one coming to see Mother. I had never seen a nun before and her black garb frightened me so much that I ran upstairs and jumped into bed with Mother; wellingtons still on! There was another funny experience when Judith was born. The nurse, who attended Mother, brought with her an eighty-year-old friend. Being quite set up with the new baby, I said to this elderly lady,
"Have you got a baby sister, because I have".

In some ways, Judith was the brains of the family, gaining her 11 plus and going on to Lady Lumley's School, Pickering. She eventually did a year's voluntary service in Germany and then studied at Manchester University- She became a social worker. She too is involved in the life of the Chapel in Lanchester, County Durham, where she now lives with her husband, Keith and two sons, Peter and James.

Judith was quite a favourite among the lads. I remember one of our dogs flew at one of her former boyfriends, biting him on the lip. Someone commented "Did you know that Willie Dunn has a dog that keeps lads off his daughter?" Another time she had a policeman boyfriend and one day he came over to see her in his uniform and patrol car. One of our neighbours, Mr. Fairburn, saw him and challenged us "Now you young devils, what's Bobby after you for?" Now it happened that earlier that week Mr. Fairburn had backed out of a road end near Hawnby into an oncoming car and he thought nobody knew about it. But we'd heard all about it. Nicholas said "Bobby's looking for a Mr. Fairburn, who backed into a car near Hawnby". Well he didn't know what to say. I think he was more surprised than pleased.

I mention Christopher and Judith together, as they were the 'good' boy and girl! It always seemed to be Nicholas and me who got up to mischief. As one of our former workmen Jack Webb used to say "I don't blame young youth, older one puts him up to it". However Christopher did blot his copybook one day by putting a red D, with which we marked sheep, on my lovely white pet goat. I tried to wash it out and landed up with a pink goat- I remember crying my eyes out and going to bed with sore eyes and Christopher going to bed with a sore bottom!

Richard was the second eldest, born with Downs Syndrome. He was cared for at home until he was 8, but his disabilities were severe, and from then on he became a patient at Claypenny hospital, Easingwold, where he died in 1969. It was always a sadness to Mam and Dad that they could not manage to care for him at home, but it was a different era with little community support from the authorities.

Nicholas is the third eldest and I think he is the one I know most about, being childhood buddies and business partners since 1975. I have often said to my wife Dorothy that I wished I could be like Nicholas who doesn't seem to have a care in the world. I was always more of a planner and worried if my plans didn't work out. I once remember saying this to Christopher and he said "I don't think our lad would worry if his backside was on fire!!!" Well he has made a good business partner. We have had our differences of opinion. He was always more open to new ideas than I was and could see easier ways of doing things.

Nicholas lives at Hagg Hall outside Rievaulx and is married to Jean. They have three children, David, who helps us part-time, Rebecca, who is a hairdresser and Andrew, who works for Mousey Thompson at Kilburn as a woodcarver. I think Nicholas has a great advantage in living away from the farm. He can switch off, whilst jobs are always looking at me. Nicholas is quite involved in the life of the Chapel, being a steward. Sunday school teacher, Shell Club helper and pastoral visitor.

Well I was the second youngest. I came on the scene on 18th May 1945. Today when babies are baptised they are generally taken to Church or Chapel followed by a celebration meal afterwards. Not so in my case. Mother told me I was baptised at home. She said, "I just put on a clean pinny (apron) and there was Dad, the maid, who is now Mary Ford, and the minister". When the minister asked Dad my name, he said "Paul". The minister said "Paul, the great preacher!" Well, the apostle Paul was a great preacher. I became one and a great talker, so they tell me! I remember someone commenting to me as a lad at a threshing day, "If thoo had as mich mustle on thi airm as on thi tongue, thoo'd be a good fella".

Three memories stand out in my mind before I started school. The first was when I was sat in the back of a cart pulled by a horse called Trimmer. Christopher and Nicholas were driving the horse and Dad was spreading basic slag out of the back. The second memory was of Joe Ashbridge from Cold Kirby fetching a sow to the boar in the back of his car. The car was a black Morris Major. I have learnt only recently that the Ashbridges used to transport young cattle in this car - it must have been a dual-purpose vehicle. Another event that stands out in my mind was when the Wilkinson family from Snape came and gave a concert at our Chapel in June 1949. The female members of the family, Molly, Ruth and Esther used to come in the afternoon to tune their instruments. 1 don't remember this as clearly as Carl and Lorne arriving in a grey wagon and I can still see Lorne taking his big bass fiddle out of the back. It is interesting to note as the years have gone by that I have become a great friend of Carl, Lorne and Esther and their families, and Paul and Gillian Ashbridge are some of our closest friends.

Taken on Scarborough sands, all the family 1953-54

Taken in 1958 and shown in a Leeds photo competition, entitled "Just 3 kids"
Left to right: Author, Judith and Nicholas

Author (7 Months)

*Christopher in the yard at
New Leys (real farmers boy)*

*Left to right: Christopher, Author
and Nicholas*

Mam and Bairns left to right: Christopher, Author, Judith and Nicholas

Family photo taken 1960.
Left to right: Christopher, Nicholas, Judith and Author

Wilkinson Family from Snape as in concert 1950.
Left to right: Molly, Mother, Father, Ruth, Esther and Lorne

Chapter 3
Primary School Days

Today parents have a lot more choice at which school their children can be educated. In my case there were only two. The nearest school was at Rievaulx, where nuns taught the children and I think Dad and Mother thought we would get a better education if we were taught by proper teachers, so they decided to send us to school in Helmsley. At that time there were three schools in Helmsley, the High School, which catered for senior pupils, the Low School which was a junior school - Church School some called it - and the one I went to, which was the Methodist School.

From our farm Helmsley is a distance of three and a half miles. There was no school transport. This meant you made your way under your own steam. If it was wet Dad would perhaps run us down in the car -If it was fine we would either cadge a lift or walk. I remember different people giving us lifts back home. Two of my favourites were Adam Gordon, the head keeper and Lady Marjorie Beckett. Both of these people seemed to make a fuss of me. Quite often we would get a ride in a haulage bus. I remember walking up out of Helmsley and a bus was coming up very slowly. When the driver was nearly up to me, he shouted out, "If thou wants a ride, thou will have to jump on as we're going. Clutch is dickey and I can't stop". Well I jumped on the step, opened the door and got in. It was a cold day and my hands were freezing. In those days buses gave off a lot of heat and I remember warming my hands over the engine. The driver was a friendly chap. He opened his dinner tin and gave me a piece of chocolate roll - quite a luxury for a lad like me, brought up on porridge, fat bacon, potatoes, sad cake and treacle!

Not all lifts were as pleasant. I remember a Saddler's bus from Middlesborough picked me up and took me well past our road end. I was frightened stiff. I literally thought I was going to land in the back streets of Middlesborough. I made sure after that experience that whenever I saw a Saddler's bus coming I jumped into the hedge and hid.

I often compare my schooldays with those of our two children, Miriam and Philip. I would say that education today is a lot better. Children seem to enjoy school a lot more. The teachers, at least with Miriam and Philip, seem to get the best out of them and are more interested in them. Children are more expressive and perhaps cheekier, answering back more. When I was a child it was a case of "Little boys should be seen and not heard".

I never liked primary school. It seemed as though you were frightened stiff of the teachers,especially if you weren't in the teacher's good books. It seemed to me that they had favourites or pets as we used to call them. I think Christopher and Judith were pets of the headmaster, Mr. Law. Well my mates and I didn't seem to get on with him so we nicknamed him "Bawry". Mr. Law was a tall man with a big nose. We used to say, "Look out Bawry's nose is going red. He could be in a bad mood". I remember one day my friend Brian Davies was having problems doing his sums and it seemed he couldn't do anything right for Bawry. I felt sorry for him and it so happened that for once I could do them so I told him the answers. He got his sums right. I remember when Mr. Law marked them he said in front of the class, "I knew you could do them when you tried, Davies".

Quite often in winter we had days off school because of the snow. As children we all used to wish it would snow, snow and snow! The trouble was we could have a lot of snow up above Helmsley and there could be nothing much in Helmsley itself. Albert Law could never understand this. I remember once talking round the supper table after carol singing, reminiscing about our schooldays. A remark was heard that every parent living in Hambleton and Rievaulx would have liked to sit Albert Law on top of a snowdrift.

Well, Mr. Law wasn't the only one who didn't understand about snow. Neither did the school attendance officer - or kid-catcher as we used to call him. The kid-catcher at that time was a man called Mr. Tain. We were off school one snowy day and he came looking for us. He came down our road and got stuck and Dad had to pull him out. We were sledging at the time. I think Joe and Bri Garbutt were with us and we shouted to Dad, "Don't pull Tain out. Let him stop. That will cap him!" Another experience with the kid-catcher was when Judith was off school one day and Mr. Tain came into class. He asked me where Judith was. I explained that she had been to Sunday school and got wet. Mr. Tain piped up and said, "Hasn't she got dried yet?" Everybody laughed seeming to make a fool of me. What I really wanted to say was that she had got wet and as a result got a death of a cold.

Although I didn't enjoy primary school, there were a few pleasant memories of going up to the playing field to play football and cricket and going to Duncombe Park to watch their nativity play. I liked the school dinners. In those days we used to get venison. We always had a good appetite as the dinners were served in the scout hut, which is at the other end of the town, about half a mile from the school.

Helmsley has changed a lot since my school days. There used to be five farms then, but not one now. It was a regular sight seeing Snowdon's and

Barker's cows coming along the street for milking. Quite often we would see Mr. Swales from Harome, with his horse and rully. He was a carrier, bringing eggs and rabbits. At that time a Mr. Lightfoot from Middlesborough would be standing with his bus in Helmsley market place waiting for carriers and farmers to bring him their eggs and rabbits. No longer do we see trailers and wagons going to the cattle mart. It has been closed for many years and is now built on. At the back of the school were fields but now there are housing estates.

I left primary school in 1956, ninth out of a class of twenty-nine. Mr. Law put on my report, "Paul has generally worked well and done his best. In spite of his disappointing results in the exam subjects, I trust he will work hard in his new school".

Taken 1952-53 when at Helmsley school. Left to right: Paul, Christopher and Nicholas

What would we do without our wellingtons! Left to right: Christopher, Author and Nicholas

Taken at Helmsley school 1955-56 with Mr Albert Law, headmaster. Author, back row, next to Mr Law

Ted Emmitt, Christopher,
Nicholas and Author, 1952

Author in 1952-53
at Helmsley school

Percy Swales. Carrier from Harome. Mentioned in Chapter 3

Helmsley Methodist School 1954

Chapter 4
Run, Rabbit, Run

Today we often hear children say "I'm bored!" or "That's boring!" It is a word I hate to hear. I don't think we ever got bored as children. One of our big pastimes as lads was catching rabbits. I have already mentioned in a previous chapter Joe and Bri Garbutt. They lived on the next farm Middle Heads. Their parents died when they were very young and so Mr. and Mrs. Wilson, their grandparents, brought them up. We used to call Mrs. Wilson, Gran and Mr. Wilson, Father. They were a homely couple and as children and teenagers, we used to go over to Middle Heads quite a lot. Mr. Wilson had a real dry sense of humour. It would be raining and pouring down and he would say, "Do you think it's going to rain?" Another of his sayings was "Little taties aren't very big this year, are they?" Another funny experience was when Mr. Patterson, the estate agent, was visiting Middle Heads and Mr. Wilson had some grass growing out of a spouting. Mr. Patterson said he ought to clean it out. Mr. Wilson said "It's strange you should say that. I'd thought of putting a sheep up to graze it off!!" Another favourite thing the Wilson's liked to do was to put a rubber cake among the real ones to catch you out at teatime.

Well, we spent quite a bit of time rabbitting together. Rabbits were certainly pests before Myxomatosis came along. They say that 8 to 10 rabbits can eat as much as one sheep.

In the late forties and early fifties, our estate, that is the Duncombe Park Estate, employed at least three rabbit catchers. There was Joe Bowes, his son Edmund, and Alf Speight. Joe was a real country character and had some droll sayings. If you were in a hurry, he would say, "Be careful thou doan't meet theesen coming back". If Joe met someone and didn't know where they came from, he would say, "Are you a Leeds man from Bradford?"

I have talked quite a lot with Alf about his days catching rabbits with Joe. Alf told me about the first day he started working with Joe. Alf was really enthusiastic and energetic, so much so that at dinnertime he gulped his sandwiches down and was ready to start again. Joe turned to him and said, "Steady up, me lad. I've been catching rabbits for thirty years and ah haven't caught them all yet and thou needn't think tha's going to catch 'em all in't dinner hour! Sit theesen down and hev thee rest".

I can remember some of the damage that rabbits did. If you had a crop of corn near woodland, you could almost guarantee that the outsides would be eaten off. One day we were bindering (cutting corn) in a woodside field and the last time round we caught twelve rabbits. It was a Friday and Nicholas took them to the road to catch Lightfoot, the huxters (game dealers) as they were going down to the market. One day we caught a black rabbit and I wanted to keep it as a pet, so I put it in a bottomless hen coup. Next morning when I went it had escaped, having burrowed its way out. It proved that the rabbit knew what it was about more than I did!

Another day we set off enthusiastically with a newly bought ferret. Being quite inexperienced we lost him down a burrow and we came back cheesed off.

Now we weren't always good lads! One day we pulled a lot of Joe Bowes' snares up and set them on our runs. I can see him marching into our yard now when he found out, as wild as a March hare, as we say. He didn't half let into Dad about the situation. Dad said, "Don't worry Joe. I'll sort them out". We got a good talking to and had to take the snares back.

In those days, rabbit catchers ferreted, snared or netted rabbits. I don't think shooting was that popular. Alf Speight told me the most he caught in any one day in his snares was eighty-four, although he said that if you set your stall out netting, you could catch a lot more on a night. One night they caught one hundred and fourteen in one hour by netting. How did they carry them back home? Well, they would cycle to work and push the bikes back with all the rabbits loaded onto them.

Not all farmers regarded rabbits as pests. In fact to many Dales farmers, rabbit money contributed to their income and in some cases paid their rent. It was normal practice every now and then, especially in slack times, for a Dales farmer to have a day rabbitting.

Rabbit was a very saleable commodity. Meat was scarce in those days and rabbit was eaten by a lot of people. It was lovely flesh - pure organic. Alf told me he often had a request to get some rabbits for a meal for the Duncombe Park boarding school. One cricket club wanted some too, as they were having rabbit pie for their club dinner.

Just as there were lots of ways of catching rabbits, there were lots of ways of cooking them. We ate a lot of rabbit in our young days. Mother would roast them stuffed with onion stuffing, not forgetting to add a piece of fat bacon to roast with them. She would boil them and then put the flesh in a pie. Really young rabbits were jointed and then fried. My favourite was a stew or casserole, which we used to have about Harvest time, and served with new potatoes. It was delicious - I guess if that was on the menu today it would be a favourite.

Rabbit skins were another source of income or pin money for the farmer's wife. It was a familiar sight seeing them hanging in the farm house kitchen. Mother once told us that when they first came to New Leys, Billy Burnside from Kirkbymoorside, who used to buy them, poked his head through the door and said, "Are you settled? Any skins?"

Well rabbitting came to an end in 1954/55 when Myxomatosis wiped out the rabbit population. There were dead rabbits laid all over the place. Alf said that one day he had moved sixty-eight off the road down our wood, a distance of two and a half miles. Both Alf and Joe became gamekeepers. They were part of the furniture of country life, walking and feeding their pheasants in all sorts of weather. If they were passing our house, we would have them in for a cup of tea - lowance we called it. Joe would give us a report on his pheasants. He would often say that before he started feeding them in autumn they were in the woods brambling! Joe was one of those chaps who were never happy unless he was grumbling. He often felt that when he was a rabbit catcher he had been treated as a second class keeper. He would comment about the young keepers and say, "All they mind is riding around in their Landrovers. They see nowt. They know nowt. I know more than them all put together".

Many hired and country people will have memories of living on nothing but rabbit. I am reminded of a story of a young hired lad who worked on a farm where they fed him on nothing but rabbit. One day they had a special guest for dinner so they bought a lovely joint of beef for the occasion. When the lad saw this, his eyes popped out like chapel hat pegs. The lad was asked to say grace and this is what he said:

"Rabbits young and rabbits old,
Rabbits hot and rabbits cold,
Rabbits tender, rabbits tough,
Thank thee Lord, we've had enough"

Mr and Mrs Joe Bowes at Crabtree Hall

Rabbiting in the Harvest Field at Oscar Park, Mr Ernest Hawkins and his two sons Thomas and William

Edmond Bowes with his catch of rabbits

Chapter 5
Fleeting Memories Of The Fifties

This chapter spans a period from 1950 to 1956. Memory is a wonderful thing. A lot of people tell me that I have a very good memory. This can have its disadvantages as well as its advantages, when we remember what people have done or said against us. It can become a grudge if we are not careful. A lot of these memories I am sharing with you have been backed up by talking to the people involved, or to people who remember them or from Mother's or Auntie Lizzie Medd's press cuttings books.

I have already mentioned in a previous chapter, Mary Ford who was our maid. She was Mary Newlove then. She worked for us from 1944 to 1946. She nursed me as a child and says she often had to smack my bottom, but now she says she thinks of me as a second son. I mention Mary specially, because in 1950 I remember going with Dad and Mother to see her. She was very ill in bed and in fact the doctors gave her up until a new drug came out. She was treated with this and eventually got better. Mary often says that God healed her. I class Mary as a real lady, a loving person who has helped many people with her wise words of counsel. Although Mary hasn't had the best of health, she has a wonderful gift of praying for sick people.

At this point I want to mention her husband, George, whom she married in the terrible winter of 1947. The bridal car got stuck in a snowdrift, making the bride half an hour late. George was born in Farndale and came to work for my grandad at Abbott Hagg. Once a group of us lads were discussing the pros and cons of striking. I think it would be when the long strike of miners was going on in 1985. George said, "Always remember this. A job is never the same to go back to after a person has been on strike. Value your job however slow or hard it is". He proceeded to tell us about the day he cycled to Abbott Hagg. He said "I passed a group of men standing at the bank corner in Helmsley, all unemployed. They would have done anything to be in my shoes, going to a job". Eventually, George and Mary took a small holding, then a 150 acre farm and finally bought it. George was a real jolly character, who had an infectious laugh. He liked telling us about the old characters in Farndale and latterly about people he had met, whether it was to do with farming or Christian things. George and Mary were a very hospitable couple and their home was greatly used for fellowship meetings.

It was a home where people could sit down and open their hearts with their problems. They were good listeners and their counsel was often sought because they had seen a lot of life, seeing both sides of the coin as workmen and bosses, which made a lot of difference.

In 1951 I remember a man called John Thompson staying with us. He was a distant relative of Dad's and had emigrated to New Zealand in 1909. He had come back to visit friends and relations. He called me a silly chump. I remember when he left everyone sang "God be with you till we meet again". He said he hoped to be back in 1955, but to me that sounded like fifty years away!

I think it was 1951 when we had our Aga cooker and a bathroom installed. Mother often said that she didn't know what she would have done without the Aga. Well it's still going strong today although it now runs on oil and not solid fuel.

Mother used to tell me I was "a droll youth" as a child. I remember walking down to the stream near our wood and saying to her, "Does the beck stop running at dark?" On another occasion a chap came to tea who had a big moustache and I said to him, "Why have you got sheep's wool stuck round your mouth?"

It was around 1952 that Margaret Wilson, Gran and Father's daughter from the next farm, Middleheads got married. I remember this bonny bride passing our road end. Nicholas and I were waiting for her. At that time we were walking on top of treacle tins with bands tied to them. We used to race one another walking on these "lame ladies" as we called them! Our cousins, John, Donald, Martin and Jean Medd, lived at the next farm to Middle Heads and the Dunn lads, along with Joe and Bri Garbutt and other children out of Rievaulx would go to their birthday parties. I remember going to one party about this time, jumping over a fence, catching my trousers on some barbed wire and tearing the backside out! As I was one of the youngest, they tended to make fun of me and call me "Peeling". They chanted:

> "Peeling went a-walking one fine day.
> Tore his breeches on the way.
> Somebody laughed and somebody cried
> To see poor Peeling in his bare backside"

Auntie Lizzie took pity on me and I went back home in a pair of my cousin's trousers.

1953 was coronation year. It was the first time I had seen television. We went as a family to Aunt Tat and Uncle Milton Leadley's house at Great Edstone to see the coronation ceremony. I remember coming back through Helmsley and seeing a procession of floats. One that especially stood out was a thatched cottage built on a wagon by Fred Handley the builder. We also had some sports at Rievaulx and George Otterburn was the organiser. One of the things you had to do was get an apple out of a bucket of water. I remember George saying to me, "Get your head down and shape yourself!"

One often asks the children, "What would we do without the telephone?" It was hard when you had to rely on the public kiosk up the road. Many a time we would go up and the number Dad was trying would be engaged. However, we got the telephone in 1955. I remember going for a ride and we decided to have fun ringing back home. We were at Stamford Bridge near York. Dad rang up and Jack Webb who worked for us answered. "Who's speaking?" he said. Dad replied, "Mr. Dalton from Stamford Bridge". When we came back Dad asked, "Any telephone calls Jack?" "Yes. A Mr. Dalton from Stamford Bridge rang. I don't know whether it was someone larking on with me!"

Well as children we did some strange things. Once about this time the granary was full of corn and we all decided we would strip off and dive about in it naked. It so happened that a relative called Colin Dowson was staying with us from Stockton and his parents had sent his bus fare home through the post and he had it in his jacket. When we did our stripping act we hung our clothes over a beam and his half crown fell out. Dad made us find it in the heap of corn. It was like trying to find a needle in a haystack but we eventually found it. I only remember us once going potato picking, when we three lads went to Mr. and Mrs. Bean's at Scawton. George Ford's small holding was nearby and so he was helping as well. Two things stand out. I had never seen red skinned potatoes before and it was the first time we tasted Cornish pasties.

Memories of 1954 are all about harvest. It must have been the talking point that year. It was very wet and I think we finished in November. I also remember our late neighbours, the Trousdales cutting some laid oats with a grass cutter and then raking them into heaps rather like haycocks.

1955 was the year we bought our first hydraulic tractor, a diesel Fordson Major. We had a lot of haytime as we hadn't many cattle due to TB testing. I remember Mother coming up the field with the lowance and she said "I have just heard Bert Harper on the wireless. He has had a good do at the Great Yorkshire Show". Bert is a show ring character and I will refer to him in a later chapter.

Dad had begun breeding Teeswater sheep and was getting contacts and making friends with the sheep people round Richmond, Leyburn and Barnard

Castle. I remember him being friendly with Willie Wilkinson from Spanham near Barnard Castle and in a casual conversation Willie asked if Dad knew of anyone who had any hay to sell. We had - lots! To cut a long story short the hay was sold to the Wilkinsons and they came and helped us bale it out of the stack with one of Isaac Weighell's stationary balers. This was a heavy machine which tied up the bales with wire. We used to call it a horse head baler. I also remember going to the International Sheepdog Trials at Darlington in 1955, when I think Ashton Priestly had a dramatic points win.

Dad and Mam didn't have many holidays. On the odd time they would spend a few days with relatives in Darlington. In those days Darlington was like London to us. Mother would say "All your Dad is interested in is sheep" and they would go calling on his sheep friends near Barnard Castle. We lads didn't have any holiday but every now and then in the summer we would have a day out as a family touring the Lake District, Swaledale and Nidderdale.

Mother must have been a very busy person at that time. There were three men living in and a hungry, growing family to feed and no electricity! There were no washing machines. Dad and Mam had to get up in good time on a Monday morning to get the copper fire on in the washhouse and Dad would use the peggy stick and dolly tub. I think Nicholas was the chief lad for turning the clothes mangle before he went to school. Mother was quite a dab hand at making fruit cakes. It was a regular thing for us lads to beat the eggs - no electric mixers. One night Nicholas had toothache. In the middle of the night he felt hungry and got up and cut into one of Mother's show fruit cakes. You can well imagine there was music on!

I think we miss out nowadays community-wise, with not being able to hire workmen. They added richness to our lives with their different characteristics. Our last three were all characters in their own right. Jack Webb was an elderly man who was a bit lame. He was the bullocky, a slang word for a herdsman. Stan Wright was a bit younger and he was the shepherd. Stanley Smith's nickname was "Cowey" because he had looked after the cows on his last farm. He was an odd job man. Jack Webb thought the world of Judith and would often read to her on a night and really make a fuss of her.

I think jealousy began to creep in with Nicholas and me as we could do nothing right for Jack as he always seemed to 'down' us. One day Jack had a difficult job starting the turnip cutter engine. Eventually he got it started and was soon carrying cut turnips away down a long passage. Nicholas dared me to stop the engine so I did. Jack come chasing after us. He couldn't catch us so he shouted, "When I get hold of you, I'll tan your backsides with my belt". Jack used to say

I wasn't to blame for the mischief but that it was Nicholas who put me up to it. Now as is often the case when you get men together there can be industrial strife. One day Mother heard such shouts she thought there was a party of hikers coming down the yard. She looked out and there was Jack with a gripe ready to strike Cowey. Cowey was shouting, "Fight with your fists! Fight with your fists!" Jack said, "I'll kill thou, thou cheeky lubber" Obviously there had been a bit of a disagreement! We needn't go to Northern Ireland to find violence - it can be and is on our doorsteps. Mother eventually got them reconciled. Stan was a quieter chap but if he got his micky up he could fly. When Nicholas left school, Stan left the farm and went to work for the Forestry Commission but when he retired he made his home with us and we treated him as one of the family.

Cowey once went on a trip to Scarborough and lost his rail ticket. The train guard asked him if he knew where he'd lost it- Cowey said, "Don't be so daft! If I knew where I'd lost it, I'd know where to find it!" As Christopher and Nicholas left school the hired men were phased out. Dad used to say, "Things will look up when we haven't got labour to pay." Well neither Nicholas nor I had a wage but in a way I don't think we missed out as it taught us to take care of our money.

1956 was quite a wet year. I remember going down to Uncle Milton Leadley's, Gt. Edstone. On his farm, where the land was strong wet clay, the binder would do nothing but bog and skid so they had to put an engine in. In the backend of 1956 Dad and Nicholas had rather a frightening experience. Dad had a bull bought for us in Barnard Castle and it was put on a train to be collected at Helmsley railway station. Dad and Nicholas would lead the bull up Beckdale. Everything went well until they came across a party of hikers. The bull took fright and got loose. I think it was loose for about two hours. Mother was worried stiff and rang Helmsley police. She had expected Dad and Nicholas back long before. She went down Beckdale, called at "Ouldrey" and got Uncle Fred Medd and his men. They eventually got the fugitive caught. Among the party of hikers was a man called Arthur Minnie, who was a Quaker. It was through this episode with the bull that he became a great friend, visiting us periodically. So you can never tell what good can come out of bad. Mr. Minnie had an important job with Rowntrees in York and would sometimes bring us some chocolates - second casts he called them - but we lads always appreciated them.

I remember in the fifties we listened to the wireless quite a lot - that is if the battery was charged up! In those days wirelesses had wet batteries - or did they call them accumulators? You used to have to take them to Sid Wilson's up the High Street to get them charged up. One of our favourite programmes was

"Have A Go" with Wilfred and Mabel Pickles. I think it was around 1956 or 1957 that Wilfred came to Helmsley with "Have A Go". Six people appeared on the programme: Colin Baldwin, Joyce Dowker, Dorothy Hildrick, Mrs. Sonley, Kit Barker and John Teasdale. At that time Kit Barker had the riding school in Helmsley, which is now run by his son, Anthony. I remember Wilfred asking Kit about the controversial subject of fox hunting. Well this is still being discussed and debated today. The man we knew best on the programme was John Teasdale from Low Woods. Teasdale is a well-known Ryedale farming name. If you remember, Wilfred used to ask people questions. He asked John, "Are you married?" "Yes". "Are you a family man?" At this the audience roared with laughter for John had three sons and ten daughters. Wilfred eventually asked John, "Would you like to ask me a question?" John said "Yes. How would you cope with ten daughters?" It was also on that programme that greetings were sent to Mr. and Mrs. John Garbutt at Hawnby who were celebrating their diamond wedding. It was John's second marriage - he was ninety-five and his wife was eighty. John had been a local preacher for seventy two years and was a well-loved and respected person.

How did we keep ourselves amused and entertained with no TV? We visited our relations a lot more and they would come and visit us. Brian Leadley, Uncle Milton and Aunty Tat's son, would come and stay with us every summer holiday. Mother used to have a special baking day for Brian - her chocolate biscuits were his favourites. I remember playing hide-and-seek and Brian accidentally knocked a tin of biscuits down the stairs, Mother nearly fainted! Brian also liked to ride our Billy goat. Anyone who knows anything about Billy goats knows that they smell terribly. Brian had got all changed to go home but he would have a final ride on the Billy goat. When he got home his sister Ruth said, "Where on earth have you been Brian?"

I think children brought up in the country or on a farm are privileged. There is always something happening with the different seasons, different animals. As I write this our son Philip is very excited. One of his goats has just kidded. I don't think we were ever bored. One of our favourite games after lambing time was running on top of the bales round the lambing pen and playing tig. We used to play "fell-to" - a slang word for hide-and-seek. If the seeker couldn't find anyone he would say, "Whistle or shout or else come out, or else the dogs won't follow". Winter nights we would play Snakes and Ladders, Snap cards, Draughts and Merrills. I used to read quite a lot, my favourite author being Enid Blyton. I just loved her series of Famous Five and Secret Seven. These books are still the favourites of our children today.

Fred Handleys cottage on his bus, coronation 1953.

George and Jane Otterburn in fancy dress, coronation 1953 at Rievaulx, as a tramp and a victorian lady

Family photo 1955

George and Mary Fords wedding 1947

Uncle Jack Thompson from New Zealand (on horse in backgound with his sheep)

29

Mr and Mrs John Garbutt on their Diamond wedding aniversary

A real craftsmans work. stack made and thatched by Frank Flintoft on his farm, Sour Leys 1955

John Teasdale with one of his prize winning horses

Chapter 6
Secondary School Days

Ryedale Secondary Modern School at Nawton will have a special place in the story of the Dunn family as brother Christopher was the first head boy. This was a bit daunting for me as teachers tended to judge one by one's siblings, in my case brother Christopher. I remember fooling around one day when a teacher said to another, "Do you know who this boy is? He's Christopher Dunn's brother. He'll never be the same boy Christopher was". Well it felt like a kick in the teeth! I suppose we all make the same mistake. If someone is an outstanding leader and someone else takes over their job and we feel they aren't doing it as well, we say "He'll never be as good a man as his predecessor!"

The first pupils at Ryedale School were admitted on 8th September 1953 and Lord Halifax officially opened it on 3rd May 1954. In his speech he made a comment that he had asked a pupil what they learned and the pupil had replied, "Everything!" It so happened that the pupil was Christopher and one teacher said he ought to have had ten merit marks!

It has been quite interesting looking back on the history of the school. According to records, tenders for the building were received on September 1st 1939 and it was hoped it would have been built in 1941. The Second World War put an end to that. It is interesting to note that it was built by the railway line as in the early forties railways were the chief means of transport.

I started at Ryedale School on 6th September 1956. For all country children, I think it was the beginning of broadening one's horizons and the start of centralisation. Ryedale was drawing on twenty-three village schools, a catchment area from Sutton Bank to Sinnington and Bilsdale to Brawby - quite some area. It was originally built for 450 pupils but had a lot more when I started, as there was a classroom in the main hall. For me it was my first taste of public transport, being collected from the road end by Sid Wilson's bus. We were often a rowdy lot on the bus as we used to argue which was the best tractor. The best being the one we used! We also used to argue which was the best football or cricket team. I supported Ipswich Town, as Stan who used to work for us, came from that area.

The captain at that time was, I believe, the now famous manager, Bobby Robson. 1 supported Surrey County Cricket team, as they were the best then. They had an outstanding number of players, which included the famous bowling "twins" Tony Lock and Jim Laker. Other famous players were Alec and Eric

Eric Bedser, and Stuart Surridge and Peter May. I think Peter May was the England captain at that time. I well remember going with my uncles John and Fred Wass and George Breckon to the cricket festival at Scarborough. Several of my heroes were playing. I saw Peter May bat and Stuart Surridge fielding. He was a very good catcher. On the way back, I remember saying to George Breckon that Peter May was my man and for years after that whenever I met up with George he would pull my leg about that statement. I was never much of a sportsman but I did enjoy playing about on the equipment in the gym.

One day when I got on the bus, it was a lot quieter than normal. It had just been announced about the Munich air disaster, when several Manchester United players were killed. There were several Manchester United supporters on our bus and the shock had knocked them for six as we say.

The other day I thought how many things had changed when I had to go and meet our children off the bus. My mind went back forty years. Then you would sometimes see a steamroller coming down the road and hear the clanking of milk cans as they loaded and unloaded the milk. It's funny how some sayings stay with you. Uncle Fred Medd after putting his milk cans on the stand would say on fine days, "Have you brought a coat today? Always remember to take a coat when it's fine but please yourself when it's raining!" There would be John Otterburn senior, and Jack and Reg Sunley coming up in their cattle wagons to go to Stokesley market. There would be Bert Jackson and Stanley Richardson travelling in their pick-up to Stockton mart. There is a tale told that Bert liked to sing a lot and Stanley wasn't that keen on it. One day Stanley said to Bert, "Don't sing so much Bert". When Bert asked why, Stanley replied, "There's many a bird been singing in the morning and cat got him by night!" Sometimes you would see small holder George Atkinson, driving a sow down to Mr. Fairburn's boar and he would have two of the pig's legs tied together to keep it under control. I don't think the RSPCA would have allowed that today. Nowadays hardly any farmers keep small numbers of pigs. They are all kept in large units. You would also see at least three farmers bringing up domestic help from the village to help their wives with the household chores. Today there is a steady stream of farmers' wives going out to work in Helmsley and the surrounding area.

I found secondary school a lot more enjoyable than primary school. There were many more subjects, more teachers, and I felt that teachers didn't have as many "pet" pupils. In the autumn term of my second year there was a bad epidemic of Asian flu. I got it twice and had nearly half the term off. There is nothing new about outbreaks of flu! Come to think of it I had quite a few days off. If Mother was ill, it used to fall to my lot to stop off school and do the housework. Mother had me fairly domesticated. Someone said I would make someone a good wife! I remember having days off to thresh. John Robson the teacher once asked me, "Where were you yesterday, little man?" I said "I was threshing sir". He replied, "You ought to have got stuck in the thresher!!!" That's what he thought about me!

I well remember marching into the hall for assembly. Several of us used to wear hob-nailed boots and when we walked in on the wood floor it made a terrible noise. One day the headmaster, George Spencer made a public example of us. He said we were all like newly shod shire horses and had to stop this clompety-clomp business.

Funny experiences stand out. One day we had a new music teacher called Mr. Pye. One lad wrote across the blackboard, "PORK PIE". The teacher was a serious sort of chap and he gave us all a dressing down about making remarks about people's names. Most children made fun of him from day one as he used to wear narrow trousers halfway up his legs and bright red stockings, and he had a Desperate Dan bottom jaw! The poor chap was a right sight and he couldn't discipline children if he tried. One class locked him in a back store cupboard one day.

One Monday morning there was an awful smell in the class, whether it was the effects of the previous day's peas or not I don't know. The teacher, John Robson, said to me, "Why are you curling your nose up, boy?" I said, "There seems to be a smell in the place, sir". "Well, get the windows open, boy. The trouble with you lad is you've had your nose too near your bum!"

I wasn't the brightest of children although I was in the A stream, generally about halfway up the class. The nearest I got to the top was second in history and I always got a good report in this subject. I was quite interested in current affairs. I liked metal work and got on well with the teacher, Mr. Clark. He was a small round chap and we called him Pop Belly Clark as a nickname.

The subject I enjoyed most was optional in the last year and this was cookery. Although we Dunn lads were quite domesticated, mother insisted that all three lads took it. I almost had a disaster with my egg and bacon pie. I got it well prepared but put it in a loose-bottomed dish and when I carried it to the oven I disturbed the pastry and a leak appeared! I had to hurry back to the table to mend it. However I was proud of my Christmas cake as I got a merit mark for my icing. One day we had to iron a shirt. I remember Miss Hey telling us to lightly sprinkle some water on it. One lad said that he was going to make a right job of his and put it under the tap. Miss Hey yelled at him, "What do you think you're playing at, boy?"

School is a place where you are called names and given nicknames. At primary school, Christopher was called Big Willie, Nicholas, Middle Willie, and I was Little Willie, after Dad I suppose and this carried on at Ryedale. Sometimes children can be cruel to one another. I remember there were some lads from one of the dales. They were always known as 'Daddies' because they came to school in hob-nailed boots, big caps, and sometimes collarless shirts with a stud. Another lad who liked a fight, was called 'Bulldog'. A lad with fair hair was called 'Wozzell', maybe because he looked a bit like a mangel-wurzel.

Every school had, has and will have its problems. I would think the chief problem today would be drugs. In my day there used to be a lot of smoking, a bit of bullying and the odd fight.

At one time there used to be a craze for marbles and conkers. My cousin Edward Atkinson, called Little Acky, was quite an enthusiastic player of marbles.

With both our children at Ryedale now we can make a comparison. I would think that Ryedale is much better now and indeed it has a good reputation.

I left school on 22nd July 1960. It is interesting looking at some of the comments teachers made. Music teacher Mr. Scarth once wrote, "Spoils his efforts by trying to be a comedian". All the teachers you got on well with gave you good comments but those you didn't get on with seemed to give you either bad or moderate reports! In the last term I helped the headmaster quite a lot with his pheasants and we got on well. I wonder if it was this, which prompted him to give me a good final report. This is what he wrote: "Paul Dunn is a likeable mature boy - one could almost say he was already a North Riding farmer and I dare say will grow up to be a very good one. He has plenty of common sense; good powers of observation, is well able to come to conclusions on his own and has good powers of selection and judgement. Whatever he tackles he does so in a whole-hearted manner and he likes to have a real job in front of him and be able to get on with it. He is cheerful, lively and not such a rough diamond as his voice suggests. He has the wit I think to cultivate a better way of speaking and he could start as soon as possible on Young Farmers' Club matters now and farming in general in the future. He could have some very good ideas to put forward".

Author, billy goat riding

Gym scene when we performed in the school concert. from left to right. Dennis Wilson, Frank Hildrick, Harold Wheldon, Geoff Andrews, Joe Ward, Ken Fletcher and Author. 1957

Pupils at the opening of Rydale School, 1954.
Brother Christopher, front row right, cousin Donald Wass, fourth row 2nd from right

Sid Wilsons bus which took us to Ryedale school

Author in Ryedale school uniform

Judith in her Lady Lumley's school uniform

Chapter 7
1958 - 1960
The Beginning Of A Day To Day Diary

In 1958 I started a very interesting exercise, that of keeping a day to day diary. Little did I think when I first started that some of the contents of my diaries down the years would be quoted in the national newspapers and on television.

They say that most of the conversation of farmers and country folk is taken up by their work and the weather. As you read my diaries these two subjects are the main topics!

In my first diaries I used to write, "Did my work". George Ford came one night as I was filling in my diary and he was reading it. He passed a comment, "What is thy work, Paul? If thou doesn't put it down, folks won't know what the work is!" So what was my work? In winter it was getting sticks and coals in, feeding my goats and lighting the Tilley lamps for the hens on a deep litter system. An old uncle of mine, commenting on this said, "Pushing nature again. Poor old hens, can't thou let them have their proper rest? Thou's expecting them to dee ower time!" In summer it would be suckling lambs on the goats and feeding show sheep. I would sometimes help Mam to collect the eggs and wash them.

In my later diaries I have made a point of describing the weather and my Bible readings. The weather plays an important part in farming. In fact the farmer is subject to two uncontrollable forces, the weather and the buyer of what he produces.

I remember somebody asking an old character about the weather and he replied, "Now then I had better tell thee there is always some sort of weather at this time of the year".

1958

1958 was a hard winter and a wet summer. Between February 25th and 28th the main Helmsley to Stokesley road was blocked by snow. March 8th to 10th we had an awful lot of snow. In fact it was reported on television that they had two feet on the level up in Farndale. Again the main road was blocked. As children, we felt it was great as we had time off school

During the March bad snow, there was a funeral up at Cold Kirby. It is interesting to record what happened as told first hand by Mary Ford. It started to snow on the Friday and the two undertakers, Alf Harper from Hawnby and Alf Cussons from Helmsley, along with their driver, Mike Harper had to go up to Mr. Chumes, the deceased man's home and pick up some document before they could collect the coffin and body from York Hospital. The two Alfs were steady sort of men, never in a hurry and when they got to Cold Kirby Mrs. Chumes was worried stiff that they wouldn't get back with the coffin that afternoon, for the funeral next morning. The undertakers were fortunate that they went for the body in a long-wheel based Land Rover and eventually got back within a mile of Cold Kirby, but couldn't get any further because of the drifted snow. All the men from Cold Kirby turned out to try and dig a way in but they had to give up and the two undertakers abandoned the Land Rover with the coffin inside. When the undertakers arrived at Mrs. Chumes' house she had nowhere to sleep them. Mary Ford was there and said, "You feed them and I'll sleep them". Both men got royal treatment, the best bed with an electric blanket.

Next morning the two Alfs, along with their driver and men from the village, set off to try and get the Land Rover and coffin. They found the road completely blocked both ways and the Land Rover nearly covered over. So they made a gap in the wall and travelled over the fields to the church in time for the funeral. The vicar, along with Mrs. Chumes' daughter, Eileen Yarker, and Alf Wight (James Herriot) walked from Sutton Bank top to attend the funeral. Afterwards the mourners went back to Mrs. Chumes' for a cup of tea. Mary Ford said that Alf Wight, soon to be James Herriot, fired a lot of questions at her. Was he gaining knowledge for his books? One never knows. In all, the undertakers spent five nights with the Fords until the road was opened out. When the news leaked out in Helmsley, they started to take the mickey out of Alf Cussons. Alf's reply was, "I wouldn't mind another funeral in a snowstorm, after all, I haven't an electric blanket on my own bed!" Snow in March is never a good thing for in-lamb sheep and I remember a lot of sheep died on the North Yorkshire Moors that year.

Back to our farm. Cattle weren't fed as hard as they are now. They were in store condition and fed out on grass in summer. In winter we would give them ground oats, straw and a few chopped turnips. That winter we had a lot of ringworm on the cattle and Nicholas caught them. His back was completely covered and I remember him crying out in agony as I brushed the ointment on.

It is interesting comparing the things that happened in 1958 to today. There were things that happened then, which perhaps will never happen again. For example, we did all our grinding through a stone mill and I have it recorded that Thackrays of Brawby came to dress the stones.

As Uncle Fred and Frank Wilson, our neighbours hadn't the telephone, they would use ours to contact the vet or AI (Artificial Insemination) and if there were any messages for them it was an understood thing that they rang us. Mam would write the message on a note and I would have to go and be the messenger boy.

If there was a lot of snow, Joe Garbutt would fetch the eggs over with the horse and sledge and us lads would have a good ride around. A lot of our stock was sold through dealers. I remember John Otterburn coming and buying five pigs. He bagged them up and put them in the boot of his car. Bob Harland from Pickering would come and buy some cattle and pigs. Rowland Weighell from Wombleton sometimes bought cattle. I think he was a sub-agent for Frank and Richard Machin of Brandsby. I remember Richard Machin coming with a small open top wagon. What a contrast with Machin's wagons today! Richard is now a nation-wide sheep buyer.

The summer of 1958 was wet and backward. There was only one week of decent hay weather, Yorkshire Show week. I remember crying because I couldn't go to the Yorkshire Show. We did make a bit of silage. All our hay was made loose, buckraked into a stack in the field and led in for the stock during the winter. That summer we never did finish haytime. We gave one bit up and turned cattle in to graze it. That year we started harvest 10th September and finished 20th October. We did a bit of combining but most of it was cut with the binder.

Threshing days were big occasions. We would have about seven a year. We used Isaac Weighell's threshing set from Kirkbymoorside. The neighbours, Hawkins, Medds and Wilsons would come and help us plus the tramp threshers. A tramp thresher was a man who followed the machine around. One such man was a chap called Ted Peacock and at lowance time he would give a running commentary on the farms he threshed at and of his days as a farm labourer on the Yorkshire Wolds. Ted took some stopping talking. One man commented that he must have been injected with a gramophone needle. It was good entertainment. We would have a good laugh and the more we laughed the more Ted told his tales. Threshing days were exciting when you got down to the bottom of a stack. We used to farm a few rats then, and one day one labourer was busy trying to kill the rodents, got his foot stuck with a fork and ended up going to the doctor. Threshing days were a busy time too for Mother. Normally two men would come and set the machine up the night before and have a bit of tea. She would have them in for breakfast next morning and then dinner plus giving drinks to the other people who helped. I can see now the big meat and potato pies she used to make. Threshing was hard work and in 1958 the wage was thirty-five shillings per day, and £2 per day for corn carriers.

Pigs and poultry played an important part in the farm's economy at that time. Much time was spent mucking out pigs and poultry houses. Again Mother had an important role. She would rear the chickens and wash the eggs. On February 9th we sent 123 dozen, top grade eggs making three shillings and sixpence per dozen. Cull hens would be about ten shillings each. We sold Christmas chickens all in their feathers at nineteen shillings each. Most of the pigs were sold as weaners to John Otterburn, £5 to £6 each, and we would fatten some of the sows up for slaughter for our own use. Pig killing days were quite an occasion. It was quite a task getting the fire stoked up under the copper. Plenty of hot water was important for scalding the pig. George Atkinson was the pig killer at that time. There was no humane killer, just mell and punch. Nicholas would hold the pig with a rope around its jaw and snout and I was all of a dother, as we say, holding the punch. We got the job done eventually and next day George would come and cut the pig up. Auntie Tamar would come and help Mother to cut fat and make the sausages and black pudding. We would sometimes have a day off school to cut fat. It was rendered down for lard and what was left we called scrappings. It was nice to have some fresh liver and some fillet of pork. What a delicious roast it was! They say there is nothing wasted on a pig except its squeal. We would make broth from the pig's head. The heart would be cooked and then diced up and boiled with swede and carrots. We called this dish "ash". As children we would have great arguments as to whose turn it was to have the brains. They were delicious especially if you had them on toast. I might be mad but I haven't got BSE yet!! What was left which included the trotters and the ears would be made into brawn. Mother's brawn was out of this world, especially if you ate it with some of her apple chutney. Of course the sides and hams were cured. I have it recorded that we sold a ham for £7. It makes you wonder how we managed without a deep freeze. We would share our pork round with aunts and uncles and when they killed their pig we would get a little back.

Here are some prices, written down in my 1958 diary:
Note, a dead sheep sold to the fellmonger, Harry Atkinson, ten shillings.
Jan. 10th Helmsley mart. 5 hoggs graded at 55lbs made £7. 4. 0d. each
Feb. 14th Helmsley mart. 9 ½ cwt heifer £6.4.0d per cwt plus
    £1 per cwt. subsidy.
5th March, newly calved red cow £52
31st Dec. Eggs 4/6d per dozen.
Farm wage £8 per week
Stock numbers as at 31st Dec. 55 cattle including 15 cows, 20 pigs, 700 poultry, 7 goats, 125 ewes and 110 fattening hoggs.

1959

For several years Mam and Dad tried to get the electricity to our farm but the authorities objected to electric poles being erected on the Harriet Air plain. Eventually, after contacting our MP, plans were passed for electricity to come to New Leys. It was a sore point with Mother that we, living in the country, were denied this necessity. She would often say when washing dirty lamp glasses, or when an Aladdin lamp mantle would get blacked or the Tilley lamp wouldn't work properly, "If these Preservation for Rural England folk saw this lot they would change their tunes!" Work started after Christmas. Poles were erected. The whole farm was wired up and on 23rd February the electricity was switched on. People used to say to Mother, "You will be able to have a TV, a washing machine and a fridge". Mother used to say, "If I get light that will satisfy me!" However we did get an electric radio and a Hoover, followed by a washing machine some years later.

What an asset electricity was for the farm! We could now have infra red lamps for the pigs and calves and an electric motor for the milking machine. Petrol engines were temperamental things at any time.

What a contrast to last year was the weather. 1959 was a really hot scorching summer. You could have haytimed and harvested from 1st June to the middle of September. In 1959 we started haytime on 13th June and finished on 7th July. We did some baling. We started harvest 6th August and finished 25th August. All of it cut with the binder.

1959 was the year I travelled the most. A day train trip was arranged from Helmsley station to Llandudno in North Wales. Neither Nicholas nor I were that impressed because all we seemed to see was caravans and rocks! It was in 1959 that I had my first night away from home. I stayed two nights at the Yorkshire Show. Jack Ripley was a great friend of Dads and we used to winter his Teeswater gimmer and tup hoggs. That year, one we wintered got 1st in its class, female champion and reserve breed champion. I well remember sleeping in a stockman's cubicle. It had been occupied the night before and the chap left his frying pan under the bed. During the night nature called as we say. I was used to a chamber pot and being half-asleep, urinated into the frying pan. I realised what I had done and emptied it out straight away. Later in the day I went back and the chap was having a fry-up. I don't know what the hygiene people would say about that lot!

Another interesting experience that happened when we were showing was at Hawnby Show. I think Dad was at another show because Bill Todd from Ampleforth brought me and the sheep back. I happened to leave an orange squash bottle in his Land Rover. This bottle contained shampoo and stuff for washing the sheep's faces. Bill felt dry on the way back and he said "I supped it up quickly". Talk about cleaning a fellow out! In the October of that year, I returned to the Yorkshire showground to a National Sheep Exhibition and spent two nights there. I remember hearing some Welsh shepherds singing. They were marvellous! At that time Dad also travelled the furthest from home. He went to the Smithfield Show in London. I think he was the most interested because Benny Nicholson a butcher from Helmsley was showing some sheep that had been bred by Bert Harper. Bert was there with them and they won! When he came back Dad said that Bert was really set up with himself. As we say, he was like a dog with two tails. That same year Dad had a farm sale for his cousin Herbert Agar at Hall Farm, Famdale- I noted some of the prices:

Dairy cows to £94

Moor ewes in lamb £6

Sows in pig £29.10s

Eggs must have dropped in price as they were 2/1d

and 3/ld per dozen.

Herbert and Annie came to live at Harome and Annie came a day or two a week to help Mam. We had some lively discussions at dinnertimes. Annie was good at recalling the characters in Farndale and we all had a good laugh.

1960

What a contrast we have in our English weather! It was what we call a mucky winter, not much frost or snow. The spring and early summer were very dry. We started haytime 15th June and finished 2nd July. The weather broke in the middle of July and it rained the entire back end. Dad said that as we had all our own labour we would cut all the corn with the binder. It was the worst harvest we have ever had. We never finished. We cut some of the sheaves loose to try and get them dry. Over half of our corn had either to be led to the cattle or led into the wood. There was a lot of flooding in Pickering and the Malton area round 9th October and the river was out in Rievaulx. A lot of potatoes were never got up until the following spring.

Now that we had all our own labour, we were given specialist jobs. Christopher was the tractor man, Nicholas the cattleman and I was the shepherd. In those days we folded the hoggs on turnip or swedes. All the swedes were pulled in heaps and cut with a Russell's mobile cutter. There were no electric fences, just wire nets. We had our hoggs in the stickiest field and as we had a lot with long wool, they got very mucky, "clagged up" as we used to say. So much so that some couldn't get up and we had to take them off and put them in a grass paddock. It was quite a depressing year. I remember John Otterburn coming to wish Christopher all the best on his 21st birthday on Dec 20. Mother said, "We've had a bad harvest. I don't know how we are going to manage". John Otterburn turned to her and said, "Always remember this, Mrs. Dunn. No matter how hard things are there's always someone in a worse situation than you are".

We had a lot of callers in those days; hawkers selling ropes and stack sheets, three mobile shops - Les Helm from Kirkbymoorside, John Sutton from Appleton-le-Moors and Broughs from Nawton - as well as lots of travellers. It made life very interesting. Here are some 1960 prices:

30th August sold 6 Masham show gimmers, £10 each.

7th September, sold a boar pig £25.

17th October, sold 2 geld cows £37. 3s 4d each

Mam making one of her hookey rugs

Author and Nicholas, taken about 1959-60

Mothers words, "get some sticks in". Judith and friend Helen Reynolds. taken 1959-60

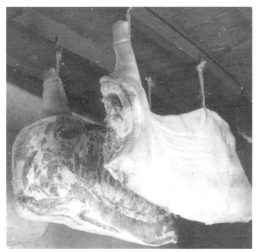

Bacon hanging in the kitchen 1959-60

George Atkinson, pig killer

Aunty Tamar making sausages

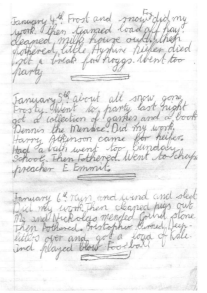

Extracts from my first diary
January 1958

John Otterburn. cattle dealer, with young John and Audrey at the Helmsley young farmers calf club show and sale. Taken in the late 1960's

Bob Harland, right centre with son in law Tom Bentley, left centre, taken 1976

Machin family, father Frank in centre, with sons Richard and John

Chapter 8
1961 - 1966
An Assortment Of Winters

1961

There is an old saying that nature has a wonderful way of providing. We wondered how we would get through after the disastrous harvest of 1960, with no corn to sell and little bedding for the stock. Well nature did provide! **January** and **February** were abnormally mild, no frost or snow. We out-wintered many of the strong cattle and fed a lot of sprouted sheaves to them. We had to bring them in in the middle of **March** as they escaped one day and got a taste of spring grass and we couldn't stop them jumping hedges. It was quite an early spring. We started seedtime on the 7th March and finished on the 29th.

There is another old saying that a speck of dust in March is worth a king's ransom, meaning if you can get your corn sown in good time, you'll have a better chance of a good harvest. The only snow we had that winter was three and a half inches on the 4th **April**. It was a good growing year, with fine crops of hay and corn. We started hay-time on the 7th **June** and finished on the 1st **July**, some of it baled and some loose. Our crop rotation at that time was grass, ploughed out and put in with oats, followed by wheat. Roots followed that, and then spring barley under-sown with a three to five year grass ley. Our corn average could vary depending on the sizes of the fields. It was mainly between 46 and 55 acres. We had around 16 to 20 acres of roots and the rest in grass. Until now we were all employed at home, although odd times Nicholas and I went turnip hoeing. Then Christopher's future in-laws had a tragic death in the family and he started working for them two days a week. We started harvest on the 24th **August** and finished on the 22nd **September**, the wheat and oats being cut with the binder and the barley being combined. As yet, tanker combines hadn't caught on except on big farms. All our corn was bagged off the combine. It is still a good way of storing corn, especially if you haven't a dryer.

John Ashbridge from Cold Kirby did our combining at that time. He came to us from the Thirsk area, where he had been combining winter barley. Up to that time we hadn't heard of such a thing. John remarked how forward our spring barley was. The variety was Freja. The weather for harvest was a bit catchy to start with and then it got out very hot and humid followed by a violent thunderstorm on the 3rd September. It started thundering and lightning about midnight on the Saturday and continued till the Sunday afternoon. It was the worst thunder and lightning I have ever experienced. We had neither electricity nor generator so we couldn't milk the cows that Sunday morning!

It was a decent open back-end until early **December** when we had some keen frosts right through the month. A lot of potatoes were frozen in store. That year we sold some cattle to John Otterburn and the customer who got them couldn't stop them jumping hedges and fences, so they had to come back.

It was in 1961 that Nicholas and I launched into pedigree pig breeding. We bought a pedigree Large White sow, Sawdon Heights East-Lass, from Herbert Dickinson of Sawdon near Scarborough. He was a grand chap and took a great interest in us. He said when he sold her to us, "I hope she does well. If I knew she was going to do badly I would rather keep her". We paid £44 for her. Dad had a sale for Arthur Robinson in Rievaulx that year:

Cows making to £71

Five month old heifer, £28

Gilts in pig, 29 guineas each

A Fergy tractor £185

And a grass cutter £63

1962

If the wind is howling at our front door we are in for some wet, mild, windy weather. If it is howling at our back door we are in for some wintry weather or dry, cold, droughty weather. All that year it seemed to be howling in the back door and we had a cold dry winter. We had nine inches of snow on 1st **January**. From the middle of **February** we had a lot of wind and the land started to dry up. On the 22nd we started to harrow. Some farmers even sowed their corn, a thing unheard of in February! We were just going to start to sow when there was some snow on the 26th. It wasn't until the 11th **April** that we got a start sowing and finished on the 25th. We started haytime on the 23rd **June** and finished on the 10th **July**. For the first time, all the hay was baled which meant an end to the job of leading hay in the wintertime. We started harvest on 13th **September** and finished on the 30th **October**. A lot of the barley and wheat had second growth in it and all had to be dried. We just bindered the oats that year. I remember the oats were growing in a field by the roadside and they always looked a good colour. One night, early July, there was a really strong cold wind and it made all the leaves go brown. It was then that some of the tents were blown down at the Royal Show at its last temporary site in Newcastle.

Winter started early in the back end of 1962. On the 18th and 19th **November** it snowed and we had 9 inches on the level and it blocked our road. Because of the storm at sea nine lives were lost in a lifeboat disaster at Seaham Harbour in Durham. There was more snow on the 13th **December** and keen frosts on the

25th and 26th December. It made quite a talking point when we were carol singing as everyone had the same problems with water pipes frozen up and vehicles that wouldn't start.

From an early age I had always kept goats and in 1962 I went into pedigree breeding. I bought three pedigree Saanen kids from Mrs. Greaves of Robin Hood's Bay. We travelled round a bit to the pedigree pig sales at York and home sales. I remember going up to Brown Brothers of Hepscott Manor, Northumberland, to their sale. Gilts made up to 250 guineas and boars to 200 guineas. We got "copped" for speeding, which rather dampened our day out.

One day we hired a car and had a day out visiting two famous Large White herds in Cheshire; JK Smith's Leighmile herd and Colton Latham's Brindeleyhall herd. We were rather inexperienced travellers and got lost. We ended up driving 380 miles, travelling into four counties and landed back at two o'clock in the morning! Here are some prices:

23rd January sold 25 hoggs dead weight, 3/5d per pound.

2nd February sold two fat heifers 2/5d per pound dead weight.

We were paying £9.11 shillings for Friesian bull calves.

1963

1963 will stand out for me as the longest and hardest winter of my life. I was shepherding and we were still cutting roots, which were just like cricket balls in the turnip cutter. The ground was that frozen you could hardly set nets. Our Williamsberg variety swedes were very small and we gave up trying to get them as a bad job. On January 10th we gave the sheep the whole field. It made life a lot easier for me. What a contrast weather can be on a sheepfold. I have known it to be wet and sticky. Now it was cold and clean. We had continuous hard frosts right through **January** and **February** into early March and when the snow came it blew about easily. The main road was blocked ever so many times. They had to get bulldozers in to open it out. We never opened up our farm road but just travelled across the fields. We finally dug our road out on the 7th and 8th of **March**. A lot of emergency supplies were taken by helicopter to outlying farms. I remember one flying some straw from John Edward Cook's High Baxtons, Helmsley, to George Robinson's at Potter House, East Moors. What a wonderful thing it is to have good neighbours! I often have it recorded that Will Wilson and Joe Garbutt from next door came to pull off tractors. I don't think we had heard of jump leads!

On the 25th March, Christopher and Hazel moved to Breck House, taking some stock ewes and lambs and some young cattle. Nicholas and I let them have some gilts cheaper. We started seedtime on 9th **April** and finished on 25th April. We helped Christopher plant his potatoes, a new experience for me. It was a backward spring and there seemed so much to do. Being a close-knit family we wanted to help Christopher all we could. Well we hired Bri Garbutt from next door for two days a week. Haytime was a mammoth undertaking. I think we had 120 acres, including Christopher's. We didn't have a baler and there weren't the good hay turners there are now. We had one grass cutter between us and we used to shuttle it between farms in the back of the van. We started haytime on 9th **July** and finished on 10th **August**. There wasn't much hay weather after the 5th August. Christopher finished haytime on the 17th **September**, the day we started to lead sheaves. We had started harvesting on the 5th September and finished on the 23rd **October**. This date seems rather late but there came a fine spell in the middle of October and we helped Christopher pick his potatoes first. It was quite an experience working up Bransdale. We got a bit of a taste of hill farming since we were used to level dry fields. There were hillsides and wet bog holes as we called them. I came to the conclusion that we mustn't begrudge the hill farmer's subsidies. He deserves all he gets.

Life is full of interesting experiences and things tend to go wrong rather than right. At that time we used to hire boar pigs from a Mr. Forsdike of Marton-cum-Grafton, Boroughbridge. One night we were coming home with one and our lights went dicky. We called at a garage and the chap said, "Don't use your headlights. Drive behind a wagon." We followed a wagon right to Thirsk. Then we switched on our headlights and they were as bright as normal. However they gradually faded and went out completely just as we got into our yard - providence was on our side. I got out and went to open the barn door but couldn't. The electric light wouldn't work either. I realised that the granary floor had come down, so went straight to the house and said "Is everybody in?" "Yes. Why?" said Mother. "Because the granary floor has come down!" Only the day before we had carried ten tons of corn up in sixteen stone bags and it was now all on the floor. What a job we had! We borrowed Mr. Fairburn's auger and sold most of the corn. It was quite some task sorting stones and mortar from the corn!.

Dad had a sale for Frank Featherstone in Farndale. Bullocks made up to £70. A grey mare made £45.

Here are some general prices I have written down:

6th March sold young Friesian bull at Otley Bull Sale, £71

8th April sold two boar pigs, £30 each.

Bought a load of wheat straw from Frank Wilson, 1s per bale.

1964

If anyone were to ask me what sort of a year 1964 was I don't think I should be able to tell them from memory. Nothing seems to stand out. In most of my records I have generally given a review of each year. This is what 1 wrote for 1964:

"One of the best years in living memory. Mild from Christmas to spring. Good seedtime. Good crops of hay and any amount of weather to get it in. Roots did exceptionally well under rather dry conditions. Harvest a bumper one, most of it done in a fortnight. A wet day very rare. Water in short supply".

We started seedtime on 7th **April** and finished on 13th April. We continued to help Christopher to plant and pick his potatoes and as we now had a baler we baled his hay. We started haytime on 25th **June** and finished on 29th **July**. This seems a long time, but what happened was this. We got all our hay baled and because it was such fine weather we left it out for a fortnight and concentrated on our root crop. As yet we had not used a precision drill and most of the roots were to hoe. They were growing like mad and had got very rank. We had to hoe alternate rows. Ted Peacock came to help us and said he could smell them growing! We all laughed at him. "It's true, it's true", he said and proceeded to tell us about his days hoeing on the Yorkshire Wolds.

We started harvest on 20th **August** and finished on 10th **September**. All the wheat and most of the oats were cut with the binder. I want at this point to mention two men, Lionel and Stephen Watson from East Moors who started to combine for us and did so for the next thirty years. They also did some of our ploughing, drilling, and other contract work.

Most farmers at that time would keep two or three breeding pigs and as word had got round that we were breeding boars, they would bring young gilts to be mated. We also kept a Billy goat as stud. All this made life rich and varied meeting up with so many different farmers.

There were a lot of reps calling in those days. There would be Peter Young of Bibby's, Mr. Hardy of Dobson's Lime, Mr. Stratchen of Clibrans Seeds, Alan Lawton from Silcocks and Alan Fenner of Cross Bone Fertilisers. Other reps would come from Bees Seeds, Nickerson's Seeds, Chapman and Freasons and Thomas Pettifer. One special traveller was Mr. Trevor Dodsworth from Bradshaws of Driffield. He had a wealth of experience in many things and you could set your clock by his coming. Even now, I still keep in touch with him. He's in his ninetieth year, a great historian and family man.

I also want to mention at this point George Breckon, another special man who has meant a lot both to me and to my wife Dorothy. On 18th March we went to George's farm sale. Why was George selling up when he was only in his mid-forties? He said to Dad, "Nobody understands me, Willie!" Dad said, "I do George. God has called you!" He was giving up farming to be an evangelist. Perhaps Dad knew quite a lot about George as he had taught him in Sunday school. George was a progressive farmer for a Dalesman, milking cows three times a day, a breeder of pedigree Large White pigs and one of the first Dalesmen to make silage. He had left Farndale to take on a larger farm in Pickering. He had only been there three years when he felt the call to give up in order to do evangelistic work. No one will ever know the impact this man has had for the Kingdom of God. I said to Dorothy on his funeral day, "I wonder what would have happened if George hadn't been obedient to the call of God!" Here are some prices:

29th January sold 12 pigs, weighed 79 pounds each sold for £9

22nd February sold hens 10 pence per Ib.

18th April sold boar pig thirty and a half guineas.

9th November bought 5 Dalesbred ewes from JB Liddle at £5.10s each

1965

This year was quite different from 1964. This is how I reviewed it:

"Coldish spring. Poor crop of lambs. Grass grew well considering dry
May and June. Fairly good haytime. Roots did well. Wet and very
difficult harvest. A good potato picking time. Very bad November.
Worst snowstorm in living memory. Altogether a very difficult year".

We started sowing on 2nd **April** and finished on 23rd April. We started haytime on 21st **June** and finished on 23rd **July**. We started harvest on 2nd **September** and finished on 27th **October**. It was a wet and muggy harvest. We had 20 acres of Capelle winter wheat. We cut half of it with the binder. I never knew corn sprout so fast and so much. We never got those sheaves properly dry. I remember there was a lot of dust on threshing day. Corn that was still standing was also sprouting. When we combined it, it was more like porridge than anything else. We had to poke it out of the combine tank. It set like concrete in the bags and even after we got it dried it had a sort of fermenting smell about it. Trevor Dodsworth said, "I'm a bit worried you won't find a buyer. I can't take it". However we did get it sold eventually. We still seemed to be short staffed. Bri Garbutt left us in August 1964 and again we helped Christopher at haytime and to plant and pick his potatoes.

I think it was the **November** snow that makes 1965 stand out. On 21st it was white over with snow. The 22nd was a snowy day and George Atkinson, our pig killer was knocked down by a car on Newgate Bank. On the 25th, the day of his funeral, it snowed and sleeted most of the day. On the 27th we had ten inches of snow on the level. This is what I recorded on the 29th:

"Terrible rough day, snowing and blowing. Christopher and Stan came for some rolled barley and got stranded on the way back up Rudland at George Bentley's. Two snow ploughs stuck up road to Bransdale. Had to make a lot of telephone calls to know where Christopher and Stan were. Six others from Bransdale were stranded with them. When they set off next morning to walk to Bransdale it was like a blizzard and when they arrived home they had icicles on their eyebrows".

After the dry year of 1964, two other things stand out. One was the water shortage in January 1965. It was the first time I can remember having to lead water. It was also the year when we altered the Bank Holiday. Prior to this it was always the first Monday in August. Now it was to be the last Monday! After the November snows one farmer said, "I blame altering the Bank Holiday. It has upset the weather!"

Here are some 1965 prices:

16th February sold 113 hens, 5/6d each.

19th May sold a gilt in pig. Beverley market £36/10s

August bought two Friesian heifer calves off Albert Robson £23 each

1966

This is how I reviewed 1966:

"Wet January and February. Very dry and cold March.
Terribly cold and wet April. Wettish May. Very moderate
June and July. A lot of poor hay got. Dullish August.
A good September. Harvest got in good condition- October
November and December very wet. Very poor year for farmers.
Store cattle and sheep very poor trade due to credit squeeze
brought out before back end sales".

We started sowing on 16th **March** and would have finished on 31st but we were held up for some seed oats. The land was already prepared and we had to wait until 26th **April** before we could sow them. I remember that there was a lot of flu around that winter. I had several days in bed and seemed to be in moderate fettle all summer. Sunshine is a wonderful thing. I remember the doctor saying, "What you need is some sunshine on your back!" Both 1965 and 1966 were sunless summers.

Changes came and our neighbours the Wilsons left Middle Heads. It was a sad day for me as over the years I'd been over there quite a lot and some nights went to watch television. Frank Wilson and Will used to play the melodeon and would entertain us with their wooden dancing doll. Their farm sale was on 23rd March and on 29th Nicholas helped with a ploughing day for our new neighbour Ray Skilbeck.

That year we had the most snow on 1st and 2nd of April. I went to an April Fools party at Nawton. A decent night when I set off but during the party we had a covering of snow. We had quite a job getting up out of Helmsley. When we got above Helmsley there was a lot more snow. I had Mike Kent and Trevor Speight with me and after taking them back home 1 couldn't get out of Rievaulx. I left the car and walked home in my low shoes over the fields.....a distance of about 2 miles. I can still hear the noise of my feet squelching in my wet shoes. I can tell you I was not only an April fool but I felt one as well!! I went to bed a very tired person only to awake to more snow. There had been quite a blizzard after I had gone to bed. Part of our main road was blocked. When it was snowy weather Mother would always ring my Uncle Fred up in Farndale to know what the weather was like up there. Uncle Fred told her that twenty people had been snowed out of Farndale and had to spend the night at Castleton. Derek Kendall's wedding had to be put off too. We started haytime that year on 30th June and finished on 19th August. We had sixteen acres of seeds wasted, no better than straw. We started harvest on 5th **September** and finished on 29th September. We only bindered eight acres of spring wheat and this took more getting than the other forty acres which we combined. This made us think. It was the last year of using the binder.

Things were beginning to change on the farm. It was the first year we used a precision drill for our roots, doing away with quite a bit of hoeing. Pigs and poultry were gradually being phased out and we were beginning to specialise in dairying. Prior to 1966 we had always milked 12 to 18 cows but this year we stepped them up to over thirty. It was quite hard work milking them through a twelve stall byre. There was no pipeline. All the milk had to be carried into the dairy.

54

There was some Foot and Mouth disease about that year and all the stock shown at The Yorkshire Show had a "stand-still" order put on it for a few days which meant that we couldn't exhibit at the Ryedale Show. All the livestock classes were cancelled at the Stokesley Show.

We still combined to help Christopher at haytime and to plant and pick his potatoes. We were still a bit short staffed and welcomed young lads who would come out from the village. Mike Kent came and helped us and our neighbour's son, George Hawkins would come and drive the tractor a bit. George once said "It's a dangerous spot to come to is New Leys. They always set you to work!"

Mother, being the hospitable person she was, always made people feel welcome. She didn't stand on ceremony but up to this time we didn't have a flush toilet and I think she felt a little embarrassed at the lack of this luxury - or necessity! - on visitors' behalf. She had been on at our agent for some years and finally said to him, "You will have to do something as we are having a French girl to stay. I think she might have a culture shock if she had to sit on a primitive toilet." The flush toilet was installed and the French girl, Sylvia Wantz arrived. She was a real grand girl and Judith still keeps in touch with her. She was with us coming back from youth club one night and the lights went out on the car. We had a torch in the front and Sylvia said, "No problem! No problem! I sit on ze front of ze car and shine ze light!" So she sat on the bonnet and we got going only to find that the wind blew her skirt up. That put an end to that!

Mother was convalescing that year following a hysterectomy, and after her operation she stayed for a few days with Alan and Addie Moss at Kirkbymoorside. We would go to see her and take her post. One day she received a letter from some solicitors in New Zealand. Mother made one of her usual remarks, "What in the world is this?" Addie Moss said, "You will have been left some money, Mary". Sure enough that was the case. John Thompson, whom I mentioned earlier on had left £100 each to Rievaulx and High Farndale chapels and £250 each to the Dunn children. We had no idea why he had remembered us in his will. All we could think of was that he did stay with us for several weeks, and when he went back Mother and I would write to him and he would tell me all about farming in New Zealand. I think he was quite a crack hand, as we say, at training sheep dogs because he always used to mention them in his letters. When he came over in the early 1950's there was quite a report about him in the Ryedale at Random column of the Malton Gazette and Herald and I quote:

"John Herbert Thompson born and bred in the moorland valley of Farndale and now at Whangarei, New Zealand, paid a visit to a slight relation, WH Dunn of New Leys farm on the occasion of Rievaulx Sunday school Anniversary. He scarcely expected to make the acquaintance of a fellow visitor from Down Under, Mr. Clifford Atkinson of Adelaide, Australia, who was born at Lydds Farm, Pickering.

Both Mr. Thompson and Mr. Atkinson were taking their first holiday in the mother country since they emigrated as young men more than forty years ago. For a short period last Sunday they recounted some of their experiences over a good tea in a North Riding farmhouse. A coincidence maybe but both these men have arranged a further meeting at the Great Yorkshire Show at Malton in July".

Uncle Jack Thompson as we called him told us round the table at New Leys that he now owned his own grazing farm of 250 acres on which he ran 300 sheep and fifty head of cattle. He was mainly engaged in the breeding of South Down cross Romney sheep. He clipped the lambs at between three and four months old and showed Dad and others a sample of the wool he had brought across with him. Uncle Jack said he emigrated at a good time and bought his farm out of his savings. He was asked how he favoured the British way of farming and replied that it was all work and no play. "We go in for more leisure out there!" He also said there was still ample opportunity for the emigrant who was prepared to work hard and rough it a little. "It is no use an emigrant thinking he is going to pick up pound notes in the big towns, but he will get on if he goes in the country and works hard. I worked hard but I was quite used to it in Farndale before I went out. I was well able to mow one and a half acres of oats a day in the Dale. I do not think I would care to settle in this country again. It is not that I would mind going back to Farndale but there are many other reasons. One is the climate. When it gets too cold I shall go back, though I would like to see some snow as I haven't seen any since I left forty years ago! New Zealand is the best country in the world. The farmer owns his own land and he is his own master. It is my home and I am proud of it!"

Author with his pedigree Saanen goat, Leith Rigg Larkspur, 1963

Our purchase from H.P.Dickinson. Sawdon Heights East Lass, 1961

Snow up Baxton Rigg, 1963

*Bulldozer used to clear roads 1963.
It not only cleared the roads, but
knocked down hedges and walls*

*Helmsley to Stokesley road, 1963. With
Ann Robson aged five*

*J.E.Cook from High Baxton on his
"Fordson Major" 1963*

Helicopter at "High Baxton" 1963

Chapter 9
Teens And Twenties

I well remember hearing a story about a lad whose school report wasn't over good. When he brought it home and gave it to his Dad, the lad could see it wasn't meeting with his approval. So the lad thought he had better get his spoke in first and said, "What do you think my problem is. Dad? Is it hereditary or environmental?" It is a fact that we are children of our parents and products of our environment.

Looking back, the Dunn teenagers lived rather sheltered lives. Life was centred round our work, the chapel, making our own entertainment and visiting relations more than we do now. Money was scarce. Neither Nicholas nor I had a wage. You worked hard and Dad paid for our clothes. Lodgings were thrown in and if you wanted anything to spend you asked Dad for it. We were always given what we needed not what we wanted! One thing we were never short of was petrol. Dad was always willing to fill the van up provided we were getting into the right company. Our parents' motto was, "Be good lads. Keep off drink. Keep yourselves straight". And this meant sex was for marriage. For three years after I left school we only had one vehicle, an Austin A60 van. We had plenty of drivers though and this meant we had to come to some compromise. Pleasing everyone was quite a difficult job at times. We would sometimes grumble at having to sit in the back of the van but a second class ride was better than a first class walk.

We were fortunate in our teens that the new minister at that time, Rev. Brian Shackleton, along with my cousin Donald Wass, formed a youth group in the circuit and it was around this that we made our social life. It was a regular thing for the next four or five years to take a van load of our family and neighbouring lads and lasses to the youth club at Nawton on a Friday night. We would have a good time playing table tennis, darts and draughts. Every youth club ended with an epilogue with some Christian input. We also began to meet in different club members' homes on a Sunday evening, calling it the Youth Squash, and it was a squash at times with thirty young people in a room for ten! We would have discussions and debates and invite various types of speaker. I quite liked being involved in the variety concerts we used to perform, all the proceeds going to charity - we were supporting the Freedom from Hunger campaign. Here we are forty years on and famine and hunger continue to be a problem in the third world. Our first concert was in January 1962 in Helmsley Scout Hut. It was an amateur building with amateur performers. The stage was made up of table tops balanced on top of some logs. I remember in the act I was involved in I stepped onto the stage and a table top flew up! Everybody laughed but me! In the Easter of 1962 we went round different chapels doing an Easter play. As usual there were funny experiences. One such happened at Rievaulx. Our main actor, Brian Shackleton, who was playing the devil shot out from behind a screen shouting "Chaos! Chaos! Can God create a world out of chaos?" and his false teeth fell out! He really did look like the devil and our organist, Annie Robinson, nearly fell off the organ stool with fright. Every month for a while we would go to a 'teen and twenty' concert in Kirkbymoorside Memorial Hall when other youth groups would come and perform. It was good, wholesome and cheap entertainment.

I think it is every young person's dream to get his or her driving test passed and to have the freedom of going off on their own. I remember having quite a struggle with my driving lessons, especially with the emergency stop. Tommy Tateson, my instructor, said to me, "When I tap on the front of this dashboard I want you to do an emergency stop." I was far too late. Tommy said, "I'm sorry. We've had a funeral and he's dead and buried". However I did manage to pass my test first time. Something I'm thankful for as cousin Audrey, who lodged with us, had passed the first time only the week before! I don't think I would have lived it down if I had failed.

Brian Shackleton was a man with original ideas and in the spring of 1963 he would have the youth club involved in some kind of mobile drama. Cousin Donald got their tractor and trailer rigged up and a cast went round several villages performing a play called 'Passion in Paradise Street' - kitchen sink religious drama! It appeared to me very professionally done, so much so that it appeared on the TV local news.

Over the years we had special nights when we would have a table tennis tournament or a talent concert. On some nights members were asked to give a five minute speech on some subject- I was very shy and nervous in those days and my first public speech was on keeping goats. Everyone laughed at me and forty years on they are still laughing at me. One night we had our local MP, Robin Turton. Another night we had a policeman and he would take our fingerprints. He said to me that if ever I landed up a criminal I would be good to tell by my prints as I had distinctive scars on my hands. We also had a series of first aid lectures given by local ambulance man, Noel Lishman.

In the May of 1963 we had a special visit to the circuit of two deaconesses from the Home Missions Department. On youth club and squash nights these two ladies would come and mingle amongst us and take the epilogues. I remember one night Sister Shirley Barker speaking clearly of what it meant to be a Christian and I felt God calling me to give my life to Him. The next week there seemed to be a tussle going on inside me and I felt very uneasy. We were planting potatoes in Bransdale and every time I had a spare moment I felt God compelling me to give my life to Him. The next Friday night I had a word with Sister Shirley. I realised I was a sinner, that Jesus loved me so much he died for me and that he was willing to forgive my sin. That night on 24th May 1963 I became a born again Christian, the most important day of my life.

I want at this point to make special mention of cousin Donald Wass who had a big influence on my life. It was his shining witness that encouraged me to become a Christian. Donald went on to become a Methodist minister. One never knows the potential you can have in a youth group. Out of Ryedale youth group came teachers, nurses, solicitors, local preachers, ministers. In 1990 one of our members was made Vice-President of the Methodist Conference followed in 2001 by becoming the President of the World Federation of Methodist and Uniting Church Women.

As we went to the District and National Congress we met up and made friends with other youth clubs and would ask them over to special youth weekends when we would have a social or walk on the Saturday night and a special service on the Sunday. We had visiting clubs from Ilkeston, Wakefield and Lower Wensleydale. Once at the District Congress we put on an act on the Saturday night concert and the President of Methodist Association of Youth Clubs, Reg Bedford,was that impressed he said he would like us to perform at the National Congress in London. I remember we did a dialect sketch, hand-written by myself. I said he would need an interpreter. Well my speech is still broad and there are lots of people who ask me to speak the King's English!

The National Congresses which were held in London were great occasions when youth clubs from all over Britain and the Channel Islands would meet for the finals of the five-a-side football and netball competitions. There would be a discussion on some topic on the Saturday morning, a concert on the Saturday night and a big service in the Albert Hall on the Sunday. It was great to be part of such a crowd of young people. Over the years it got to be quite well known that our local youth club did concerts and it was great to go round to the different places giving good, clean, humorous entertainment. I remember entertaining the British Legion in Helmsley and going to the disabled children at Welburn Hall School and the Multiple Sclerosis sufferers at Barmoor Lodge, Hutton-le-Hole. Other places we went were Masham, Sand Hutton, Sproxton, Stape, Rievaulx, Hawnby and Pickering, all for charity.

One of our favourite songs was one written by another minister, Arthur Windridge, for a District Congress in Hull. It was called "Ryedale in Spring" and sung to the tune of 'The Ash Grove'

Oh tell me my brothers, you lively young farmers
Who work from the dawn till dusk doth come in,
Why will you so labour
In shirts like pyjamas
For only a pittance
I count it a sin.

Oh go to the city and make you some money,
And find you a sweetie and buy her a ring.
For this is the challenge
That comes to young farmers
Oh stay you not lonely
In Ryedale in Spring!

We may not be 'Beatles' or even the 'Seekers',
We're not 'Pretty Things' and we're not 'Rolling Stones'
We can't cast a 'Shadow' or find ourselves 'Searchers',
We've all got our 'Animals' so we can't be those
We're the latest from Helmsley,
We're 'with-it' from Rievaulx,
We're the greatest from Farndale and also Fadmoor
We'll get in the charts boys
The top spot we're hitting
and then we will knock them
In Ryedale in Spring

From 1963 to 1965 we had three big money raising events for Methodist Association of Youth Clubs projects. Garden fetes were held at Nawton Towers, home of the Countess of Feversham, Abbott's Well, Rievaulx, home of Lady Marjorie Beckett, and at Ravenswick Hall, Kirkbymoorside, home of Major Holt. For several years at Christmas we would put on a party for old folks in Ryedale School, providing tea, games and entertainment. One year we had to put it off because of the snow and we would hold it the following Easter. Guess what? We nearly had to put it off again because of snow!! Yes, at Easter!.

We weren't always doing things for others. From time to time we would arrange club trips to the open-air theatre in Scarborough and trips to see films like 'Ben Hur'- I will never forget seeing those wonderful white horses. I remember when we got home there was a note on the table asking if we would fasten up the hens. I went to fasten them up only to find that the hen house slide had dropped down and all the hens were outside. We had quite a job getting them in and it put a bit of a damper on a good night out. We once took a bus load to a pantomime at Stockton when The Seekers singing group, at that time unknowns, were appearing. After that night I became a Seekers fan. I thought their singing and type of music was marvellous.

In 1965 we helped to form a youth club up at Fangdale Beck, Bilsdale, along with Freda Ainsley, catering more for a country type of young person. Again we would play games and have speakers. Stanley Carr from Sherburn came and gave a film on hunting and fishing. Wilf Dickinson from Sawdon, near Scarborough, came and gave us a talk on shot-guns, showing some of his marvellous collection. Susan Smith, a local lady from the Dale came and gave a hairdressing demonstration and said, "I will make this girl so beautiful that all the boys will want to take her home!" Again we made contact with other clubs and young people from Carlton-in-Cleveland, Scorton near Richmond and Snape near Bedale.

By now we had managed to run a car and a van but we gave Dad and Mam priority with the car. We used to pack young people in the back of the van, like sardines in a tin. One night we had twelve in, more heavy-weights than light-weights, and ran out of petrol coming up Newgate Bank. What a performance we had pushing our old A60 van up the hill! We eventually got to the top and free-wheeled a bit. Providence was on our side. A passing motorist stopped and had some spare petrol in a can. A wiser man than we were! It's surprising how the news got around because the next week in Helmsley a chap said to me, "Is Methodists so greedy they can't put petrol in now? Are they expecting their vehicles to run on nowt?"

In 1969 we had a 'do' as they say, putting on a concert up at Chop Gate village hall, We had hardly as good a talent as the Ryedale club but we did our best. Three fellows dressed up as ladies would sing this song which brought the house down. It was called 'Three Old Maids' and went as follows to the tune of 'Three Blind Mice.'

Three old maids, three old maids
Why we don't know, why we don't know.
I'm the eldest, I'm sixty-three
For years a bride I've longed to be

But none of the fellows would look at me
We're three old maids.

I'd like a man with plenty of cash.
I'd like a man with plenty of dash.
I'd like a man with a little moustache
We're three old maids.

I wanted the butcher who lives down our street.
He took her home from a Sunday school treat.
She wanted his heart but he gave her pig's feet.
We're three old maids.

I went to keep-fit class to try to get thin.
I bought a pump roller to massage my skin
But still she comes out where she ought to go in.
We're three old maids.

I asked Will Featherstone to think of a plan.
I've got seven and six and all I want is a man.
I'm going to be labelled an also-ran.
We're three old maids.

I proposed to Wilf Lynas, I gave him a scare.
I told Arnold Leadley he was my maiden's prayer.
I'd ask Stan Carter if only I'd dare.
We're three old maids.

And so to the audience we make our last plea.
Do you know a man who'd take pity on me?
In fact we'd be grateful for one between three!
We're three old maids.

Our priorities began to change and we attended both youth clubs less. Perhaps it was because we were no longer young people. Deep down inside myself there was a hunger going on. To quote Pastor George Breckon "we were hungry for God"

RYEDALE METHODIST YOUTH GARDEN FETE

July 1963

Members of the Ryedale Methodist Circuit Youth Club at their garden fete at Nawton Tower on Saturday. — (G & H)

Garden fete, July 1963

Cousin Donald Wass's wedding 1963

THEATRE ON WHEELS. Fourteen scattered villages on the North Yorkshire Moors will see this theatre on wheels. It has been built by members of Ryedale, North Yorkshire, Methodist youth club on an agricultural trailer. Yesterday they started towing it round the villages. They are presenting " Passion in Paradise Street," by P. W. Turner. It was described by the Minister, the Rev. Brian Shackleton, as " kitchen sink religious drama." Proceeds will go to the Freedom from Hunger Campaign. The players hope to raise £50.

Members of Ryedale Methodist Youth Club in their Easter-week half-hour play, Passion in Paradise Street, which they presented on their tractor-towed trailer. With pyjama dressed collectors (in foreground) they toured villages in the Ryedale area at Easter, raising money for the Freedom from Hunger Campaign.—G & H).

Youth squash, early 1970's

Chapter 10
Hungry For God

There is an old saying that it's your company that determines your character. We were blessed that a group of us, with plenty in common, knocked about together. In particular we were all hungry for God. We were all farmers and hadn't as much money as other young people but we never begrudged ourselves money on petrol. Mother used to say, "You don't smoke or drink, so don't deny yourselves money for petrol." There was my brother, Nicholas, John Mattison and Arthur Bennison from Bilsdale and George Moules from Hawnby. Eventually all three gave up farming to take a new direction in life. John went to Bible College and afterwards went to be a mechanic with the Church Missionary Society in Uganda. Arthur went to live with Jim and Cynthia Wilkinson and became a key man at Hollybush Fellowship. George went for a year to Cliff College, did a lay pastorship term at several churches and then went to help John in Uganda, later going on to do missionary work in Pakistan.

In May 1966 I noticed an advert in the Darlington and Stockton Times that there were special centenary services being held at Houghton-le-Side Chapel, near Darlington. The special preacher was Tom Butler from Sheffield. I suggested to the rest of the gang that we have a run up. We went, and the chapel was packed, mainly with young people and we had to sit in the pulpit. We met a man called Fred Sowerby, the main leader there and he was on fire for God. Once a month in the nearby village hall they had special rallies. They would have a gospel beat group or folk singing group and an evangelistic preacher. For the next few years we would go to these meetings and Fred Sowerby came down and preached at the opening of our new Sunday School. Fred was a real live wire and I always said it was a good job we extended the pulpit - the old one couldn't have contained him.

In June 1966 a group of us went down to London with Lorne Wilkinson to hear Billy Graham. On coming back, Lome said to me, "What you lads need is to get into a Bible Study". So we met at Lorne and Mary's home periodically for this purpose. Tom Butler had a crusade in Northallerton and we went over a lot and were blessed by these meetings.

On January 1st 1967 I remember listening to the Sunday Half Hour Singing on the wireless. It was from an Elim Pentecostal Church and I had never heard singing like it. It was live and real. I was warned to keep clear of these Pentecostals - as being extreme and way-out; emotional and clap-happy people.

How mistaken can one be?! 1 realised they had something I hadn't. They were filled with the fullness of the Holy Spirit.

Travel is a wonderful thing and especially when you are meeting God's people. We would travel all over. If there was a Cliff Mission we would be there to support it whether it be Pateley Bridge or Pocklington. In those days we were young and daft. I am still daft but no longer young. Time of day didn't bother us then. Once we went to a Cliff Mission at Westhouse near Carnforth and our car broke down between Ingleton and Hawes. We arrived back next morning at 6 o'clock just in time to start milking. Another time Arthur and I went to Hesketh Bank near Southport to support Tom Butler. Arthur was a real night hawk, in other words he hadn't the sense to get back home. That night we landed back at 2.30 in the morning and Arthur came in and sat on with me until 5 o'clock and then let me go to bed. Because of that day John Mattison said "I have a text for you Arthur, 'Don't stay in your neighbour's house till he grows weary of thee'" It has often been one of my favourite quotes. When I have gone visiting people I always try to make a point of not outstaying my welcome.

We would also from time to time travel in to York to the Bible studies at St. Michael's church, taken by David Watson. In July we would try and have a day out at the Keswick Convention and in September we would occasionally have an evening at the Christian Holiday Crusade at Butlins Holiday Camp, Filey. As a result we were getting contacts for good speakers and singing groups to come to take our Saturday night meetings at Rievaulx. Somebody said to me once, "How on earth do you get to hear about all these groups and speakers?"

At Rievaulx some very talented groups led meetings, for example the Paul Brecht singers from Hull, the Wesleyan Gospel Beat Group from Newcastle, and the Heralds from Gateshead. I often think that if these groups hadn't been Christian they would have been very popular in the night clubs and show scene. It has been great to hear over the years of people who have been challenged, blessed and helped through these meetings. One such lad was Paul Wells who came over from Danby. One night he was challenged in one of these meetings and as a result went to be a student at Cliff College and stayed for a number of years on the staff as an evangelist. I remember a group of us taking a bus load down to hear Billy Graham in 1989 and one of the chief leaders and organisers was Paul Wells. At times we sometimes have to encourage ourselves, and I said to our group "Did you know that the start of Paul's discipleship was in Rievaulx chapel?" We never know what influence we can have.

Neither myself nor Nicholas had any holidays until 1967 but from then on we took it in turns having a week off in alternate years to go to the Derwent convention at Cliff College. Here again we met a lot of people. We got good practical teaching and it was good to hear Bible studies taken by men like Maurice Barnett, Reg Walker, Alf Lawson, Ken McDougall and Don English.

In May 1969 we started going over to some meetings at Hollybush Farm, near Thirsk, led by a farmer called Jim Wilkinson. There have been two books written about this fellowship, and they tell a remarkable story. In 1968 Jim felt led to buy Hollybush farm, and start a fellowship there. Jim and his wife Cynthia had had a second blessing from God and were eager to share it with others. They are a lively charismatic group and when I first went I was very put off as they were too lively and noisy for me. In fact I said this scene isn't for me, I will never go again.

My tune had to change because in the June of 1969, we had a visit from a team of Cliff College students to the Circuit. At the final meeting the student preacher spoke from Acts 19:2 'Have you received the Holy Spirit since you believed?' I remember after the meeting talking to Esther Dennis from Burythorpe who I regard as a very balanced Christian. I asked her, "What do you make of this Holy Spirit business? At Hollybush they seem to put a lot of emphasis on speaking in tongues". Esther said, "I speak in tongues but I wouldn't get carried away with that particular gift. Follow your Bible and you won't go far wrong". This was good advice.

The next month I went to Cliff College to the Derwent Convention. An unknown speaker to most of us, Rev. Ken McDougall, took the Bible studies and his emphasis was on the Holy Spirit. I knew there were areas of my life that God needed to deal with. I entered into the chorus singing and teaching and the fellowship of other Christians. On the final night he issued a challenge - are you going away a better person than you came? I wasn't. He said "There are lots of people who need God to deal with their lives. You can come out for ministry or have a word with a cousellor or you can sort it out on your own." I went into the chapel at Cliff College and got hold of the Methodist hymn book, turned to number 559 and read:

Come O my God the promise seal
This mountain sin remove
Now in my fainting soul reveal
The virtue of thy love

I want thy life, thy purity
Thy righteousness brought in
I ask, desire and trust in thee
To be redeemed from sin

Anger and sloth, desire and pride
This moment be subdued
Be cast into the crimson tide
Of my redeemer's blood

Saviour to Thee my soul looks up
My present saviour thou
In all the confidence of hope
I claim the blessing now

'Tis done Thou dost this moment save
With full salvation bless
Redemption through thy blood I have
And spotless love and peace

Nothing spectacular happened but a tremendous peace came over me and I was given victory over sins that had bound me. Some people might call it the baptism of the Spirit or the second blessing, or being filled with the fullness of God. Terminology doesn't bother me. I began to read my Bible more and wait upon God in prayer. It is wonderful how in the late sixties and early seventies Renewal spread through most of our main line denominations. I am a firm believer that no denomination can contain the whole truth and every denomination has their own particular and precious emphasis. I have often quoted this "All word and you dry up, all Spirit and you blow up, but if you have the word and the Spirit you grow up".

Things started to happen in our Saturday night meetings and I could sense no matter what area I travelled in that there was a wave of spiritual renewal abroad. I had at this point done quite a lot of local preaching and I eventually became a fully accredited local preacher in 1970. Opportunities to preach came my way from this time until the mid eighties in the circuit and in North Yorkshire and South Durham. I took quite a few specials like Chapel Anniversaries and Harvest Festivals in the Lancaster area. I believe it was a season in my life. From the mid eighties opportunities to preach outside the circuit declined, and it was just as well. I had the responsibility of being a circuit steward and had a wife and family to look after. It is great to look back and think of all the lovely Christian people I have met, some who became lifelong friends. Denominations have never bothered me. I have had the opportunity of preaching among most denominations including Baptists, Comgregationalists, Pentecostal, Free Evangelical, Anglican, Salvation Army and Brethren.

I have mentioned Cliff College quite a lot in this chapter. Where is this place and what is it? It is situated in the Peak District of Derbyshire, not far from Chatsworth House. It is a Methodist lay training college and was raised up to train lay people for a year so that they would be better equipped for Christian service, to go back to their local churches (though alot of students do go on to be full time Christian workers.) Even though Cliff is Methodist based it is interdenominational, and there is always a sprinkling of students from other main line denominations and other countries

What was the reason for me taking a year out of farming and going there? I believe God called me. How do I define a call? In 1967 I attended the Derwent convention and felt that God was calling me to be a student. I remember talking to a counsellor, Norman Herbert, and he said, "If God wants you at Cliff, He will see that you get there in His own time". From that time I began to pray a lot about this, but I never believed God would open the way. We were struggling financially on the farm and I think if the truth were known. Mother didn't want me to leave home. Parents can sometimes be a bit possessive. People would say to me, "Have you ever thought about having a year at Cliff?" Well God has ways of giving us a nudge. In September 1971 I happened to be in a fellowship meeting at Lorne and Mary Wilkinson's and a man was leading it. I had only met him once before. He said to me, "I feel I have a word from the Lord for you, that in the future you will become a full time disciple". I wondered what this meant. Did it mean I had to offer for the full time ministry? The word was a word of prophesy. The Apostle Paul said, "Despise not prophesy but test all things". I shared this prophesy with Esther Dennis and again she gave me sound words of advice: "Don't do anything in a hurry, the Lord will reveal it to you in His own time". To cut a long story short I applied and was accepted, and on 15th September 1973 I set foot in Cliff College as a student. In fact there were three others from our circuit who went with me: Celia Bowes and Peter Jackson from our own chapel at Rievaulx and Stephen Heath from Kirkbymoorside.

I remember Mam and Judith took me, and when they said goodbye I cried my eyes out. It was a new experience for me, I had never been away from home for any length of time before. Mam said, "You will be alright honey" and I settled in straight away. It was good to mix with such a cross-section of people of all ages and all occupations. It was good to see life from another's perspective whether that person was a nurse, teacher or social worker. There was also a mixture of overseas students which was an added ingredient in the life of the college, along with a sprinkling of farmers and it was two of these, Bill Cornall and Jim Hutchinson from the Lancaster area, who became my closest friends.

Our day at Cliff began with a rising bell at 6.45. We all met at 7.45 in the college chapel for morning prayers and devotions taken by a different student every morning. After breakfast it was lectures all morning consisting of Old and New Testament, Theology and General Studies, which included Sociology and Comparative Religions. Our afternoons were spent with private study and writing essays. On a Tuesday and Thursday afternoon it was manual work varying between gardening, domestic work and library work. Saturday morning was also a manual time and we were free on a Saturday afternoon. I used to go and cheer along the college football team and I went ice skating in Sheffield occasionally.

College life was very full as it was quite a hectic programme. Tuesday night was the prayer meeting. Thursday night was the class meeting. Friday night we had an outside speaker followed by house groups. Sunday could be a very busy day if you were out preaching. If you weren't out preaching it was an opportunity to go to visit and worship at other churches in the area.

Preaching has always played an important part in the training at Cliff. On a Thursday morning a student who was training to be a preacher would lead a service and preach a sermon. This would be examined later in the day by students and tutors. It was called the sermon clinic. One of the questions that had to be asked was, "Did the preacher speak clearly?" I remember when I did my sermon and they discussed this, everyone laughed as I have a rather broad Yorkshire accent. Howard Belben the Principal encouraged me by saying, "We do take regional accents into consideration, and I think you are a preacher full of promise Paul".

Evangelism and mission played an important part at Cliff. There were three missions a year. One Autumn weekend mission in late October I went to Moston Manchester. They were warm hearted people the Mancunians. There was the 10 day Pre-Easter Mission when I went to Northwich in Cheshire and the monthly Summer Mission which found me in Melton Mowbray in Leicestershire and Grantham in Lincolnshire. At all these places we endeavoured to spread the good news about Jesus whether it was through children's meetings, schools work, house groups, open-air services or rallies.

One of the wonderful things about mixing with God's people is that you make friends and I still keep in contact with some of the people I met whilst on mission at Northwich and Melton Mowbray.

Evangelism isn't easy. We are in a battle. I remember going into a youth club. Most of the kids 10 years and upward smoked, were abusive and fought one another. Another time a gang of rough lads came in who had police convictions. We couldn't get rid of them, so we invited them to stay, while we had a prayer time. They stayed and made fun of us. In one of the corners was a box of cauliflowers and they were throwing them at us. However we kept praying until after midnight. They eventually left and I'm glad to say nothing was damaged. A very hair-raising experience.

One never knows the good we can do when we sow the seed of God's word. I remember being on mission and I felt we had wasted our time. Nothing seemed to be organised by the church and nothing seemed to go right. However, a year later I met up with a lad who was then studying at Cliff and he recognised me and said, "Do you remember you and your team from Cliff coming into our youth club? It was after you had spoken that I decided to become a Christian".

We must never forget in the church, whatever our denomination, the gift of the evangelist. Methodism owes a great debt to the following Cliff evangelists: Herbert Silverwood, Tom Butler, Ernie Steel, Malcolm Pears, Alec Passmore and Sandy Roger.

A picture of Cliff wouldn't be complete without mentioning the Celebration Weekend, held at Spring Bank Holiday, and the Derwent Convention held the last week in July. Celebration Weekend is a gathering of thousands of Christians who come to hear some of the great preachers of the day, men like Billy Graham, David Pawson, David Watson and Arthur Blessit, not forgetting past students who have become great preachers like Paul Smith, Steven Wilde and Rob Frost. The Derwent Convention is a much smaller gathering of people for a teaching week, and I owe a great debt to past Derwent Conventions I've attended.

While I was a student at Cliff it was hard to forget my love of farming and I would regularly go down to Farmer Dalton's who farmed next to the college and have a look at his Farmers Guardian. I remember myself, Bill and Jim at the Newark Agricultural Show. When we approached the car park we found people selling entrance tickets at half price. Being a Yorkshireman I was out for the cheap, but we realised afterwards they were fake tickets. Our Christian conscience worked on us and I had to inform the officials who were extremely grateful for this. This fake ticket business had been going on for several years.

Both Bill, Jim and myself would talk about farming and would share what was happening on one another's farms. Bill had been talking to his Dad and they wanted a Teeswater tup. I said in my customary salesmanship style that we had some good ones and could fix them up. One Saturday we came up home and had a look at them and Bill bought one. Word got out at college that we had been up home and that I had sold a tup to Bill. Ever after that we were named the Tup Farmers. We had some good laughs quite often at my expense. I got put into the bath fully clothed on my birthday. At the college Christmas concert we three farmers did an auction mart scene, me acting as the auctioneer. I trust it wasn't a reflection on our manners but the table in the dining hall where us farmers sat was nicknamed 'the trough'. If there was any spare food it was always 'take it to the trough, they'll help to eat it.'

We also had good fun at a sponsored snip when four students would sacrifice their beards for charity. I said "Before we start we must do it in Cliff style and sing a chorus". So I wrote the following words sung to the old chorus tune 'Rolled Away': 'Snip away, snip away and the hairs of their beards snipped away. Every hair, has to go 'neath the shaving flow, Hallelujah, snip away, snip away and the hairs of their beards snipped away'.

We had our happy and humorous times. We had our serious and sad times. One of the saddest things was when an overseas student went missing. Several of us with the Police and a Peak District National Park warden spent three or four days combing the countryside around Cliff with no clues whatsoever of his whereabouts. Several years later his body was found in a wood quite near Cliff. What we think happened was that he had been suffering from Malaria. When Africans get it they go into the bush country to rest. This student had gone out and being the winter months had died of hypothermia. I'm still mystified that we didn't find him, as he was relatively near the college.

One of my greatest surprises was when I was voted in the last term to be the college chairman, a job I felt inadequate to do. I followed two outstanding chairmen and had a sleepless night or two worrying that I couldn't do the job. Well, God reassured me through His word and the encouragement of a fellow student who said, 'Be yourself, that's all that matters, you are the man for the job'. Being the college chairman taught me a lot about people, leadership, and myself and the running of the college. I look back on my year at Cliff with gratitude, for many things. Firstly to Dad and Nicholas for holding the fort on the farm back home. For the fellowship and encouragement of my fellow students. To the Principal and his wife, Howard and Jean Belben. To the tutors.

Dr. Skevington Wood and David Sharp. To God for providing my material needs, as the college fees were paid in full by the North Riding Education Committee. We are all as Christians called to be disciples. I remember very well David Sharp saying in one of his lectures that to be a disciple is to be a learner. It suddenly clicked with me that the prophesy I had been given in 1971 had come true. I had been a full time learner. I didn't feel any particular call to any full time Christian service. I was the tenant of our farm back home and felt that was the place where God wanted me to be.

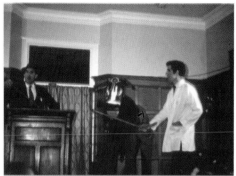

Christmas concert at Cliff College. The farmers auction market scene, 1973

Fun time, sponsored snip, January 1974

How would you like to spend your holiday in these huts. They were used at Cliff College from after the war till 1973, happy memories of pillow fights

Here I am giving my chairman's speech, at the prize giving, Cliff College June 1974

Coach park at the Cliff College anniversary 1974. The mode of transport has since changed, people now come in cars

A drama scene on mission, Northwich, Cheshire. Easter 1974 (Author 4th from right)

Tom Butler, a man God greatly used at Cliff College

Our beloved principal and his wife, Howard and Jean Belben, at the Christmas meal 1973

THE METHODIST CHURCH

CLIFF   COLLEGE

This is to certify that

Paul S Dunn

has completed a full-time one-year course of study at the College

has satisfied the External Examiners in the following **four** subjects

Old Testament
New Testament
Theology
General Studies

and has taken part in the following

Manual Work
Missions
Preaching
Social Work

Howard Belben

PRINCIPAL

Certificate No. *335* Dated this *4th* day of *August* 19*74*

CLIFF COLLEGE · CALVER · SHEFFIELD

My Cliff college certificate

78

Our year at Cliff 1973-74

79

Cliff College present day

Chapter 11
1967 - 1970
The Beginning Of Modernisation

1967 was a very good farming year on the whole in this locality. Not so good in others, especially up west. In the Penrith area a lot of crops were never harvested. Cheshire, Shropshire and Derbyshire were hit by a terrible Foot and Mouth epidemic. There were over two thousand cases and a stand-still order on all movement of animals from the beginning of November1967

A very mild winter, dry **February** and **March**, fairly wet **April** and terribly wet **May**. It dried up all at once, making fallows hard to work. There was a dry June, July, August and September, good harvest weather. October was very wet, November reasonably dry. December was reasonable. The pound was devalued.

We started sowing corn on 15th March and finished on 11th **May** with some turnip land. We had our last threshing day and I would say it was one of the last in the district. In a way it was rather sad as threshing tended to be a bit of a social occasion as well, when you got some chat with your neighbours and a general talk about what was going on. On the other hand I wasn't sorry as I was usually in the caff hole and it was a mucky, dusty job! I think if the Health and Safety men had been around they would have ordered everybody to wear a dust mask.

On the 29th April that year we opened our new Sunday School room at Rievaulx on a brilliant, warm, springlike day. Two days later it was as cold as winter with a covering of snow.

I have recorded that on 26th May, Dad, Nicholas and I went down to the bank to sign a partnership agreement. It was no longer W.H. Dunn but W.H. Dunn and Sons.

That year we started to spray some of our corn for weeds. Thistles were the biggest problem. In odd fields where they weren't too bad, Dad would hoe them out. The term we used to describe this was "looking" corn. I suppose this word was used because you were looking over your corn. It wasn't the pleasantest of jobs, stooking or loading sheaves that were full of thistles.

We started haytime the 17th **June** and finished the 10th **July**. It was good weather for harvest. We started the 30th **August** and finished on 14th **September**, all but the four acres which had been sown late. This was combined on 29th September and taken straight to Peter Young's of Pickering where it was dried and sold to him. Unfortunately he went bankrupt and we got very little for it. I think half a crown in the pound was paid out. As far as I can remember we have been very fortunate as that was the only case when we were "let in" for money.

This was the first year we didn't grow wheat and the first year we sowed a smaller acreage of oats. We started to store some of our corn in polythene bags. We were told you could put it in these bags at any moisture. One day we started combining. The corn wasn't fit but it was interesting to see other combines from neighbouring farms come out. The moral is don't follow your neighbour, he might be crackers, and we were that day ! One of the regular jobs, I think twice a week, was washing the milking machine. It meant taking all the rubbers off and giving them a scrub with hot water and detergent. We weren't pestered in those days with red tape and officialdom like we are today. Two things have been done away with that happened then. One was the ministry men coming to pass stirks for a headage subsidy. The other was an inspector who had to come and inspect a bull or boar pig to license it worthy to be used for stock breeding purposes.

We still continued to help Christopher with haytime and planting and picking potatoes. Another interesting thing this year was Judith going to Germany on V.S.O. For those unacquainted with these initials it meant Voluntary Service Overseas. Well, Nicholas and I were on V.S.A.H. - voluntary service at home!

With the Wilsons leaving Middle Heads Farm, I had further to walk to watch television, to Uncle Fred's and Aunt Lizzie's further along the valley. So we decided, rather reluctantly on Dad and Mam's parts, to get a television. Old Amos who writes in the Dalesman said most of man's inventions were time-savers. Then he invented television, which is a great time-waster. Another time I heard a character say, 'There used to be family circles. Along came television and now we have semi-circles." Television has done a lot of harm in degrading marriage and family life. It has also done a lot of harm to the farmer and butcher by blowing things out of all proportion with food scares. On the other hand it has made us more informed and a lot of people appreciated the series "The Dying Breed" in which I was involved. More about that later. I always appreciated good Christian worship on TV - at the end of the day they were invented with a knob and we can turn them off as well as on.
Here are some prices:
1st May: sold 10 Masham hoggs and their lambs to Tom Spence, Brompton, these made £12.10s for each hogg and lamb pair.

1968
This is how I reviewed 1968. Quite a good farming year in this locality. Very poor in others. Very mild January and February and March. A good seedtime. It was cold and dry the backend of April and the beginning

of May. There was a warm wet spell, shifting grass. Then another dry spell until 10th June. We had a shocking haytime, which took up the backend of July and the beginning of August. The backend of August and the first fortnight of September there was good harvest weather. A very mild and wet backend.

The 14th and 15th **January** were terribly windy days. A stack of our hay bales blew over and there was a lot of damage done in Glasgow. When you get a lot of westerly winds it's generally a sign of an open winter. On **February** 4th it was snowing and blowing all day. Whitby was completely cut off and Shap Fell was blocked. We started seedtime on 14th **March** and finished on 11th **April**. I remember haytime was a wet catchy time. We started on 13th June and finished on 1st August. We had been going seven weeks. It must have been a wet time, as we had three attempts to sow our soft turnips. John Aconley from Brecks Farm, Pockley, used to sow them with his precision drill. His first two attempts were on 22nd and 25th June and he finally got them sown on 1st **July**. These turnips must have grown fast as we scruffled them ten days later. On 2nd July I was working in our stackyard when within minutes it came in very dark, almost like night. It was the darkest I have ever known in daytime. A storm had brewed up on the west coast and was bouncing across the country. It caught the Ripon area the worst. It was so dark that people thought the world was coming to an end. There was a terrific hailstone shower and the area was white over. The hailstones were as big as marbles and stripped the leaves off potato crops, the heads off corn and in some cases crops were ruined.

We started harvest on 27th **August** and finished combining on 14th **September**. I remember it was a very backward time up the east coast. Whitby and Filey areas had a lot of sea-fret. Dad went to Egton Show on 29th August. The sea-fret was so heavy he was almost soaked through and when he got home he could hardly believe his eyes to see us combining in brilliant sunshine. The corn was rattling nicely which meant it was dry. We grew a variety called Vada which dried up easily. You had to think about such things when you hadn't a drier. All the corn was still stored in bags, either polythene or hessian, except for a small tonnage that was augered into a store near the mill. As we began to keep more cattle, we needed more straw and bought quite a lot out of the swath down Nunnington way, all to be carted home in little bales. We had a massive stack the length of the Dutch barn and it was quite a job keeping the water out. Whatever people tell us, you can't beat having your fodder in a shed. A bit of good threshed wheat straw was the best for thatch. Without it we had to use Polythene sheets which were expensive, and hard to keep on the stack in windy weather

For several years we as a family always went up Bransdale to Christopher and Hazel's for Christmas dinner. This year it was just like spring, mild and with the sun shining. Dad said, "There's an old saying, 'If the sun shines through the apple trees before dinner on Christmas Day we are in for a fine harvest'" Mother said, "Watch out, my nose end is a bit cold, we could be in for some snow" Sure enough, two days later on 27th it was snowing and blowing. 28th **December** had been a rough night. Most roads were blocked on the Wolds and round here. We had no milk away and no postman. On 29th December we had eighteen inches on the level. It had been an abnormally mild backend and the council men hadn't even thought of putting snow ploughs on and this, doubled with the fact that it was bank holiday, meant they were very unprepared. On 30th December we managed to get two days milk away. It was around that time that the American spacemen came down from circling the moon- Joe Bowes said that he blamed them for all the snow!

Dad had a sale for John Ward up Snilesworth in the middle of December. In that sale was an old trumpet which we bought for an antique dealer. For some reason we took it up Bransdale on Christmas day. Our nephew, Simon, was only five but he could blow this trumpet like a man. In fact he was more interested in this trumpet than all the toys Father Christmas had brought him!

We continued to work hard on our farm. Our cow numbers were up to forty, still milking through the byre. The collecting yard was a very unhygienic affair as it didn't have a concrete floor. We only cleaned it when we were forced. It soon became smelly migg. I remember slipping in it one day and I thought about the song cousin Donald Wass used to sing in our youth club concerts: "Mud, mud, glorious mud! There's nothing quite like it for cooling the blood. So follow me, follow, down to the hollow and there let us wallow in glorious mud!" We rectified this by using five loads of ready-mixed concrete, and concreting the adjoining shed to the byre and an area outside. It was grand to have a sweep-up every day even though it was a brush and shovel and barrow job!

Mike Kent had now left school so Trevor Speight out of the village took his place. I don't think I knew anybody as strong for his age. Dad set him on one day to dig a soak-away out of solid rock and he did it! He was only thirteen. We were still managing to work the farm mainly on our own, except that David Dowkes from Bilsdale came an odd day now and again.

I seemed to have quite an eventful year with my goats. I sold a newly kidded one on 20th January for £14. One day I had two racehorse trainers here wanting to buy a goat. They had a very good horse that wouldn't settle and they had been told that if you put a goat in with it that would do the trick. They bought one and sure enough it worked! I don't know if the horse won any races - horse racing was something I could never get interested in. Granddad Dunn used to have a saying, "Fast women and slow horses have beggared many a man". I decided to get rid of my goats and took some to a show and sale at Pannall Mart, Harrogate. I remember topping the sale for an in-milker at sixteen guineas.

Friendship is a wonderful thing. I don't think you will have problems making friends, providing you take an interest in people and don't bore them with your own talk. I want at this point to mention two families who feature in my 1968 diary. Firstly the Jacksons of Cottingham, near Hull. They happened to be camping at Rievaulx, came to chapel and Mam and Dad asked them over for supper. This was the start of our friendship. Peter, their son, who was twelve at the time, eventually worked on a nearby farm when he left school, and later went with me to Cliff College. Peter is now a policeman on Teesside and we are still close friends. The other two people I want to mention are Bill and Jean Cowley from Potto in Cleveland. This friendship goes back a long time before Mother was married. Bill was a hiking enthusiast and one day he was hiking up Farndale and happened to be coming through the yard at Horn End. It was a really hot day and his tongue was hanging out - he was as thirsty as a fish. He knocked at the farm door and asked would they be so kind as to give him a glass of water. They invited him in and he ended up having a lunch of roast rabbit and bacon. Bill was what we called an educated sort of a person, not backwards at coming forwards. After studying at Cambridge University and working overseas in India, he eventually went into farming in the Cleveland area. He was in great demand as an after-dinner speaker. Bill did quite a lot of broadcasting on the North Countryman programme and latterly the Northern Farmer. He interviewed Dad twice for this programme. Bill was also a regular contributor to "The Dalesman" magazine and was very interested in Yorkshire dialect, writing several books on this subject. He was an enthusiastic member of the Yorkshire Dialect Society and I remember him coming with some Finnish friends to tape record me and Dad. Perhaps he is best known in the Cleveland area for being the founder of the Lyke Wake Walk in 1955.

Here are some prices:

16th July went to York Friesian sale. Top price bull 300 guineas
Top price heifer 210 guineas.
23rd September sold Teeswater tup lamb £25
4th October bought 20 Dalesbred ewes at Bentham £9. 7s. 6d each
Stock number Christmas 1968:
3 fat bacon pigs; 7 goats; 138 breeding ewes; 50 gimmer hoggs;

160 fat hoggs and fat ewes in sheepfold; 6 tups; 43 dairy cows
and 67 followers. In comparison to ten years ago the poultry had been
completely phased out, the pigs nearly, but the cattle numbers were up.

1969

This is how I reviewed 1969. This was a disastrous year for many farmers due
to the excessive wet. A lot of land on heavy clay was never sown, but due to a
remarkably fine summer this was fallowed. On some hill farms up to 40 per cent
of sheep went down owing to the snowy, blashy wet weather. A lot of ewes died
on the lowlands with Fluke Liver disease. A special plea was made to the
Ministry of Agriculture to give a fallow subsidy to those who could not sow
their crops, mainly in Yorkshire and Lincolnshire.

To move on to a more cheerful note. This was not a bad year at all in our
locality. Corn yield was average, about thirty hundredweight to the acre. Roots
did extremely well. It was a very good summer for milk, although flies bothered
the cows and there were a lot of sore teats. In some areas it was a bad year for
summer mastitis. We had a very good crop of lambs but then lost a lot. The end
total wasn't too bad. Cows were a good trade, calves and stores moderate, sheep
fair and pigs very good.

We dug our road out on 3rd **January** and it was mild and wet until 7th
February when it started to snow and blow. There was a keen frost the morning
of the 8th, the day of David March's sale at Featherholme, Bilsdale. I remember
the auctioneer saying, "Bid sharp, gentlemen, then we won't freeze to death".
From llth to 20th we had quite a lot of snow and our farm road was blocked.
There was a real blizzard on 20th and the main road was blocked. I want to
mention another character called Bill Cowton. Bill hailed from Hawnby. He was
a bit of a roadster, a simple man. He would spend quite a bit of time in the
Salvation Army Hostel and St. Mary's in Scarborough, but they couldn't keep
him in long. He liked to be roaming around this area and sleeping rough. One
day he turned up at our farm, no socks on, no top coat, looking just like a
snowman- I said to him, "What on earth's tha doing here, Bill, on a day like
today?" Bill said, "Ask thee Mother to give me a mug of tea and then I's going
down t'wood, back to Scarborough". One night I was coming slowly down the
main road in the car when Bill jumped out from behind the hedge and started
singing, "Pass me not, O gentle Saviour. Hear my humble cry. While on
others thou art calling, do not pass me by". He got in and told me all about
his roamings and wanderings and that he was sweethearting the local GP Doctor

Downie! Bill could turn up anywhere. One of his favourite activities was attending funerals. I think he smelt the funeral teas. One day he turned up at Rievaulx Sunday School Anniversary and Dad asked him over to the farm for tea, (and was greatly admired for doing so).

March was a terrible month. A lot of blash, rain and wet snow and from the 12th to the 19th, heavy snow. I can see it now settled on the electric and telegraph wires. A lot broke under the strain. I remember knocking the nets on the sheep fold and ice just dropped off them like glass. There was a bad forecast on the 11th and we had to take a Guild meeting at Topcliffe on the 12th. Mother was always an alarmist about snow and said we were venturesome setting off. There was no sign of snow going but it was a different story coming back. We had Sutton Bank to grit, and the car to push part of the way up. When we made the top there was a real blizzard. That night a lot of roads were blocked. On the 18th I remember going up to Reg Bosomworth's sale at Cold Kirby. We bought some ewes and John Otterburn brought them to our road end. We had to drive them over on foot. On the 28th we had one of the keenest frosts for the time of year. What grass there was turned blue! On the 31st it was a terribly wet snowy day. Poor sheep, I think it knocked their ends in.

April by and large was cold and wet. There was a dry spell from the 8th to the 16th when we started and finished sowing our corn. I want to mention two things that we were doing on our farm that winter which we seldom do now. Dad was hacking turnips on the sheepfold. What was hacking? It was using a turnip hack which was like a strong pointed hoe to pull up the remains of the turnips which the sheep couldn't get at, so that nothing was wasted. Another job was burning thorns. All hedges now are cut with a flail hedger breaking all the thorns up. An uncle of mine said it is a lazy way of going on!

May was a little warmer but terribly wet. I remember going down to see Mam's cousin, John Waind at Normanby, on the 13th. He was on strong land and hadn't sown a grain of corn. We had had about five months of bad weather but things changed and from the 12th **June** the weather 'took up'. Rains came at the right time and everything went well. Nature has a wonderful way of providing. We started haytime on 12th **June** and finished on 19th **July**. We bought a new type of hay turner, the first in the district. As usual there were a lot of sceptics but they caught on and are now commonplace.

Things began to take a more modern look in the way we stored our corn. That summer we erected a hundred ton Simplex sealed corn silo. Langtons of Northallerton promised to have it up for the middle of **August**, but didn't finish it until the 4th **September**. We were quite frustrated as it was fine weather.

Everyone was harvesting except us and they finished before we even got started. That takes a bit of swallowing in a farming community. Patience did run out. We started on 2nd September bagging most of the corn up and then augered it into the silo afterwards. Harvest went like clockwork. It was properly ripe and dry. We had forty-eight acres, all barley, cut in only three days with an ordinary Massey Combine; a good clean job, with no corn thrown over the back. We finished harvest on 8th September, a record for us, taking only six days. The saying that Dad had quoted last Christmas had come true! It had been a fine harvest indeed!

Some prices this year - 1969

> 25th April - bought 8 acres of eatage at Finghall near Leyburn at £18 per acre.
> 30th April - sold hoggs and lambs in Northallerton - £13 per hogg and lamb pair
> 21st August - sold newly calved cow in York - £108
> 22nd August - sold two Charolais bull calves - £24 each
> 23rd September - bought 10 Masham gimmer lambs off Ralph Liddle at £11.15s, others up to £17 at Masham Mart.

1970

This is how I reviewed 1970. This was the worst farming year I can remember since 1960. A cold dry spring was followed by drought in May and June. The hay yield was down by two thousand bales and there was a terrible lot of green corn. We put it all in the silo where it set like concrete, the estimated yield being twenty-two to twenty-five hundredweight per acre. There was half as much straw as usual. Roots did well considering the chance they had. Big hoggs were a poor trade until late spring, but store pigs, calves, cows and cattle were a good trade. It would appear over the years that I have had my fair share of flu, as the first week of this year I was off work with it.

The first ten days of **January** were frosty with some snow on 7th. It was the coldest night since the hard frosts of 1963. The second half of the month was a complete contrast, mild, mucky and very wet - terrible for the sheepfold. The first fortnight in **February** was frosty and fine with a bit of snow and the second half was wet and windy. There seemed to be discontent among farming folk. A lot of farmers were demonstrating, demanding better prices for what they produced. Local NFU branches staged a demonstration in Scarborough with a convoy of tractors and vehicles. Some farmers in other areas withheld livestock from auction marts. I remember NFU members in the Boroughbridge branch withheld stock and were harshly criticised by the auctioneer. As a result some took their stock elsewhere. When you are a public servant you have to be careful how and when you speak.

I am reminded of a little verse:

'If your lips would keep from slips,
Five things observe with care.
Of whom you speak
To whom you speak
And how, and when and where'.

I have always been a member of the National Farmers' Union albeit not a very good one as I haven't gone to many meetings. A lot of farmers criticise the NFU. Some of these critics never go to meetings, and some aren't even members. It seems rather a shame that those who aren't members get the same privileges as those who are. I sometimes think the NFU is a weak organisation, - No Flaming Use! as one farmer put it - but on the other hand we would be worse off without it. The average farmer doesn't recognise the unseen work they do. There is a real discontent as I write this in February 2001. We have seen in past months farmers and hauliers demonstrating, all independent of the NFU about high fuel prices, and low produce prices. I remember a similar situation in February 1970, when Dad, Nicholas and I went to what was called a farmers' action meeting, led by a Devon farmer called Wallace Day.

March was a cold month, fairly dry, but it didn't seem to dry up to get much sowing done. We started sowing on 26th March and finished on 22nd April. The 1st of **April** greeted us with a real taste of winter - four inches of snow on the level and up to four foot drifts. Our road was blown in. The next nine days saw a covering of snow but then it gradually warmed up. The last few days of April were dry and warm. **May** was an abnormally dry month. We only had five hours of rain on the 7th. It was so hot you could see the grass beginning to burn off on thin land. We were fortunate that for the first time we had grown grazing rye for the cows. It was ideal grazing conditions and the cows milked well on it. **June** was abnormally dry and hot. We started haytime on the 9th and we baled it on the 12th. It was almost too dry to bale as it was half hay before we cut it!

On 21st June I had a very interesting conversation with a well-known farmer, George Edmund Lumley, who was born and bred on the farm next to New Leys called Harriet Air. He lived then at Wrelton, near Pickering. Out of his pocket he produced a matchbox and said, "I have something to show you, Paul". I thought he was going to show me some rare insect, but no! Inside were grains of barley. Mr Lumley proceeded to tell his story. He had sown a field of barley late April and it had never germinated properly because it had been too dry. The grains Mr. Lumley showed me, he had dug up out of the ground the day before. Mr. Lumley would have been in his late seventies then and had never experienced anything like it before.

The weather broke on the 27th June with a tremendous storm, hailstones and thunder and it knocked off some heads of corn. We changed our rotation a bit by not having as many acres solely for roots but began ploughing out grass that had been grazed. We put in white turnips and also followed on our rye land with either kale or swedes. **July** was quite dry, just enough rain to green the grass up and keep the root crops going. We finished haytime on the 18th.

I want at this point to mention a man with whom we have done a lot of business - Brian Otterburn. He has supplied us with Zetor tractors and milking parlours. Anybody who has come across Brian knows he doesn't beat about the bush! One day I went down and he said, "What's thoo want thoo little weaster?" When I replied that I only wanted a machine belt, he said, "T'only belt thou wants is a belt under t'lug!!" His wife Joan, reprimanded him, "Don't be so rude to your customers Brian!" I took it all in my stride! I mention Brian at this point because on 20th July Brian and his gang came and in the next four days gutted the cow byre and put a six-stall abreast parlour in. No milk pipelines, still milking into units. What a job we had temporarily milking with one unit in the shed next door! It wasn't much better when we first started milking through the parlour. It was thundery type weather and the flies were keen. The cows seemed to be skittered to death as we say. I was covered head to foot with cow muck. What made it worse was that Nicholas went on holiday so I was left to it with some help from a lad called Andrew Graham, a Methodist minister's son from Helmsley. I don't think his parents would be too pleased when he walked into the manse all covered with cow muck!

August was reasonably dry, as was **September.** We started harvest on 28th August and finished on the 12th September. With it being such a dry May and June there came a lot of second growth in the corn. We were told that you could put it in the silo whatever the moisture. It seemed queer stuff when we were putting it in. The corn augers were blocking up and we burnt a motor out. Well, we were reminded of an old saying regarding making hay: 'If you put queer stuff in the stack, you'll get queer stuff out!' The corn heated up and turned brown in the middle. It was difficult to get out and the last few tons in the bottom went rotten.

What we should have done was to spray it with a ripener before combining or alternately, sent it to dry and sold it straight away. The old saying came true! If we had known then what we know now we would have acted differently. **October** was very dry and on the 27th we had the most rain in six weeks. **November** was very mild. At the end of the month we still had sixteen dry cows, nine bulling heifers and three young stirks living outside. **December** was also very mild, so much so that we laid concrete on the 18th and 21st. However, winter did come in the last few days and on the 31st it was snowing and blowing all day, blocking our field road.

Some prices for 1970

    14th January, sold 6 geld ewes, £7. 4s each, six hoggs graded 62lbs £8. 6s each

    6th February, sold a Charolais bull calf, £25

    26th February, sold a newly calved cow in York for £107

    29th April, sold hoggs and lamb in Northallerton, £15. 5s per hogg and lamb pair

    28th August, sold Teeswater tup lamb, £25

Bill Cowley, taking part in 'This is your life' at mams 80th birthday. Bill's wife Jean is on his left

Bill Cowton, Stan Wright and Me

My sister, Judith working in an old peoples home in Nagold in South Germany 1967-68

Not all work, Judith taking time off to go skiing in Germany, 1967-68

Our road end 1969

Digging road out, 1969

Nearer the top of the telegraph pole than the bottom

Mam and dad, snow 1969

Snow is always a problem especially when you are producing milk - New Leys Farm road

Cousin John Medd from neighbouring Ouldray farm's children: Stephen and Katherine, 1970's

Always good to see Cook's milk wagon, 1970's

Chapter 12
1971 - 1974
Repairs, Renewals, Rents And A Recession

This is how I reviewed 1971.

Every farmer will tell you there are never two seasons alike. What a contrast 1971 was to 1970. 1971 was a very good farming year with good crops and plenty of fine weather to get them in and a good trade in stock.

Ours is thin limestone land. We need plenty of rain. There is an old saying, 'A wet May for long-tailed hay and a droppy June suits our tune'. To compare 1970 to 1971, in 1970 we had 3820 bales of hay and in 1971 we had 7430. In 1970 we had 1763 bales of straw and in 1971 we had 6600. Overall in 1971 then we had nearly twice as much hay and nearly four times as much straw.

1971

January was very mild. We still had twelve cows outside feeding on hay and potatoes. We were doing quite a bit of concreting of the back yard, so you can imagine how mild it was. From the late sixties to the late eighties we did a lot of building and concrete work, supervised by a local builder and handyman, Geoff Kent from Rievaulx. **February** was also mild. The only snow we had was two inches on the 28th. **March** was good growing weather. We started sowing on the 30th and finished on the 7th **April**. Things grew well in April although we had keen frosts on the 26th and 27th, perhaps the keenest of all the winter months. **May** was another good month for growth. **June** greeted us with a sharp frost. We started haytime on the 15th and finished on the 22nd **July**. It isn't often you have both plenty of crop and good weather to get it in. On the 15th July it was too windy to bale hay. I remember we got all baled up before we led any. Christopher and Hazel came and helped us along with Stephen Watson and we led 7430 bales in four days. I was the stacker handling every bale.

I went on holiday the next week to the Derwent Convention at Cliff College. I was that tired I slept through most of the first few days' meetings! At the end of the week I was busy trying to get thistles out of my fingers. I haven't many happy memories of haytime!

August was a good month. Rains came at the right time for a good show of grass and roots. **September** was an excellent harvest month. We started on the 1st and finished on the 20th. **October** was fine and mild and we did a lot of ploughing. We had plenty of snow in **November**, with five inches on the 9th. On the 10th our road was blocked. More heavy snow on the 22nd with drifting and our road was blocked again. Then **December** was mild with little frost.

Two things happened in 1971 that affected everyone. In January we had a postal strike for a week- Post Office staff were demanding higher wages. They got them. Post Office charges went up and as a result a lot of firms we dealt with no longer posted their bills. Reps brought them round on their regular visits. Decimalization came in this year and everything you had to buy went up from that moment onwards.

1971 was a year of accidents both in our family and in the locality. In April I broke my leg and was off work for several weeks. When you are laid up it makes you think. In August there was a terrible coach crash just outside Helmsley. A coach carrying a load of old people got out of control. Eight were killed and thirty-nine injured. Dad had a 'near-do' as we say - during harvest a tractor got away with him, overturning. In December a local lad, Paul Worsley, who knocked about with us quite a lot was involved in a serious car accident. His eldest brother was killed and Ruth Imeson (my sister-in-law, Jean's sister) was also seriously injured. Much prayer was offered on behalf of these young people. Here are some 1971 prices:

Good halfbred geld ewes, sold February made £8.20

Hoggs graded at 50lbs £11.45 each

Hoggs and lambs making up to £17 for each hogg and lamb pair

March 11th sold a newly calved cow in York, £127

Charolais bull calf £37

Geld cows up to £9.15 per cwt.

For some reason I noted some feeding stuff prices:

All Bradshaws products

No.1 dairy nuts £39 per ton

No.8 high protein pellets, £56.60 per ton

Pig meal, rearer and porker £41.80 per ton

1972

In many ways 1972 was a similar year to 1971 - a good high side season suiting our farm. **January** was very mild and very mucky on the sheepfold. Sheep hadn't done any good since Christmas. There were odd days when we had snow. On 17th it started to snow and blow, blocking our road. Dad went to a Teeswater sheep breeders meeting at Reeth, got snowed out at Ampleforth and had to sleep at Heb Sunley's. He never lived that down because if ever it was like snow Dad and Mam would say, "You're better off staying at home." And we would kindly remind Dad we hadn't got snowed out yet, not like somebody we knew! They say if the cap fits, wear it!

Things were beginning to take on a look of modernisation on the farm. This month we treated ourselves to a meal mixer and Cormall Plate Mill, the mill being worked by the power take off - a real Brian Otterburn job! Both machines are going strong today so have been a good investment. Prior to this it was mixing by hand with a shovel in the middle of the barn floor. Wearing both goggles and masks we looked like spacemen.

February greeted us with rough snow showers and when it was blowing, it blocked our road. Otherwise it was a mild mucky month, terrible for sheep on roots. The miners went on strike on 9th February and it went on for several weeks. A lot of disruption was caused by daily power cuts, sometimes three a day. This month Brian Otterburn came and fitted milking jars and a pipeline in the milking parlour. We didn't know we were born now. No carrying milk into the milk dairy

March was very mild with a lot of rain. We started sowing on the 23rd and finished on the 19th April. It isn't often there's much grass in March but this year there was a good show. The first half of **April** was wet and coldish, then cold and dry. We had a good lambing time. It was the first time I could remember all the ewes were in lamb.

May was fairly dry, cold and windy. On the 3rd it was white over with snow! It came some rain in the last few days. Crops were looking well.

June. This was the coldest and wettest I have known. The records show that it was warmer on the 21st December than the 21st June. We started haytime on the 20th June and finished on the 29th July. We had thought and dreamed about going on to bulk milk. One of the conditions was that you had to have a hard, solid, good road with no potholes. Our road wasn't suitable until April this year when the estate decided to repair and tarmac it. So we could now think about it. Our dreams became a reality on the 1st **July** when we went on to bulk milk. No more carting churns down to the main road; no more milk returned. It was quite a job keeping the milk sweet in churns, particularly in hot weather and if it was collected late. My Uncle Fred from Farndale often told the tale about two farmers in Farndale. One was having problems in the days of the milk churn with his milk going sour. "Nivver maand" said his neighbour, "T'pigs 'll be smilin!" meaning they would be having a good feed on the sour milk.

We started harvest on the 23rd **August** and finished on the 27th **September**, with very good yields. We had some very bright days with white frosts. In fact on the 26th September, I have it recorded as being quite keen. It was a very mild open back end except for the 17th **November** when it snowed heavily and we wondered about Nicholas and Jean's wedding next day. In fact it was a lovely clear sunny day, with no more snow.

1972 will go down as a year of repairs and renewals. Because of some tax saving, the estate did more repairs than usual. New doors were fitted to the buildings, roofs were repaired and a long hard look was taken at our cattle accommodation. Both we and the estate thought it wasn't worth repairing so it was decided to knock down the original fold yards and construct a new set-up. We knocked all the old buildings down by mid-October, fully intending that our new accommodation would be ready by the end of November. It wasn't until late January next year that it was up, and only the shell at that! Providence was on our side - we housed the milk cows in the few existing buildings, including a deep litter house, and most of the other cattle were out-wintered. It must have been abnormally mild as we only slept the milk cows inside from the 15th November onwards.

There seemed to be an upsurge in the price of things we needed to buy. If I remember rightly, the price of our building went up ten per cent from the original price. Decimalisation last year and 10% VAT introduced this year these were the main factors contributing to the rise.

1973

January and **February** were quite mild, just the ticket for us, not having our proper cattle shed yet. There was a really fine spell in February. Our neighbour, Ray Skilbeck, sowed some corn on the 8th February. February sowing was unheard of in our locality! **March** was cold and dry. We started sowing on the 9th and finished on the 17th, all but four acres of turnip land.

I want at this point to talk about our relationship with the Duncombe Park Estate and the Feversham family. As a tenant of one of their farms, Dad had been very forward in his thinking, from time to time trying to get me and Nicholas as joint tenants but without any success. We started to put a bit more pressure on, especially when we erected these new buildings at our own expense. Quite out of the blue in March the Estate offered me the tenancy provided Dad would relinquish his. We gave it some thought and prayer and decided to go ahead. From the 19th of March 1973, I became the tenant.

I was now the third generation to have had a farm on the Feversham Estate. Dad always said, "The Fevershams have been good landlords to granddad and myself. Treat them with respect". He stressed, "Whatever you do don't touch game". This is no temptation to me as I have never shot a bullet in my life. I am dead scared of guns. We have always tried to respect the Estate, whether it be their workers, gamekeepers, or their agent. Life is all about establishing relationships and I try to be part of the solution rather than the problem. Levels of rents can be a problem and every farm is different. A landlord has his job to do - to get the best rent he can, while the tenant wants it as reasonable as he can. It is all about talking round the table and both parties realising the earning capacity of that farm. I have found our agent reasonable and helpful at rent reviews, but there have been times when I have employed an outside valuer to advise and help me. As the saying goes, two heads are better than one, even if they're only sheep heads!

It is unfortunate that we are seeing the landlord and tenant system slowly disappearing. It has given many families a start on the bottom rung of the ladder. Because of the economics of farming today, we are seeing farmland that once would have been let to a new tenant, added to existing farms, while the farmhouse has been sold or let to someone outside farming.

To get back to the 1973 season- There is an old saying that if you get a mild January and February, you will have to pay for it later! **April** was very cold and we had the most snow of the winter. On the 2nd I have recorded that it was the worst I'd known for lambing. Dad must have been in touch with his sheep friends at Reeth. They told him they had twelve inches of snow on the level. We had to fetch all the lambs into the Dutch barn and new shed. On the 8th I recorded the coldest April night for years. **May** was cold and dry early on. Then it came a lot of damp, growing weather. Corn grew that fast, it got too big to spray. We started haytime on the 16th **June**. We had the first field flail mowed. In modern terms it would be conditioned. We finished haytime on 27th **July**.

Both June and July had fine spells interspersed with very wet weather. On the 16th July it came some very heavy rain, the most for four years and a lot of corn was laid. **August** and **September** were decent months with some very hot days. We started harvest on 16th August and finished combining on 24th. Most of our corn was laid and was a very light lean sample. Late September, **October** and **November** were quite wet and some potatoes never got lifted.

1973 was another year when we did quite a lot of renewals. We block-walled and concreted out the new shed, put feeding troughs in and fitted sliding doors. It was hard work; no ready-mixed concrete, just a shovel and mixer. I have noted that on several mornings we got up at 5.30 to get milked and foddered and make a flying start on our building and concreting jobs.

Here are some 1973 prices:

Charolais bull calves up to £75

Masham hoggs and lambs up to £29 per hogg and lamb pair

November, milk 23.6p per gallon

Barley £57 per ton

Sheep have gone up,
Hoggs in December graded at 55lbs made £17.20

1974

January, **February** and **March** were wet and relatively mild with odd frosts. The ground dried up in **April** and we started seedtime on the 2nd and finished on the 10th. That week, the 3rd to the 10th we had lovely sunshine but the Stokesley/Northallerton areas were foggy all week. **May** and **June** were very dry. In fact, Dad would say in his letters to me at Cliff College that if it didn't rain soon it would be too late for the corn crops. Hay crops were light. We started on 20th June and finished on 24th July. On the 2nd **July** I took a day off from my Cliff College course to go to the Royal Show at Stoneleigh and guess what? It rained most of the day and I hadn't an overcoat with me. This rain saved our corn crops, as it was the most we'd had since it was sown in early April. July was quite damp and there was more rain in that month than the previous three. **August** was quite wet at times. We started harvest on 28th August. The weather turned bad the next day and continued wet and stormy for nine days. Many heads of corn were knocked off. We finished combining on 14th **September** and got all the straw bales in by the 19th. The weather took a turn for the worse again on the 23rd and we had three weeks of wet weather. **October** was wet and cold; **November** and **December** were wet and mild.

Mother, like other people of her generation, had experienced the slump of the 1930's and used to tell us that those days could come back. Late September, October and November we were the nearest to recession that I had known. There was a total collapse in the beef sector. Some guaranteed subsidies were done away with and calves could hardly be given away! Store cattle prices slumped. In fact I remember on 9th October, Uncle Milton Leadley had his farm stock sale. The bidding nearly stopped; big bullocks were only making £90 each. My brother, Christopher, sold some 18 month cattle at less than he gave for them as calves. Afterwards he said that if he had another year like that he would have had to sell up. It also affected the sheep prices. Moor ewes were half the price of last year and gimmer lambs were down £5 a head. There was a shortage of confidence, money and fodder. Straw was very scarce and at the height of its trade could make as much per ton as a ton of grain, something that has repeated itself several times since. However, this recession was short-lived. Things began to improve. The bullocks that were sold for £90 in October 1973 were the following February making up to £270. That year we had quite a lot of sheep on keep in the Sand Hutton, Skipton Bridge area, near Thirsk. You always want to make it clear to your haulier exactly where they have to go. I gave them instructions to take a load of sheep to Sand Hutton and they landed up at Sand Hutton near York, 30 miles away from where they should have been!

We were short-staffed on the farm from September 1973 to the end of July 1974 while I was away doing a year's studying at Cliff College. I did what I could during my vacations because I was ready for a change from study to farm work. Dad and Nicholas did a great job of managing the farm. From time to time we had the help of local school lads and while I was away we were ably assisted by Graham Speight from Rievaulx and Russ Bainbridge from Cold Kirby. Every farmer at one time would encourage a lad to get work experience. It is a sign of the times that there are fewer and fewer jobs to set a lad on with. Farming is getting very skilled and complicated. 1974 ended up on a sad note for this locality. On the 28th December, a terribly windy day, Mrs. Robert Fenwick from Ashberry, Rievaulx was killed and her daughter-in-law seriously injured, when a tree blew down on top of their car as they travelled to Helmsley market.

Taken July 1963 before we started our renewals

Taken 40 years later in 2003

In March 1971 we had a coffee evening and merrills competition. Nicholas studying the game

Signing my broken leg, same evening, 1971

Dad overturned the tractor, 1971

End of milk cans for us

Chapter 13
1975 - 1978
Snow, Sun, Silage
And A Change In Sheep Systems

1975

January, **February** and **March** were a continuation of the Autumn weather of 1974 - mild and wet although there were odd dry periods. There was straw never baled after the 1974 harvest, and our neighbour Ray Skilbeck baled some straw at Sproxton on 7th January 1975. Generally when you get a mild February and March you get winter in **April** and 1975 was no exception. The first ten days we had wet snow and on the 8th there was a real blizzard, so much so that we had to bring all the lambs in. Dad always used to say that if you get snow in April it was a sign of a good summer to follow. We started sowing on 25th April and finished on 28th. The first ten days of **May** were dry and droughty then very changeable with extremes of heat and cold. It was marvellous how things grew. On 16th May there was a terrible keen frost with ice.

In a previous chapter I've mentioned our friendship with Trevor Dodsworth, Bradshaw's rep. In many ways he was our advisory man, having a wealth of experience, mixing with farmers of all types. He was always saying to us, "You lads ought to make silage!" so this year we decided to make an all out effort to build a silage store and go the whole way to put all our grass into silage. We began clearing the site in January and from 22nd May till 21st June we worked like slaves, setting posts, block-walling sides, fixing sleepers at one end and concreting an area 36 feet by 100 feet. All this was done by Nicholas, Geoff Kent and myself. On 2nd **June** we were white over with snow and had snow showers most of the morning. I had some friends from Cheshire who told me afterwards that they had wanted to go and play cricket in Derbyshire that day but couldn't because the road was blocked over the tops with snow. I don't think you will find that happening very often - snow putting off cricket matches!!! On 9th June Trevor Dodsworth came and said "Do you think you will have this silage spot ready for this season?" I think he had his doubts. The weather had turned really hot. People were beginning to make hay and I said to Nicholas, "I am beginning to think the same as Mr. Dodsworth that it will never be finished. The weather is good so what about leaving it this time and making hay?" Nicholas said, "If silage is as marvellous stuff as they say, lets press on!" This we did and we started silaging on 23rd June and finished on the 30th. The crop was very bulky and mature and some of it had got so dry we had to make it into hay. I have often said that silage has been one of the biggest breakthroughs on our farm. You can farm your grass a lot better.Looking back to 1968 we were haymaking for 7 weeks. This year, 1975, we got our silage in 7 days. Nicholas commented that if we kept progressing at this rate our grass crop wouldn't be gathered in seven weeks or even seven days, but seven hours! Guess what? This year, 2001, fifty-three acres of grass were gathered in four hours!

I want at this point to mention our silage contractor, Stuart Dean, who has given us very good service over the last twenty years. I don't know of anyone who can work to time like he does, but he expects you to do the same. One of our neighbours said, "You will get something done when you call speedy Deany in!"

July was like June, hot and dry. A remarkable rain came on 9th which saved root and corn crops. **August** was hot and dry although we had a day's rain on the 16th. We started harvest on the 21st and finished combining on the 28th. We had finished leading bales by 1st **September**. The month of September was even drier. Grass was burning up and root crops mildewing. **October,** **November** and **December** were relatively dry months, so you can guess people were talking about a water shortage. The Midlands and South of England had experienced a bigger drought than in the North and a lot of hay and straw was carted down there. Dad's saying about snow in April had come true. We'd had a fine summer.

I summed up 1975 weather-wise as being a remarkable year, considering the extremes of wet in the spring and such a dry summer. Land cracked a lot which is natures way of draining. Things began to look up in stock prices. There was a new confidence abroad. Calves that were making 25pence last backend could make up to £25 for export. I remember going to Hawes market on 16th September and noting that everything was a good trade.

This year Dad had started to draw his pension, and we were trying to twist his arm to change the sheep system we had at that time - twenty pedigree Teeswater ewes, forty-four Dalesbred ewes and one hundred and forty Mashams. Teeswater and Masham sheep were his great love, but I could see the Masham was losing its popularity. There was less demand for Teeswater tups. Our sheep system seemed very complicated when we had to have different fields available for the three different breeds. We decided to sell all the Dalesbred ewes and put the Teeswaters to the Suffolk tup. Dad could see what we were getting at. He has always been flexible with his sons. However he did ask to keep a few show sheep and then he was happy.

Here are some 1975 prices:

Our best geld cow made £213.

We were paying £200 - £264 for newly calved cows.

Big, fat hoggs graded at 58 Ibs could make £21.

We paid £26.25 for Norman Peel's top Masham gimmer lambs at Masham mart

1976

Early to the middle of **January** there was a lot of wind and much damage done up and down the country. Often when you get a lot of West winds it's the sign of an open winter. On 15th it was a tremendous grand day and the land was drying up nicely. In fact we were cultivating some stubble that had never been ploughed. There wasn't much winter this year except for the 25th and 26th of January when we had about twelve inches of snow on the level and it blew a lot. The main road, and many minor roads were blocked. This snow storm only seemed to hit the northern parts of Ryedale. We didn't seem to be that keen on opening out our farm road - we had it blocked for ten days which meant leading the milk out each day in an emergency tank. The first thirteen days of **February** we had a lot of fog, with quite mild weather the rest of the month.

It was an early spring. We started sowing on 4th **March** and finished on 8th **April**. With last year being so dry our roots were quite small, so we were short for the sheep. We bought a load of washed stockfeed carrots. I had never seen such big carrots before. Evidently only small carrots were wanted by the canning industry and the biggest were thrown out! Our neighbours found it quite a joke, seeing a great big heap tipped up in the stackyard. They made very good feed. I remember asking Eddie Cook if he could lead us ten tons of carrots. "What on earth do you need carrots for?" said Eddie. I replied that our cows were bad on their eyesight!!

Grass seemed to grow better than average in March and early April, but received a set-back when we had some keen white frosts. It set in very dry towards the end of April. Dad, Mam and Judith went on holiday in Scotland and when he came back, Dad remarked, "There's less grass now than when we went away!" We had a heavy lamb crop and there seemed to be a lot of mouths to feed. Quite on the spur of the moment we decided to buy some grazing from our friend, Mr. Peacock at Finghall, near Leyburn. As it turned out this was to be our salvation. **May** and early **June** was a very growy, damp month. Corn was shaping to come into ear on 1st June. We had some very heavy rain and then it set in very dry. We started silaging on 12th June and finished on 22nd. It was a frustrating time as there were a lot of light showers - enough to bother us with our silaging but not enough to do any good. I would think 1976 was one of the best hay times in living memory. There was lots of grass and day after day of hot weather. Hay seemed cheap and we bought quite a few wagon loads out of the field. Again it was Providence because as the summer progressed there wasn't a blade of grass. All our pastures were burnt up. The countryside looked like a desert. We started feeding hay to the milk cows early **July** and continued until the end of **September**. I have never known our farm land so eaten up and bare. Most of our sheep had to be taken to grazing in other areas, some as far away as Bowes near Barnard Castle. I can tell you we had a big haulage bill!

We started harvest on 5th **August** and finished combining on the 12th, with all the straw baled and led a week later- 1976 will stand out for me as the driest summer on record. We hardly had any rain from 1st June until 9th September. It all changed on 10th - 12th September. It rained non-stop. Stokesley High Street was under five feet of water and the committee of Stokesley Show were considering putting the show off. I remember we had a load of baled straw outside which got wet through to the bottom course. It also rained a lot early to mid **October** and much land was flooded. Stokesley town was threatened again. The best and driest of the weather came towards the end of **November**. **December** was wet with odd periods of frost, and finished on the 30th with snow blowing our road in.

We were beginning to realise that our dairy herd was the mainstay of our farm. At that time we were buying cows at farm sales and newly calved heifers at Otley mart, putting them to the beef bull. We were experiencing mastitis problems and were advised to have a self-contained herd. Quite by chance I noticed some pedigree in-calf heifers advertised in The Yorkshire Post. These were from the Winyates herd, belonging to John and Joanna Dawson of Ripley near Harrogate. We already knew Joanna through Methodist circles and when I contacted her she said, "Oh, I would like you to buy them!" We went to see them and agreed on a price on the condition they weren't paid for until 10th November. They'd had a good year and their financial year ended on 9th November. They wanted the money in the next financial year. I said, "Are you sure? I believe in paying for things straight away". Mr. Dawson said quite firmly, "That is the condition". It suited us fine as we were a bit short of cash. So God provides in wonderful ways. The six pedigree heifers arrived and they were the start of the Newsley herd of pedigree Friesians. Now, twenty-six years later we have had over fifty cattle registered from one of the original purchases. We began to make other purchases from Lancaster and from Tom Spence's Miresdale herd, near Northallerton.

There seemed to be quite an upsurge in sheep prices:
In April hoggs graded at 73 Ibs made up to £32.40
    In October lambs graded at 49lbs made up to £29.60
    We paid £39.50 at Kendal for Bob Bindlass's top pen of Masham lambs
    A good geld cow could make £250
    Hereford cross bull calves were making up to £55.

1977

On 2nd **January** we had a very keen frost, the keenest since 1968. The rest of the month we had a real mixture of frosts, wet days, coverings of snow and on 14th we had a rough night of wind and snow and a lot of minor roads were blocked. **February** started and ended with very keen frosts but in between we had a lot of wet days, a real February fill-dyke. **March** came in like a lamb, with a mild spring-like day. It ended up going out like a lion, a terrible stormy day, with rain, sleet, snow and wind. There were periods of dry weather in the month and we started sowing on 9th March and finished on 6th April. On many **April** mornings we had a slight covering of snow which gave way to fine afternoons. April was quite a growy month with a good show of grass. We turned our cows out on the 12th, one of our earliest turn-outs. April ended up with a real grand day, just the ticket for our centenary services at Rievaulx Chapel. The 1st of **May** greeted us with a keen frost, followed by good growing weather. The month ended up dry with 28th being one of the hottest May days on record.

I have always said that farming is subject to the whims and fancies of politicians. We were encouraged at that time to go all out for production and the government introduced what were known as farm development grants. You had to put a seven year plan forward as to how you were going to improve your stock, buildings and equipment. Grants are good things but if you are not careful you can spend money unnecessarily. We were cautious and our plan was to put a roof over the silage pit, (which we did in May), install a new milking parlour, increase milk production, put a sheep handling unit in and purchase a bigger tractor.

June greeted us with a very keen frost. The postman that day said that the windows of his van had to be thawed out before he could set off. It was quite a busy month as it was our Judith's wedding. We were busy painting and tidying up. We all remarked that it was a good job such occasions came or we would never get tidied up!

On llth June, her wedding day, there was torrential rain, with hailstones and thunder and lightning. I think we all had a bit of a sweat on, as we say. As a bride she landed half an hour late. However we all had a great day, a good service and a lovely atmosphere.

From 14th to the 17th we had very cold windy days, more like Christmas than June. We started silaging on 18th June and finished on the 23rd.

July started wet but the 3rd to the 6th were very hot days. Judith and Keith were now living in Rugby and I took Mam and Dad down for the weekend and went to the Royal Show. It was far too hot for the pigs and they had to spray them every day with cold water to keep them cool. We were very late that year shearing sheep, not getting finished until the 6th. July was a good haytime month with plenty of crops and good weather to get them in. The first eighteen days of **August** were dry and sunny, some days being hot. We had some very heavy dews which helped keep the root crops growing and with three wet mornings towards the end of August things grew extremely well. We started harvest on 29th August and finished combining on 9th September. We finished leading bales on 16th September. **September** was a good harvest month but also a good growing month. We had gentle rains which kept the grass and root crops growing.

October was a real mild, muggy month. It is surprising how you make friends with different people. The last weekend in October I took Mam and Dad down to our Judith's at Rugby and on the Saturday we went to a farm sale. We met up with a Christian farmer called Ray Ellis from Towcaster. We struck up a friendship and he asked us along to his church. He and Dad would often phone one another over the years exchanging farm and church news. **November** was a decent mild month with two wet and windy days. **December** was a very mild month. On 25th and 26th it was more like spring than Christmas. How changeable English weather can be! This year it was as cold as winter in June and springlike at Christmas!

Changes were again on the horizon with our sheep systems. 1976 had been an expensive year with haulage and grazing. This year we found the sheep were competing with the dairy herd in summer. So this backend we sold all except twelve of our breeding ewes and decided that in future we would fatten more lambs on the roots in winter.

Here are some 1977 prices:

November milk, 10.874p per litre

30th March, fat hoggs 27 $\frac{1}{2}$ Kg graded weight made £38.80.

We paid £51 each for Bill Croft's top pen of gimmers at Masham mart

1978

January was a continuation of December's weather, odd bits of snow and some wet days. It started off just like spring and ended up with a keen frost and three inches of snow. **February** started off very wet and mild but between the 8th and the 13th we had about fourteen inches of snow on the level. The main road was blocked up Bilsdale. It came in warm for two days and then we had another spell of wintry weather. There were reports of terrible conditions in Devon, Cornwall and Somerset. There was a rainy thaw two days later and these counties suffered bad flooding. February ended with mild wet weather. **March** greeted us with a damp, miserable, showery day, but the 2nd was a really grand day, cheering everyone up. There were odd periods of dry weather but the land didn't dry up much. We started sowing corn on 29th March and finished on 15th April. We had typically **April** weather with odd warm days. On the 10th and 12th it was very, very cold with snow showers fit to skin you to death.

At this time, John Pickersgill from Wrelton did quite a bit of our cultivation work and up to this point we used the rotovator a lot. In April this year John persuaded us to use a new machine he had bought. He called it a 'roto harrow' and it was a great success. The roto harrow is now the power harrow and goodness knows what we would do without it today! Our neighbour's son, George Hawkins used to say, "You are always trying something new at New Leys! I call your place 'Rievaulx Experimental Farm'" This was the first year I had seen tram lines in corn fields in the Midlands. I was quite ignorant -I thought they had some drill coulters blocked!

May was a real growy month with some hot days, but in **June** we had some very windy and cold days. We started silaging on 9th June and finished on 16th. It was so windy you couldn't hold the silage sheet down and we had to get up early to put the sheet on before we milked. The next few days were quite hot and droughty but towards the end of the month we had a lot of rain which made the silage aftermaths grow. Early **July** we had a lot of showery weather. On 5th it was terribly wet and stormy. For some reason we had a lot of dull, foggy days interspersed with really hot droughty ones, so much so that when we were scruffling dust was flying as we went up the rows. On the 10th I had quite a pleasant surprise. My friend Carl Wilkinson used to fly a small aeroplane and he was often teasing me and saying, "I will come to thy spot and land down and give thee a ride". Sure enough, there was quite a buzzing and Mother looked out and said, "What in the world is that plane doing, circling to come down in our field?" I said, "Carl has come to give me a ride in his plane". He landed down and I jumped in, never having flown before. I took to it like a

111

duck to water. We had a grand sky view of Kirkbymoorside, Fadmoor and Bransdale including the sight of Bransdale cricket team playing at Ankness farm. Carl was especially interested as he had farmed there briefly.

On the 13th Nicholas and I had quite an interesting experience. We went to Lancaster Friesian Sale. We landed just as they finished judging and I said the 3rd prize heifer was the best one, but we would never be able to afford it. However, when it came into the ring the bidding stopped at 720 guineas. Nicholas said "Pop one in!" and we got it for 740 guineas. Afterwards we went to see the heifer milked out. Two chaps came to me and said, "Will you take a bit of profit on it?" It seemed there had been a bit of a misunderstanding as one of them had agreed to stand out so they wouldn't bid against each other, but both had stood out! Would we take £100 profit on it? I said, "No!" as it isn't often you get something good and reasonable at the same time.

From 30th July to the 10th **August** there was an awful lot of rain. After that August was a very mixed month. We started harvest on the 28th of the month and finished combining on the 15th **September**. Round, big bales were just coming into fashion and we baled some of our straw into them. All in all 1978 was a nice backend. There were two particular spells of really warm weather - the first ten days in October and the first nine days in **November**. On 7th November we were harrowing with the spring tined harrows and it was more like spring than the backend. We had our first taste of winter on 28th November when we had three inches of snow and our road was blown in. 1978 ended up with three very wet days on 26th-28th **December** and there was a terrible lot of flooding in the North East. The 29th - 31st we had snow and blizzard conditions. Every ten years I note our stock numbers:

Year end 1978, 85 cattle, consisting of 52 cows, 33 heifers
539 sheep including 12 breeding ewes,
27 show hoggs and
500 fat hoggs on roots

One of my favourite photos, Author and nephews Simon and Timothy at Judith's wedding in 1977

The first aeroplane I rode in piloted by Carl Wilkinson 1978

Above, Trevor Dodsworth, known as Doddy

Rievaulx chapel and new Sunday School, 1967

New Life Baptist Church, Northallerton, where we worship now

Chapter 14
Chapel Life

From an early age life centred around the farm and our Methodist chapel at Rievaulx, the Helmsley Circuit, (now the Ryedale Circuit) and the other circuits where Dad went to preach.

Rievaulx chapel has always had a name for being an active cause. Let me share with you our calendar of events. On a Sunday it was Sunday school at 2.30pm and a 6.30pm service at night. As children we all went and we never rejected it or rebelled against it. On reflection we perhaps lived a rather sheltered life, not knowing anything else. However, as Nehemiah the prophet said, "The good hand of the Lord was upon us".

I can remember some of the old preachers, especially an old man called Willie Richardson. He was what we call an auxiliary. That means a preacher who wasn't qualified. I don't think he was even a Methodist. He was a saintly old character, and his face shone. He used to thrill us with his stories. We used to sit on the back seat and if we got a bit restless he would say, "I know I am rambling on a bit lads, but I am telling you for God's glory and it's true". After the service he would come and shake hands with us and say, "Keep coming lads, we're on the victory side".

When Dad and Granddad lived in Farndale they were used to midweek meetings and were surprised that there were no midweek meetings at Rievaulx. Eventually they got the people at Rievaulx persuaded to have one. So the Thursday night Fellowship meetings were formed. Different members of the chapel and community were responsible for organising an evening. It could be a slide show, a singing party, or a talk on some subject. I remember the late Fred Handley giving a talk on "Yorkshire: The most wonderful county." He was describing some of our local villages and then, he said, we come to Lastingham. "The old church stands there still". Me and Nicholas were sat together and I saw the funny side. I said to Nicholas, "Lastingham church would look queer moving about wouldn't it"? Both of us got the giggles.

We also used to have a Ladies and Gents evenings, when the men and women would seperately use their talents in recitation and song. There was a time when both the Ladies and Gents choirs would go out giving evenings of song in other circuits. The Fellowship sessions always ended up with a rally, when we got an outside speaker. We did a roll call and we were supported by other chapels.

In May we had our chapel anniversary when we had two services on a

Sunday and an afternoon and evening meeting on the following Tuesday.

Dad being a widely travelled preacher, and having good contacts amongst Christians in the farming world, was always on the lookout for preachers and singers and we used to get them from a wide area. People like Kit Calvert and Willie Preston from Hawes, Alf Suttill and Dick Simpson from Leyburn, Edwin Coates from Cockfield, Arthur Bainbridge and Fred Moore from Barnard Castle, Malcolm Skidmore from Hellifield, Bill Parkinson from Preston, Brian Thomas from Scarborough. At our 150th celebration we had Rev. Howard Belben, a past principal of Cliff College as the preacher on the Sunday and Rev. Frank Thewlis a gifted mission hall speaker on the week night, both from Sheffield.

The Sunday school anniversary held on the 3rd or 4th Sunday in June was always a big event in the chapel. Not only did the children take part but there used to be an adult choir as well. Members past and present would come back to help us. It was an occasion when both scholars and choir members, especially the ladies, would make a point of getting a new frock or hat. It was often a point of conversation over teas, "What did you think of so and so's turn out"? I am reminded of a rather humorous story about an old preacher who treated himself to a new suit. He went to preach and said to one of his friends, "Wat's tha think ti mi suit? It's yan o' them meead ti measure." His friend replied "Thou'ed better a gitten yan o' them meead ti fit."

We were well drilled as children for the anniversary but we weren't always co-operative. I remember Annie Robinson the organist stopping the practice and saying, "You want your trip, you want your presents and books, but you won't sing". Our superintendent Sidney Bowes would say to us when we were rehearsing our recitations, "Now shout up and say it slowly". Not bad advice too to anyone who has to do public speaking. I well remember helping with a dialogue with Christopher and Nicholas and I broke down in tears. I was a shy, timid lad then! The anniversary would be followed on the Monday when we had a tea in the village hall and then we would be let loose in the Abbey grounds playing Hide and Seek or Tig. In the evening we had a singing party which would have included the Wilkinson family from Snape, the Milner family from Bowes and the Neatstead Girls' Choir from Great Ayton. Sometimes we would get the Salvation Army Songsters from Middlesborough.

I would like to mention my Aunty Tamar (Mother's Sister) and my two cousins Edward and Rosamund, who were all dwarfs. I would describe them as little people with big hearts, and a great sense of humour. Each year Mam would spend a day at Bridge farm, Lastingham, helping Aunty Tamar prepare for the Sunday school anniversary. I would sometimes go with her and as I hadn't a bike it was a great opportunity to use Edward's.

Edward and Rosamund were star performers, good singers and good reciters. They were much in demand helping other anniversaries who were short in number including Rudland, Appleton-le-Moors and High Farndale. Rosamund was only telling me recently that once, Edward got up to sing a solo at Rudland and couldn't get a word out. His voice had broken on the spot, so Rosamund had to sing instead!

Edward was always special to the Dunn cousins. Like us he was interested in people and farming. He had a hard life as he had polio when he was 13 and got skin cancer in his fifties. Despite his disabilities he was always cheerful and liked to crack a joke. Edward died in 1999 aged 57. My brother Christopher gave the tribute at his funeral and quoted two of his jokes. Edward would say, "Did you hear about the chap who swallowed an electric light bulb? They took him to hospital and rang up the next day to find out how he was. The nurses said he was a little brighter". "Did you hear about the gamekeeper who met a lady and asked her, 'Are you game?' She said 'yes' and he shot her". Edward had an infectious laugh and we would all see the funny side.

Most Sunday schools would organise a trip to the seaside and from Rievaulx we would go to Scarborough. At one time there would be two or three coaches from Rievaulx and the area. I remember once getting lost on a trip. I cried my eyes out and eventually wandered into a toy shop. The owner tried to comfort me and gave me a small toy. Eventually I wandered off and Dad and Mam found me sat on a car running board playing with my toy.

I think our Sunday school anniversaries at Rievaulx are much better now, more interesting and more helpful. There is no longer an adult choir but the children do drama, written by one of the teachers, Trudie Sanderson, and the Sunday school is ably led by Sheila Foster.

One day in 1939 Dad and two of our neighbours Ernest Hawkins and Frank Wilson were washing sheep when in the course of conversation Mr. Hawkins said, "Don't you think it would be a good idea if we had an Open Air Service on Newgate Bank Top"? The idea materialised and for over 60 years there was a service there on the first Sunday in August. We always tried to have a gifted speaker which in times past included Professor Cecil Pawson of Newcastle, Leslie Newman from Brighton, Tom Butler from Sheffield, Ernest Steel from Newcastle, Alec Passmore from Preston, Malcolm Pears from Suffolk and Fred Wilson from Preston. In the early days our singing would be led by the Bilsdale Band, and the Dobson family or Farndale Quartet would sing. For some years we used to have a public tea at Mr. & Mrs. Hawkins at Oscar Park farm.

117

Being a farming community, Harvest Festivals played an important part. Two services on a Sunday were taken by a Christian farmer and on the following Tuesday evening there would be a service followed by a supper and sale in the Village Hall. Dad was the auctioneer in the early days and later I did the honours. It is interesting to note that many an auctioneer started out at harvest festival sales, including myself.

At Christmas the Sunday school would put on a Carol service with recitations and songs. This to me was more enjoyable than the anniversary. For one thing there were less rehearsals which I was never keen on. I remember singing a duet, Mary's Boy Child, with Tucky Symons. The Sunday school rounded off the year with a party where every child received a present. Christmas was always a busy time. Chapel members and friends did the annual rounds of carol singing ably led by Stan Wright who was a dab hand at starting a tune. Now it's a lot easier - we are accompanied by Sheila Foster on her accordion. Over the years hundreds of pounds has been raised for different charities by carol singing. It is interesting to note that when Dad first went singing in 1935, £5 was raised. Now it is well over £500.

Music and singing played an important part in country Methodism and especially in the Dales. It would be a regular thing to have a sing song around the piano of course. There would be very little radio and no television. Farndale people were famous for their singing and when Dad and Mam moved to New Leys they were asked if some of the people from Farndale could come and give them a night of song. Eventually this materialised and in 1943 four people came: George Breckon, his sister Hilda, Herbert Carter and my uncle Fred Wass. This was the beginning of the Farndale Quartet party who travelled all over the north east giving sacred concerts, often under the chairmanship of Dad. It was fitting they came back to Rievaulx to do their 300th performance which was in 1957.

Rievaulx was often a launching place for new choirs coming into the district, and the famous Cockfield Male Voice Choir came there in around 1953. They have given a lot of concerts in the district since and they appeared on 'This is Your Life' when Hannah Hauxwell was interviewed on that programme. In later years we have had visits from the Orton Male Voice Choir from Cumbria, the South Yorkshire Crusade Choir from Doncaster and the Forum Choir from Stanley circuit, County Durham.

In the late fifties it was felt by several members that we needed an extension to the chapel and so the idea of the new Sunday school building was born. Money raising efforts were put into operation. We had a two-performance concert at Helmsley given by Sandy Macpherson of the radio programme

'Chapel in the Valley', a garden fete at Lady Marjorie Beckett's and a big auction sale at High Leys by kind permission of Sidney and Mary Bowes. In addition to these big events we had market stalls and of course there was direct giving by a lot of people.

The Sunday school building was opened in 1967 and has been a great asset to our activities. Prior to the opening of the Sunday school I would say we had a lot of activity where perhaps the spiritual side was neglected. In the late sixties and early seventies quite a move of God's Spirit came upon us. At that time it was felt we ought to use the premises more and we organised monthly gospel rallies. At these rallies we would have gospel beat groups or folk groups followed by a message from an evangelical preacher. Young people flocked from all over. A crowd draws a crowd and young people like to meet with other young people. Many young people were blessed by these meetings; some became Christians, some had a second blessing, some met their marriage partners. One memorable meeting was when Rev. David Watson from York came to speak and both the chapel and Sunday school were full with over 200 people there.

Not only did the young people benefit but there was a move of God among the middle-aged folk. As a result bible study and prayer groups were formed. In October 1971 we had a mission led by our minister, Neil Graham, with special guests. Patrick Hinton from Middlesborough came as a Christian businessman, PC Stanley Wright from Hull came and testified about life as a Christian policeman. Michael Brooks came and shared about his life as he had been a professional wrestler.

I think seeing a lot of young people using their talents in singing groups gave us inspiration to form our own group called "The Proclaimers'" where we went to other chapels giving a performance of gospel music.

Perhaps as you read this account of our activities you will say 'How marvellous'. Yes it is but we haven't been without our problems. We are human-there have been disagreements, people walking out of meetings etc. Through it all we have learned to forgive and forget. Love conquers all things.

As I write this in 2001 the Foot and Mouth epidemic has had a big impact on the calendar of events, with many cancellations. I think Rievaulx members will, like any other country chapel, have to ask themselves these questions: 'Have the activities served their purpose?' 'Do the events need to be looked at in a new light?' I once heard a quotation, 'People are good at starting things but not very good at ending them when they have fulfilled their purpose'.

I often remember some words said by the late Ted Emmitt, a pillar in Rievaulx chapel for many years. He said, 'We need more circuit-minded people at

Rievaulx. People don't want to hold onto office too long and never have too many of one family holding office'.

In the Methodist Church I have held most offices. I have been a Sunday school teacher, local preacher, church council secretary, local preachers secretary and circuit steward, which has given me an insight into the running of the Methodist church. I think it is good advice not to hold office for too long as it gives other people chance to use their talents. We all have to learn some time. If we are not careful one individual can land up running the show. I often think my role isn't so much as a leader but an encourager.

What about the future? We are seeing great changes. The congregation at Rievaulx is now made up of very few people from the village, but people commuting back to their roots. It is no longer a local chapel, but a centre where people congregate.

I have seen great changes in the Ryedale Circuit. Once we used to have 26 chapels, now we only have 7. Many people would say this is a bad state of affairs. We have seen a similar thing happen with schools, shops and post offices. Whether we like to think of it or not, centralisation is here. What a lot of people are not aware of is that if chapels hadn't been closed and sold we couldn't have financed our circuit and the repairs of the existing chapels. Today, you see, when a chapel is closed the proceeds go into what we call the circuit advance fund. A fund where we can draw on 50% of the cost of repairs to the existing chapels and part of the interest of this fund helps towards the minister's stipend.

Since my time as a circuit steward and my experience of travelling in other rural circuits I have asked myself several heart searching questions- 'Does God want it this way?' Where we see dwindling ageing congregations sometimes meeting in chapels that are poorly heated, seats that are uncomfortable, when we could meet in a centralised place where people with their talents and gifts could give and receive more, I think we all have to remind ourselves of that hymn that says 'To serve the present age, my calling to fulfil, oh may it all my powers engage to do my master's will'. In many cases we have to face it, the average village chapel has fulfilled its role and in the next few years we will see more chapels closed.

It is interesting to note that in 1955 the then president of the Methodist conference, Rev Dr Leslie Weatherhead, challenged the Methodist conference to consider closing four out of five churches, then to plough considerable financial resources back into personnel and church planting. We have to face facts both in rural and urban areas - we have millions of pounds tied up in property. Some of it is outdated, some in the wrong place, some there for the wrong reasons. I would think Dr Weatherhead got a lot of criticism for his statement but to a certain degree he has been right. The sad thing is that we haven't closed churches by choice, but by circumstance. In many cases the undertaker has done it for us.

I am reminded of a funny story about an undertaker who was a local preacher. He went to speak at a chapel anniversary and the minister would take the chair for him and lead the prayers. The minister prayed for the preacher not knowing he was an undertaker. He prayed, 'Bless his home, bless his family and bless his business, may it prosper'. At this point the preacher interrupted and said, 'Steady on brother, I am an undertaker!'

Methodism numerically is on the decline. Ten years ago we had a membership of 450,000. Today that figure is 330,000. Where are the members going? I have noticed that in the past 20 - 30 years quite a few of our younger members have been leaving to join Pentecostal and Free churches. I have tried to tell our leadership both at national and local levels about this but it seems to fall on deaf ears. The Methodist church at this present moment in time prides itself on being a broad church, accepting beliefs of all kinds, which I believe are contrary to scripture. Our leadership in these past years has spent a lot of time discussing and debating homosexuality, ecumenism, and multi-faith relationships at the expense of neglecting prayer, evangelism and scriptural holiness. But we have to be thankful for God raising up a man like Rob Frost and the gatherings of Easter People which are a blessing to people of all denominations. As a young person I accepted everything traditional in the chapel, but our children and youngsters are different. They know what is real and if they are hungry they want to be where the life is, and meet other young people. We see this happening in centres like St. Michael's Anglican Church in York, the Elim Pentecostal Church in Malton and the New Life Baptist Church in Northallerton.

For the past few years I thought and prayed much about my position as a member of the Methodist Church, especially as Miriam and Phillip were becoming teenagers. They were starting to rebel and reject what the Methodist church was offering. Miriam by now had got involved through a school friend with a Crusader group in Ampleforth. I have great admiration for the Crusader movement. It is an inter-denominational youth organisation and it was at an area camp that Miriam became a Christian. There is an old saying 'You can't beat bairns and fools for the truth'. Miriam kept telling us things about traditional Methodism which we didn't like to hear, but which were true.

For the past 30 years both myself and Dorothy have had close links with the Baptist church in Northallerton, both because of Dorothy being a member there originally, and the two of us knowing the pastors George and Rodney Breckon.

This fellowship had outgrown its original building and was now meeting in temporary buildings. In 1998 they bought the old cinema and converted it into a modern church. At Easter 1998 Dorothy and I were guests at the opening. Little did I think that in two years time we would be worshipping there full time, as I have always believed that if you are a member of a church you put your heart and soul into it, and are loyal to it. I always believed that worship at Rievaulx chapel was a priority for us all.

However, at that time when there was no service at Rievaulx, we would go along to New Life Baptist church. We were made very welcome, there were lots of young people of Miriam and Philip's age, and we felt we were receiving Bible-based spirit empowered preaching and teaching. Dorothy and I were beginning to feel uneasy as God had been giving us nudges before to move us on, but we were dithering. If we left our own chapel what would people think of us? Perhaps that is one of human nature's biggest problems. We are too frightened of what people think about us.

In July 1998, Jim and Cynthia Wilkinson came for a meal and we were sharing our concerns about the spiritual welfare of our children and ourselves. I said to Jim when be was leaving, 'Have a prayer with us'. Jim prayed and he said 'I feel I have a word from God for you. You won't be where you are now in five years time'. After Jim and Cynthia left I said to Dorothy, 'What do you make of Jim's word from the Lord. Does it mean we have to leave Rievaulx Chapel? It doesn't make sense, I have just signed a four year tax covenant to give money to Rievaulx chapel. No, we must stay where we are.' We are all good at making excuses. With farming being so bad the next year we couldn't pay our covenant. We could no longer make that excuse. I then began to say 'I can't move, I'm the chapel secretary, who would take it on?" Somebody did take it on, so I couldn't make that my excuse.

I began to make other excuses. 'What about my preaching? Can I leave my Methodist roots?' I began to pray earnestly about the future. I wanted God's best for us as a family. We were praying 'Lord, show us the way'. In many ways we were seeing the way but hadn't the courage to take the step of faith. In early September 2000 I happened to be talking to a Christian farmer friend at a farm sale. I knew that he had been faced with a similar problem to ourselves. He had left his own local chapel to go to a larger church for the good of his family. His advice to me was, 'You must think about your family and do the best for them'. When I got home I shared this with Dorothy and we both agreed we mustn't dither any longer but make a decision to move. I shared this first with my two brothers and sister and my Dad and was quite surprised that they supported our decision. So in late September 2000 I made it known publicly at our circuit meeting, local preachers' meeting and church council meeting that from January 2001 we would no longer be members of the Methodist church but partners in the New Life Baptist Church at Northallerton. When you make a decision like this you expose yourself to criticism and misunderstanding.

I think it came as quite a shock to many people in the circuit meeting and it was unfortunate that I had to rush away afterwards to see to some cattle. I did ask Nicholas the next morning what were the comments and reactions of people. Here are some: Would they know anybody in this new church? Would they settle? Is Paul getting out of the sinking ship of Methodism before it goes down? Paul has made a hasty decision. (Little did people know that we had been talking and praying about it for the last three years.) What were we doing leaving the circuit when we had just appointed a youth worker?

But Nicholas made some encouraging comments: 'You have been one of the most faithful members of the circuit and in many ways a pioneer man both in Rievaulx chapel and the circuit, proposing the gift day and the united churches witness tent at the Ryedale Show. Some people will be glad to see you go. You told us truths we didn't like hearing'. There were times when I felt that I was ploughing a lonely furrow but I stuck to my convictions. I think the prophets felt like this and I am reminded of a passage of scripture from Isaiah 30: 10-11 They tell my prophets, "Shut up. We don't want any more of your reports." Or they say, "Don't tell us the truth tell us nice things, tell us lies. Forget all this gloom, we've heard more than enough about your Holy One of Israel and all he says". Nicholas encouraged me by saying 'It isn't really what people think or say about you, but you doing what you feel God wants you to do. I think you have made the right decision and are the bravest man in the Ryedale Circuit'. I felt I had to be more open in our local preachers' meeting and asked my fellow local preachers two questions: 1. Where are the children of the parents we are preaching to now? 2. Are we being good stewards of our time, talents and buildings in the circuit?

I felt I had to say that the role of the local preacher could be changing. They would have to think more about pastoral visiting and leading fellowship groups in the villages.

Here we are now, 2nd January 2002, having had a year in our new church.

We have been made very welcome and have got involved with its life. It is an outward looking missionary church. Yearly visits are made to Romania with relief aid and one of our partners visits Ghana periodically on mission work.

We have a great church of young people, several taking a year out to go on mission and church work. A lot of outreach takes place among the young people especially in the schools. This last year a full time youth worker has been appointed. One of the highlights in 2001 was a meeting where over 300 young people listened to the testimony of the gold medallist Olympic triple jumper Jonathan Edwards. It is great to be involved in a church like this. There is such a cross section of people consisting of doctors, health visitors, nurses, teachers, policemen, electricians, lawyers and of course farmers. Much prayer has been offered by the church in these last months for the farming community in respect of the foot and mouth epidemic. As a church we have also subscribed to the Addington Fund, set up to relieve farmers in financial crisis. We are thankful that our new church seems to cater for most age groups. Whether it is through youth meetings, house groups, mens breakfasts, womens meetings, pensioner, and Alpha groups.

No church is perfect, and there are certain elements of the Methodist church I miss. For example the singing of the old hymns, but as our children remind me, I am old fashioned and should get up to date with some modern choruses.

One of the chief criticisms we have had is that as it is a long way to travel to Northallerton, 21 miles, had we thought about the cost? My reply to that question is this: 'We are living in an age of commuting, whether it be education, employment or shopping, and there are members in the Ryedale circuit commuting back further than we are travelling anyway. It will be worth it all if we as a family grow in the Lord. I am reminded of something I read lately, 'The church that is alive is worth a drive'.

When I gave my notice to leave the Methodist Church I tried in the last three months to be faithful in my preaching, attending the different meetings, assuring people we wouldn't be leaving the Methodist family altogether, and that we would still keep our channels of communication open. Having said that, life is very full with our new church and that is our priority. I was quite touched by a card given to me at my last local preachers' meeting which said: "We wish you well as your Christian pilgrimage takes a new direction, thank you for your fellowship as a preacher, and for faithfully fulfilling your local preacher's appointments over the last 30 years."

Farndale Quartet singers at Rievaulx, 300th performance, 1957

A crowd when the new Rievaulx Sunday school was opened, 1967

Ladies play an important part. Here they are at the 300th performance of the Farndale Quartet singers, 1957

Cliff college trekkers, who visited Rievaulx in 1949

Cockfield choir around 1955

One of the early teas at Oscar Park, following Newgate Bank Top open air service. W.H. Dunn fourth from left

Rievaulx carol singers 2004

One of our crowded gospel rallies, Rievaulx chapel early 1970's

A variety sale held early 1970's at Rievaulx village hall opened by Mary Wilkinson

Early Newgate open air service

Counting the collection, Sunday school opening 1967. Backrow: Arthur Robinson, Sidney Bowes, Ted Emmitt and W.H. Dunn. Front row: Stan Wright and Nicholas Dunn

Tot smith from the Malton area. He was a great favourite with children especially when he played his accordion or, as he called it, the old squeeze box

Chapter 15
1979 - 1980
Snowy, Exhausting Winter, Followed by A Trip To Uganda

1979 will stand out for me as the snowiest and most exhausting winter that I have ever experienced. We had snow laid about most of **January**. We had to lead the milk to the road for 15 days. On the 5th, 13th and 14th we had some very keen frosts. Diesel was freezing up in the tractors. This wintry weather was nationwide. They had 12 inches of snow in Birmingham and bad blizzards in Devon and Cornwall. There was also a rail strike on odd days which meant more cars on the road. We were still getting our feeding stuffs from Bradshaws of Driffield and over the years they have served us well. However, on 6th January they were supposed to deliver six tons of dairy cake but they didn't turn up and couldn't contact us on the phone. What had happened? No lorries had left Bradshaws that day - they were all picketed as there was a Transport Union strike. Strikes never achieve much. People need to use common sense and talk round the table. Sometimes you can get trying days when everything goes wrong. We had one such day on 31st of January. I set off to go to Pannall Mart with two geld cows and got stuck with the Landrover and trailer. John Otterburn would fetch a load of straw to the road end which meant transferring it to our trailers and the load "pigged". We also had an unfortunate experience with our emergency milk tank. We were unloading it off the trailer and caught it on some harrows that were nearby and put a hole in it. Fibre-glass and iron aren't the best of friends.

February was a continuation of January. Snow was laid about all month with some very bad days in the middle. This is how I have described them in my diary:

12th   Wintry day, snow, sleet and rain, blowing quite a lot. Nicholas, Jean and I went to the National Milk Records dinner at York. Got 2nd in 'The Improved Herd' competition. I had to take the tractor down to Helmsley, couldn't have got back with a car. Drifts nicely across main road.

13th   Very moderate day, sleet, rain and snow and very strong easterly wind.

14th   Terrible day- Gale force winds and snow, in fact a blizzard. Bad reports about weather especially in the North East. Nicholas landed to work late as on his way here he met a stranded motorist and he pulled him down to Helmsley with the tractor. Nicholas set off in the afternoon with the tractor to go to Helmsley for the post. William Wood from Bilsdale was stuck below our gate and Nicholas towed him to Thirsk road end to find a bus across the road. So he towed him back to Newgate Bank Top. Watched weather pictures on television and had a good sleep over the fire.

15th   Terrible day. Gale force North East winds blowing and snowing. Worst day I have ever experienced and frosty and cold. Messing on trying to thaw water off. Succeeded at finish. Nicholas went down in the afternoon to Helmsley with the tractor, towed a stranded motorist down who was on his way to Scotland for his holidays and couldn't get any further than Scotch Corner. What he was doing down this road I just don't know. Grand to sit over fire and get your feet up!

16th   A lot better day, still blowing a bit and light snow showers but a king to yesterday- You can work in this. I had a good start. Got milked before Nicholas landed. Main road blocked. Nicholas had to leave tractor at Rievaulx Bank Top. A lot of roads blocked all over Eastern part of country. It seemed hard work.
Snow does cause a lot of hard work. We had our milk to lead out for 14 days in February and straw and feeding stuff to lead in.

It came a real good thaw on 2nd and 3rd **March** with some warm Westerly winds. You can't beat warm winds for shifting snow. It was typical March weather of winds and frost and we started to plough on the 6th. We hadn't ploughed a furrow since before Christmas. We thought with all the snow we had in January and February this would be the end of winter but it returned again with a vengeance from the 16th - 18th. This is how I described it in my diary:

16th March
    Terrible day snowing and blowing all day. Several vehicles blocking road in afternoon.

17th   Snowing and blowing all day. Main road blocked. Terrible reports about snow in North East. We were supposed to have a furniture sale for Arthur Robinson in Rievaulx. It had to be postponed.

18th   Grand and calm. Then it got up cold and fairly windy. It has snowed and blown for at least 48 hours non-stop. Most snow blown about all winter. Terrible reports about weather in Durham, Cleveland and Newcastle area. Main road was blocked. I happened to be talking to Jessie Bainbridge from Eggleston, Barnard Castle, and they have had the worst blizzard she had ever known today.

We had the milk to lead to the road end for seven days. Right to the end of March we had a lot of rain, sleet and short periods of snow. But March went out like a lamb, a really lovely day on the 31st. **April** was a mixture of dry spells and very wet days. There was still quite a lot of snow about behind walls and hedges on high land. We started sowing on 17th April and finished on 1st May.

May greeted us with a bright cold morning, one of the coldest on record. We had about half an hour of snow in the afternoon. On the 3rd and 5th we were white over with snow. The rest of the days in May were a combination of wet and fine periods with four days of really hot weather from the 12th to the 15th and from the 27th to the 30th excessive wet with floods in the West country. I remember going to my friend, Tom Spence, near Northallerton. Brompton had been in flood and he, like a lot more farmers, had to bring his cows back in again.

June greeted us with a real grand warm day and the rest of the month was above average - a lot of fine days. We started silaging on 21st June and finished on the 27th. **July** was a really dry month. This good weather was experienced only up the eastern part of the country. I was talking to a judge at the Ryedale Show from Cumbria and they had had only five days of fine weather through summer. What a contrast to our weather! **August** was a good month, mostly fine days. **September** was above average. We started harvest on the 6th and finished on the 26th.

For the past two summers we had ploughed out grass after silage and sowed it with soft turnips for the fattening hoggs. It had been a big success, but this year it was a complete failure. So at the end of September, we decided to sow it with winter wheat. Sometimes we question failures but this failure was to be a blessing in disguise. Store lambs were a good trade but the following spring 1980 fat hoggs were a mucker as we say. We never bought any. We had a relatively easy winter, 1979/1980. It was as well as I had overdone myself, what with the hard winter and doing most of the selling at our furniture sales. I began to suffer from physical and nervous exhaustion, which can leave you with

131

depression. Over the years this is something I have had to battle with - a family weakness. We have to face it. We are only children of our parents. I have learnt as I have shared with my doctor and close Christian friends that this is a common condition, and people need to open up to one another. You see life from a distorted point of view when you are depressed but if you share it, people can bring you back on course. Always remember a problem shared is a problem halved. I find a lot of people bottle up problems inside themselves, which can lead to thinking they are the only one with the problem and can in odd cases lead to suicide. We have to learn that it is no greater shame for people to suffer with nerves than it is to suffer with a broken arm or leg. We have to learn to encourage one another rather than discourage. Sometimes the best way to forget your problems is to help someone else to solve theirs. I find a good laugh is good for you. As it says in the book of Proverbs:

'A merry heart is a good medicine'.

I find it is good to get away from your work and have a holiday. I think, as farmers, we don't get away enough and in some cases we are fools. If we employ somebody, they have holidays and we pay them as well. I always remember Teddy Wilkinson from Snape saying to me, "Money spent on holidays is never a bad thing, me lad. Biggest job is getting through the yard gate - then you've made it". When I was single I took Mam and Dad away on holiday several times. Dad was quite happy travelling round the local shows, but Mam liked to see different parts of the countryside. So the three of us went to places such as Scotland and Devon, but usually fitting in visits to marts and other farmers. No wonder that I sometimes found it difficult to switch off and relax!

Two other special friends were Bill and Carole Cornall. I first met Bill in May 1970 at Cliff College. Our coaches were parked together and I saw Bill, thought he looked like a farmer, so introduced myself to him. We struck up a friendship not knowing at that time that we would both land up as students at Cliff and that I would end up being the best man at his wedding. Bill was a great help to me at Cliff. He had a similar background to me - strict, hard-working and loving. Bill used to make the bullets and I had them to shoot!!! Bill used to say that Cliff should never have been a mixed college as girls were a distraction. However, Bill succumbed to temptation and fell in love and married the principal's secretary, Carole Ormisher. I mention them because they went to live at Westhouse, Settle, Skipton, and this backend, in early October 1979, I went to spend a week with them. I visited quite a few of my friends in that area and it was obvious they'd had terrible summer weather. I remember talking to a friend of Dad's, Joe Townley from Caton near Lancaster, and he said that this last 12 months weather had been the worst in his farming experience. It was a good open backend. We had a keen frost on the 19th **November** and towards the end of **December** we had a lot of rain, causing floods in Wales and the Carlisle area.

This backend, 1979, we started to modernise our dairy set-up by enlarging the feeding and slurry area. The milk dairy was altered and we erected a building complete with a herringbone parlour. We wanted life a bit easier. It was taking us to long to milk through the abreast parlour we put in in 1970 It doesn't matter how modern your set-up is, dairy cows need feeding and milking twice a day, something some townspeople seem to forget. I am reminded of the Dairy Farmer's Lament:

I long for a cow of modern make
That milks five days for leisure's sake.
That sleeps on Saturdays, snores on Sundays
And starts afresh again on Mondays.

I long for a herd that knows the way
To wash each other, day by day.
That never bothers to excite us
With chills or fevers or mastitis.

I sigh for a new and better breed
That takes less grooming and less feed.
That has the reason, wit and wisdom
To use the seat and flushing system.

I pray each weekend long and clear.
Less work to do from year to year
And cows that reach production peak
All in a five-day working week.

I look for officials by the mob
To guide the farmer at his job
And show these stupid breeders how
To propagate a five-day cow

As I write this in December 2001 all auction marts are closed and have been since the end of February due to the Foot and Mouth epidemic. You miss the talk and friendship with other farmers. One such farmer is Gordon Teasdale from Skiplam. Gordon used to be an expert at feeding big bullocks. He once had one weighing one tonne 305kg - some bullock!! This year in April we had some big bouncing hoggs weighing 35 ½ Kilos graded weight. Gordon eyed them over and said, "You have some good hoggs mister," I said to Gordon, "You can beat us with big bullocks, but we can beat you with big hoggs!" There weren't many good hoggs around in 1979. We gave ours hand food twice a day. We had fat hoggs making £49 each; our Friesian bull calves averaged £74 each and a 570 Kilo geld cow could make 60.5 pence per kilo coming to a total of £344. Here we are 22 years later in 2001 when those fat hoggs would make £8 less. A lot of Friesian bull calves are being shot at birth and we are only being paid 49pence per kilo for our geld cows. These figures tell us farming is in crisis.

1980

What contrasts our British weather displays. This **January** we had very little snow compared to last year. We had very keen frosts on the 1st and 2nd followed by slight frosts most days. What snow we had seemed to turn off with rain. **February** greeted us with a keen frost and the rest of the month was very mild and dry with only one wet day. Grass was beginning to grow, the promise of an early spring. We had now completed the building work for the dairy set-up, ably done by Geoff and David Gamble. The new Herringbone 12-12 milking parlour was now in use, installed by Brian Otterburn and his men. **March** was colder and wetter than February. We had the most snow of the winter on the 17th when we had 8 inches on the level. The grass that had grown in February was taken off with some keenish frosts. **April** greeted us with a real grand day and the rest of the month was fine and dry with some cold draughty days. We started sowing on the 5th and finished on the 11th.

Here I will write about my trip in April 1980 to Uganda, where my friend John Mattison was working as a mechanic and handyman for the Church Missionary Society. I had written to him from time to time and quite often, because of the inconsistency of the African postal service and the effects of the Amin regime, my letters would never arrive, and I realised that John was having a hard time. John was supported much by prayer and in practical ways by the Hollybush Fellowship at Thirsk and I knew two members were going out in early January to see him. Now it happened that the leader of the Fellowship, Jim Wilkinson, was taking a Bible study at our Chapel at Rievaulx at the end of January and naturally I asked Jim how they had found John. Jim replied that they had had to postpone their trip but were hoping to go in April. He suggested I go with them, as I was "off the same moor" and would be a help and an encouragement to John. I knew there and then that God wanted me to go. I shared it with Dad and Mother and I can tell you they didn't encourage me - rightly so - as there had been several articles in The Yorkshire Post about the famine and mass murders in Uganda. "If you go, you'll do well to land back alive," they said. Well, I did go and am still alive and kicking to tell the tale.

On the 19th April, Arthur Bennison, Brad Thurston and myself boarded the plane at Heathrow and landed in Nairobi nine hours later to be met by John. We had a good look round Nairobi and John took us round the Wild Life Park. Lions were laid out in the sun just like cattle in our country. We experienced some wonderful Christian hospitality and worshipped at a Baptist and Pentecostal Church. Quite naturally they asked us what we were doing in their country. I said we were going to help and encourage a missionary friend in Uganda. They said, "You will have to be careful. There have been ever so many people shot in the capital, Kampala, and it is now under curfew." This was where John was based. Talk about fear coming up in my spirit. I was beginning to wonder whether I would land back alive but I put on the Shield of Faith and from that moment was never fearful although we had every reason to be frightened as everywhere you went in Uganda towns and villages were guarded with soldiers carrying guns.

John began to share with us. Only a fortnight ago he'd had to move from Kampala. He had nearly got shot but things had quietened down a bit. John was now living just outside Kampala and it was about 200 miles from Nairobi. It took us two days to get there. No wonder - most of the African roads were no better than cart tracks. These mud roads were alright when it was dry but terrible and greasy when it came a thunderstorm. You were sliding all over the place and you needed a substantial vehicle. We broke our journey by spending the night at the Testimony Faith Homes in Eldoret. This was an orphanage run by faith on the lines of George Muller Homes. John was quite involved there helping them in the workshops and doing general repairs. We did some repairs to the car and then travelled on having a lot less trouble than we had anticipated with the customs on the Ugandan border, and eventually arrived where John was living. The next day we travelled into Kampala and saw the destruction that had happened under the Amin regime. Buildings had been knocked down all over. At the first roundabout the central light pole had been knocked down and was part way over the road. Traffic just went round it. John said it had been this way for the last year. We spent two days helping John to make a seed hopper and set off to deliver it, travelling into the bush country. We were met at one of the villages by the Bishop of Soroti who took us round his diocese. It was obvious that they had been told we were coming. Everywhere there were great crowds as some people hadn't seen a white person before. There is a saying: one doesn't know how the other half lives.

It was a real eye-opener. We visited a leprosy centre and a hospital where they only had the bare essentials. Patients were occupying beds that weren't fit for animals to lay on. For the next few days we travelled round with the Bishop to several villages, speaking and sharing at meetings. At all these places we received a great welcome from all the VIP's of the area. African people are very warm hearted and would always would try to give a small farewell gift.

It was quite a climate change for the three of us. It was very hot and sometimes humid, with a very different diet including a lot of hot meat. They would often have a village roast by killing a goat, hanging it up in a tree and roasting it over an open fire. Arthur and Brad said they had been given the text: 'Eat what is set before you' I replied, "You lads can please yourselves but I am using to a bit more caution". I told our hosts when they were trying to put all this food before us that I was sorry, but I was on a diet and I was not a big eater! I tried to keep to an orange drink, chicken, and hard boiled eggs, but I got a surprise one day when I cracked open an egg to find a chicken inside! Towards the end of our trip, Brad and Arthur went down with a violent sickness and diarrhoea bug. They looked like death warmed up as we say. It was left to me and the Bishop to hold the fort at the meetings. The last few days we travelled into the Northern part of Uganda, Karamoja. Talk about poverty and famine. I have never seen anything like it. People were half hungered to death. Quite a few children had no clothes. There were queues of people waiting for seed and food. There was also a shortage of clean water and diesel. Crops couldn't be sown because there was a shortage of fuel for their tractors. On our way back to Nairobi to catch the plane we ran out of diesel, but Providence was on our side. A man in a break-down truck came along and stopped to help so we siphoned some diesel out of his vehicle. Evidently this is common practice. Most people with vehicles carried a piece of pipe with them for this purpose. We arrived back at Nairobi and boarded the plane, and as I sat there I began to reflect on our trip. We had received wonderful hospitality. I saw some beautiful scenery. I saw poverty that I had never seen before. I saw a richness and depth in the African people. I saw also the dedication and skill of my friend, John Mattison, and was determined more than ever to pray and encourage those on the mission field. As I travelled up in the train from London to York, my thoughts went back to home and to farming. I had been away for 23 days. What would things be like? Our crops would have grown. As I began to view farmland out of the train window a lot of spring corn hadn't germinated properly. There was less grass than when we had travelled down. There hadn't been any rain. When I got home and began to mix with my farming friends, everybody's tale was the same - we need rain badly! People were talking about a drought. We hadn't had much rain since 31st March. I used to say to them, "Drought? We know nothing about it! They have had a drought in Uganda for the past 18 months". On one of the farms I visited there, 500 cows out of 1400 had died due to drought and no food. I began to count my blessings. We might grumble about our English weather but we have a lot to be thankful for. Uganda to me could be a very fertile country if they could put an irrigation system in operation and develop some of the farming skills we have learned in this country.

May was a dry month and cold at times. It began to affect the livestock trade. Everybody's tale was still the same - we need rain badly! It came on a wet morning on the 20th. We started silage on 5th **June** and finished on the 7th, our earliest yet. However they were very light crops. They were beginning to burn off. In the late afternoon of the 7th we had a violent thunderstorm. The thunder and the lightning were the nearest I have ever known. It blew a plug out of a socket right across our kitchen. It seemed that the rest of June we had a lot of thunder and lightning and from the 12th onward we had a lot of rain.

I want to talk about some unexpected guests who came to visit us. A man, his wife and son came into our farmyard and saw Dad. He said, "Are you Willie Dunn?" When Dad said yes, the man replied, "My neighbour used to talk a lot about you and your family". "Who was your neighbour?" asked Dad. "Jack Thompson from New Zealand". Mr. and Mrs. Allison and their son were visiting this country. They were on their way up to the Royal Highland Show, where Mr. Allison was judging Devon cattle. They stayed and had a bit of tea with us. Then we took them for a ride up Farndale from where Jack Thompson had emigrated. We met up with the Allisons again at the Royal Show and they came and had a meal with us all at Judith and Keith's in Rugby.

July was a very catchy month. We cut some grass for hay on the 10th and baled it on the 22nd. It wasn't very dry and what was most annoying, the next four days were the best in the month. **August** was very mixed till the 18th and then we had 11 days of decent weather. We started combining on 23rd August and finished on 26th September. We finished leading bales on the 2nd October. The first 9 days in **September** were decent, the rest were very catchy. This was the first time we had grown wheat since 1966 and didn't we know it.

We had it all to lead to David Cusson's dryer, near Kirkbymoorside. This wheat always looked a picture and several people said it would yield well. When we got our weights back we were a little disappointed - two tons to the acre. I remember sharing this with a friend of Dad's called William Houlston from Northallerton. William said, "Perhaps you have had it too forward". And he proceeded with this rhyme: "Winter proud wheat and a summer proud wife will beggar a fellow for the rest of his life!"

Once the weather broke in the middle of June it was a tremendous good growing year for grass. This was the first time in our experience that we had taken three cuts of silage and our third cut taken at the beginning of October was put into big bales, I think the first in the area. Big-baled silage has been a great asset to many farms. It costs twice as much as damp silage but is ten times cheaper than wasted hay. The first fifteen days in **October** were real grand days but towards the end of the month we had some very wet days.

I want to mention another unexpected person who turned up in our farmyard. This person knocked at our door and Mother answered it. He said, "Are you the place that does Bed and Breakfast?" Mother replied, "You have got the wrong place. You need to be on to the next farm, but come on in". He noticed that we had some Friesian catalogues on the table and remarked, "Oh, you are in Friesians are you?" Well he and Mother had a good natter, as we say, and Mother said, "Do you know anyone round here?". He said, "1 only know of a person called Paul Dunn who preached at a barn rally in our area. Do you know him?" Mother said, "I ought to - he lives here!" This person wouldn't let on who he was but I happened to come into the house and mother asked if I knew who he was. I took a look at him and I said, "Yes. I saw you leading a bull round last October at the Lancashire bull sale. You are a Huddleston from Lancaster way!" I was dead right. We struck up a friendship with George and his family and we still keep in contact today. He stayed with us several days and over the years my nephew Timothy has bought blue-faced Leicester tups from them. Friendship is a wonderful thing.

November was above average with some very fine days. Winter came in on the 28th with a blizzardy day followed by more snow the next day. **December** wasn't a bad month. We had 8 inches of snow on the 7th followed by a keen frost- The month ended up with three mild windy days.

I mentioned earlier that fat hoggs were a mucker. We had two left. They weighed 41 kilos graded weight and made £29 plus £6.71 subsidy each, an easy £15 a head down on last year.

Our bathroom in rural Uganda

Three moor jocks from Bilsdale in Kenya. Left to right, Author, Arthur Bennison, John Mattison

The Bishop of Soroti extreme left, who took us round his parishes

The guest home that was built especially for Author to stay in in Uganda

The vehicle we travelled round with: John Mattison's mobile workshop

Nice to see a bit of British farming. Red Poll Cattle in Uganda

Goat being slaughtered ready for our meal - Uganda 1980

Gordon Teasdale with one of his big bullocks

Proof that we had been there. Arthur Bennison and Author

Chapter 16
1981 - 1984
A Trip To Israel
And A Birmingham Bonanza

1981

The beginning and end of years are good times to reflect on how we could do things better. Experience is a great teacher and what applies to one farm or farmer doesn't always apply to another. We had had a bellyful, as the saying goes, with our wheat crop: high drying costs, sack hire, and a disappointing yield in 1980. Spring barley has always done us reasonably well. It is relatively easy to harvest, most of it blown into the self-seal silo, and we had a ready sale for it. Plus the fact that we could use some to feed to our cattle and sheep. There is something to be said for a simple system. I was once talking to a friend of mine, Geoff Bean from Salton, and I have thought quite a bit about what he said, "I go for the K.I.S method Paul, that means Keep it Simple". We were also finding that ploughing out grass and sowing it with roots wasn't the best way. We were finding that it was better to grow a straight crop of roots, getting your stubble sprayed for wicks in the autumn, getting it mucked and ploughed and getting some frost on it. Muck and a good frost tilth are the next best thing to irrigation.

January 2nd, 5th and 12th were three very windy days- 7th, 15th and 16th had keen frosts. There was very little snow which always turned off with rain. **February** was relatively mild. We had two very windy days on 6th and 7th and some snow on the 2nd and 28th. The first ten days in **March** were quite wet, a real bad time for sheep on roots. On the 21st we had a terrible wet day followed by a real storm the following morning. A gale force wind with heavy snow. The last five days in March were more like spring, fairly fine and dry. April greeted us with a wet day. The 8th and 9th were warm, springlike days. We started sowing on 10th **April** and finished on 21st. April 1981 will always stand out to me as one of the worst snowstorms for the time of year. On the 22nd it came in as cold as Christmas. On the 23rd we had 2 inches of snow. The next day it snowed and blew all day. We had about 8 inches on the level and didn't get any milk away. The postman couldn't get in. To crown all we had an electric cut at night. The next morning it was snowing and blowing first thing, and the rest of the day was windy and cold. We had to take our milk to the road end in the emergency tank for three days, the first time we had had to do this in April. On

26th we had a real cold northeasterly wind. The winter storm had moved down south causing chaotic conditions. Dad always liked ringing his sheep friends up North and heard a lot had lost quite a few lambs. There was nothing the lambs could do as they were smothered with drifting snow. **April** ended up with some wet days.

May greeted us with better weather. A real fine dry day, but the next morning we were white over with snow. On the whole May was quite damp and growy. People said to me after my visit to Uganda in 1980, now you have got the travel bug you will never be at home. On the 9th May 1981, my nephew Simon and I went on a 10 day conducted trip to Israel. On the Sunday we went to a service in the garden tomb area. It was tremendous to be in the company of so many believing Christians. I remember us singing, 'He lives. He lives, Christ Jesus lives today. He walks with me and talks with me along life's narrow way. He lives, He lives, salvation to impart, you ask me how I know He lives. He lives within my heart'. I had a pleasant surprise just as I was coming away. I met up with four other Yorkshire people who were on a trip with another travel company: Mr. and Mrs. Alan Abel from Wath near Ripon, and Mr. and Mrs. Leonard Webster from Knaresborough. Over the next few days we visited many areas and places of biblical interest. Here are some extracts from my diary:

May llth

Went to the garden tomb and the place of the skull, had a communion service, very moving. There is no doubt that it was here that Jesus rose again. Visited the place where Jesus taught his disciples the Lord's Prayer. It is written in 60 different languages. Visited the dungeons where Jesus was imprisoned before He was tried by Caiphas. It must have been cruel for him before he went to the cross.

12th May

Visited the church of the Nativity where the bells broadcast from on Christmas Day- Visited the Shepherd's cave.

13th May

Went down to the Dead Sea. Went by cable car to the Fortress Masada. Talk about height - 1400 feet above sea level. It really gave me the jitters.

14th

Visited the glass works at Hebron. Went to market at Beersheba. Spent some time by the Mediterranean sea.

15th May

Had a walk around Jerusalem Old City with our leader. We were in the place where Jesus was tried by Pilate. Went to the wailing wall.

16th May

Went to Nazareth, saw Joseph's workshop. Visited Cana in Galilee.

17th May

Had a walk around the shores of Galilee. Had a biblical meal of five loaves and 2 fishes.

18th May

Went on a coach ride round the shores of Galilee, visited the Mount of the Beatitudes. Went on a boat ride across Galilee, visited a Kibbutz, which means a collective communal dwelling where people live together and have no wage. A child lives with his parents for the first 6 weeks then they are raised in a group. Had a look round the cattle unit, all Holsteins. A normal cow gives 2,000 gallons of milk fed on a complete diet of maize and bananas etc.

19th May

Left Tiberias, viewed Mount Carmel, heard a talk about architecture and visited a diamond factory. Toured around Joppa, then we came to Tel Aviv.

All good things come to an end. We arrived back at Heathrow. As we travelled back up in the train, what a contrast to last year, when we had drought. This year I wrote in my diary, "I don't think I have known things grow so fast. We have had a marvellous holiday, good food, good fellowship - a holiday with a purpose." One of the questions I was asked by several people: 'What is it that stands out about a tour of Israel?' There is no doubt in my mind - the Garden tomb. A tour of Israel is very hectic especially if you do it in ten days. You only have half a day to yourselves. On this day most people go back to the Garden tomb. It is a wonderful atmosphere where you sense the presence of the Living Lord Jesus.

June started off with a real grand warm day and in many ways was like May, a real growy month. Rains came at the right time, interspersed with some warm days. We started silaging on 15th and finished on 18th.

July was a continuation of June weather, rains coming just at the right time. 23rd and 24th we had quite a lot of rain. 26th-30th were real hot days. One of the features of this summer was that our second crop of grass was made into hay. We cut some on the 27th and baled it on the 31st. This was outstanding stuff. 1 remember taking it to Bilsdale show and it got first prize. I kept saying to myself, I wish this hay could be entered in a national competition. However, the following year they put a competition on at the Birmingham Fatstock Show. We sent two bales and got first and second, winning £60. The prize money was more than it was for livestock.

August was a continuation of June and July's weather. Rains coming at the right time with some very hot days, making it quite easy to get the rest of our second crop hay. The first ten days of **September** were fine, and we started harvest on 7th September. We had some rain on the llth, the first we had had for three weeks. We finished combining on the 23rd. It was one of those years when harvest seemed to be a struggle. We had given most of our corn a second dressing of nitrogen and it didn't seem to be ripe when the fine weather arrived. The rest of September was quite catchy. Straw seemed difficult to get dry. We baled our last straw on l2th October. The month of **October** was a combination of autumn weather. On the 16th we had a very keen frost, the keenest October frost for 56 years.

Friendship is a wonderful thing and I heard that a young couple had come to live in Kirkbymoorside. I went to visit them. That couple was Gary and Glennis Hobbs. Little did I think at that time that Gary would be the man who would put together Dad's book 'Down Memory Lane' and that his wife Glennis would type my writings on their computer.

The first six days of **November** were fine - above average for the time of year. The rest of the month was fairly mild with odd keen frosts. **December** started off with three grand fine days, very mild. Within the week it was the opposite extreme. 8th, 9th and 10th were very keen frosts, llth was extremely keen and 13th the keenest of the lot. Then it came on a real blizzard towards night. This is how I described 14th December in my diary:

"Been a very bad night, blown snow a lot but silent today. Bad reports about weather. Two people perished in cars. A lot of people stranded at Ripon and Skipton. No roads out of Whitby. Simon Bradshaw couldn't get as there wasn't a road out of Driffield. This is the worst snow I have known before Christmas."

More bad weather was to follow. Got emergency tank fettled up and took milk to road 15th, 16th and 17th, keen frosts. 18th was a blizzardy day. 19th, been a very keen frost. First time fold yard troughs were frozen up.

Keenest frosts since 1963. Blizzards came back on 20th. This is how I noted it in my diary 20th December: Talk about a rough day, snowed and blew from 7 o'clock this morning till about 3 o'clock in the afternoon. No let up. Nicholas got over but went back after dinner. Tried to get milk to road but couldn't get out of paddock. Talk about snow being blown about. One consolation, it is warmer. No chapel or carol singing, bad reports about weather on wireless and TV. Eleven people lost their lives on the sea in Cornwall. 21st December, been another rough night but a lot warmer and calmer day, though it snowed until about 3 o'clock. Bad reports about weather especially in Whitby area. I don't think I have ever seen so much drifted snow at bottom of paddock. Such big drifts we decided to take milk down Beckdale to Helmsley.

The next three days we had frost and snow showers. Christmas day we made our customary trip up to Bransdale for our Christmas dinners. We had to go around by Kirkbymoorside as the Helmsley road was blocked. It came warmer on the 27th and the next four days it began to thaw with rain at times. On 29th we had to get John Pickersgill in with his Drott to open our road. We had led the milk out for 12 days in the emergency tank.

On 1st December I happened to be talking to George Ford and he said, "Put this down in your diary - it is the first time in my farming experience that everything in the farming world is a good trade. Things have never been so dear for the time of the year".

Here are some prices:

29th April 29 Kg hoggs £47-80,

Friesian bull calves averaged £70,

665 Kg geld cow, 76.5p per kilo made over £500.

November milk 14.14p per litre.

1982

There is an old saying 'When the wind is in the East it is neither fit for man nor beast'. Although it was thawing a bit, the wind was in the East, the wrong quarter for it to thaw properly. The first two days in **January** we had frost. I have never known so much ice about- What with paddled snow and rain on top plus frost, our yard and stackyard was more like a skating rink than anything else. On the 3rd and 4th of January there had been a lot of rain during the night and it had melted snow causing flooding down York and Boroughbridge. The river Ouse was 15 feet above the normal level. On the 5th

145

it was what we call a pig of a day- This is what I recorded in my diary:
"Wet morning, came on to snow in the afternoon and a very strong easterly wind. Very bad reports about blizzards in Scotland, Northumberland and Durham. Floods in York, Cawood and Wistow near Selby worst in living memory. River Ouse 16 feet 3 inches above normal level, much higher than the all-time record in 1947."

On the 7th we had the keenest frost of the winter. TV says it is the keenest for 27 years. 8th we had more snow and blizzard conditions, blowing our farm road in. Very cold weather in Scotland, 27 degrees of frost. Very bad blizzard conditions in Devon and Cornwall, llth January. I would think this has been the keenest frost I have known - all water frozen up in the middle sheds. I spent all day fettling a relay pipe up to the big trough. At one point it was freezing running water through a three-eighths pipe. Coldest night for 42 years. We had very keen frosts on 13th, 14th and 15th. The next 10 days were quite mild with some fog. Winter came back on the 27th with snow and blizzard conditions but it was short lived. It came on to rain and most of the snow went. On 29th and 30th we had a lot of wind and the last day ended up with a grand day like spring. **February** was a decent month with no snow, some frost and fog. With the hard frosts of December and January, all of our swedes went rotten, for the first time in my experience.

Over the years we have had some good fleshy hoggs and people have often remarked, 'What do you feed them on?' My reply always was 'Give them some bag' We rarely feed them any hay or silage except when swedes are too frozen for sheep to eat them. If you are feeding big bales I don't think there has been an efficient rack feeder made yet for feeding sheep outside. I often see ring feeders on sheep folds stuck in the mud and sheep mucked up to the eyeballs. As one man remarked, 'Alright for farmers in general but no good for a dedicated shepherd'. We always try to have a good run back either with grass or where the fodder beet and mangles have been. We put the troughs on these areas and give them barley and protein. I don't think you can get sheep to weight without giving them handfood. Some people say it is expensive but remember barley has been cheaper than hay.

Sheep folding has always played an important part on our farm and it was becoming a lot easier as we went on to the three strand electric fence system giving them some fresh roots each day. The three strand electric fence system has been a big breakthrough. We normally drill our roots the long way on and give them two or three rows a day. As a shepherd there's nothing I like to see better than good Suffolk Cross hoggs grazing the

146

length of the field and going back later in the day and seeing them all laid down. Content sheep make a contented shepherd. Sometimes you can get problems trying to keep the sheep in. You can get ring leaders who teach the others bad habits like jumping or clambering underneath the wires especially if you try to make them clean up the patch too much before moving on. They always know where the food is!

March started off wet. On the 6th it was a terrible wet day, it rained and sleeted non-stop for 14 hours. The rest of March was a combination of rain, sleet, wind and odd springlike days. We started sowing on 26th March and finished on 13th April. **April** was a good grow month, considering it was dry. We only had rain on the 8th and 9th. **May** started very dry, cold and windy with frosts on the 5th and 6th. All the month we had some warm growy, spring like days, but very little rain came, Some fell on the 18th and 22nd, just plenty to keep things going. June started off with a warm humid morning, came on a terrible thunderstorm and torrential rain. Heaviest rain Dad had known. Telephone and electric were cut off. We started silaging on the 8th and finished on the 11th. **June** was quite thundery with heavy rain most of the month. I noted in my diary on the 28th: "We have had about eleven days now of real wet weather. Land is the wettest I have known for this time of year. On the last day it was a tremendous grand day, the best day we have had for a fortnight. The heavy rain we had on the 1st had caused some damage to our swede crop- They were drowned out as we say and we had to redrill with yellow turnips."

July started off droppy. We started hay month on 6th and finished on 12th. On the whole July was a good hay time with 16 days of real good weather, interspersed with nice gentle rains. **August** started off with four very hot days. In fact August was very much like July, some good days and just the right amount of rain to keep things growing. We started harvest on 14th August and finished on 9th September. The weather must have been quite good because like last year we made all our second crop grass into hay - 1,740 small bales. **September** was a repeat of July and August, some good fine days and rain at the right time. This was the first time we sowed any winter barley. **October** was an above average month, some good fine days. Two keen frosts on 23rd and 24th. **November** was an open month with quite a lot of fog ending up with a keen frost on 30th. **December** was very open, odd keen frosts and odd wet days. The last eight days were very mild, in fact I have it recorded that 'This weather is unbelievable'.

This has been a good year for our farm. One of the best yields of grass and corn, livestock prices buoyant. Here are some prices:

Our Friesian bull calves averaged £90

650Kg geld cow at 88.20 pence per kilo made £573

Fat hoggs, Pannall 14th April 28Kg made £55.50

Masham hoggs and lambs in Northallerton made £86 per hogg and lamb pair

We paid £100 each for Maurice Ryder's Top Pen of Masham gimmers

A record price for Masham mart. I said to Dad, 'This could be our last time for showing, don't begrudge yourself.' Somebody said he had taken his cheque book and left his brains at home!

1983

January was a continuation of December's weather, very mild and windy. In fact, from the 15th to the 18th they were all very windy days and then from the 26th to the 29th there was very little frost and some snow on the 30th. **February** started off terrible and windy. It was so windy we couldn't feed sheep, troughs were blowing over. There were very bad reports of wind damage in Morecambe and Blackpool. We had a lot more winter in February than January. From the 2nd to the 5th we had keenish frosts and on the 7th and 8th slight coverings of snow. On the 10th it was snowing and blowing most of the day and continued right through the night. Main road was blocked. We had the milk to lead to the road four days. For the next days we had raw frosty days, thawing a bit until the 26th and then it began to be windy and drying. **March** greeted us with a fine spring like day, and it was quite drying for the next ten days. We started sowing on the 10th March and finished on the 9th of May. From the 16th to the 29th was wet. No land work done. The 31st was most like spring and then very wet.

April was a very wet month. There was a drier spell on 14th - 18th when we sowed some corn. We now had only eight acres of turnip land left to sow. We intended getting it sown on the 28th. We got it harrowed up and then it came on to rain and sleet. We had another go at harrowing up a week later. Just got it harrowed up and it came onto rain. A fortnight later it came a drying weekend and I went to have a look at the land. It was dry on top and I said, 'Let's have it drilled'. I just got the corn drill pulled out and it started to dampen. I said to myself 'let's have it in'. It came on very wet, but we got it sown, or should I say, we paddled it in. It was interesting to note that in the next field over, our winter barley was coming into ear. I put a note in my diary at the end of April - I don't think I have ever known such a wet and cold April. Land is saturated. Things, including human beings, need sunshine on their backs. **May** was a very wet month. There was a bit of respite in the weather 16th - 18th. Then wet again, and another drier spell from the 23rd - 26th. A lot of dairymen turned their cows out,

148

then on 27th it was a rainy stormy day, just like winter. Didn't turn our cows out. The next day was wet in the morning. A lot of dairymen had to fetch their cows back in until the second week in June. I remember going to Cliff College for the Anniversary. It came on very wet. Everywhere was saturated.

June greeted us with a real cold, wild morning and came on very wet. On 2nd June this is what I recorded in my diary: Showered on most of day. I don't think I have ever known it so wet for the time of year. Cows bags this morning were terrible and mucky. Had to fence a fresh track for the cows as their existing path was so mucky and paddled. It took up on the 4th, and for the rest of June we had some very good weather. We started silaging on 14th and finished on 17th. There was very little rain. Some showers on the 26th, 28th and 29th.

July greeted us with a good hay day and dulled in late afternoon, came onto rain, gave things a drink. July was again a repeat of June. Some very hot days and very little rain, only odd showers. Tremendous grow weather for roots. On the last day of July it came a grand steady rain, most since 2nd June. **August** was a repeat of June and July, some very hot days. We had a tremendous grand rain on the 16th, the most since 2nd June. We started harvest on 5th August and finished on 7th September. We made all our second crop grass into hay. I reckon we did something unique with our grass seeds. They were cut for silage on 14th June, cut again on 13th July, made into hay, cut again on 26th August and baled on 30th for hay. All these crops had no rain water on them. The first four days in **September** were showery followed by four good drying days. The 10th and 11th were wet and stormy days. First taste of backend. The rest of the month was good weather for September. Some good drying days and odd wet days which were needed.

October was almost a repeat of September, some nice rains and some grand days. Grass greened up a lot. **November** was a grand open month with some very mild days. There were three keenish frosts on 2nd, 23rd and 24th and the end of the month landed up very mild. On **1st December** I have it recorded that it was a real grand mild day, more like spring than anything else. These mild days were a characteristic of the month from 17th - 24th when we had a lot of wet. Christmas day was a tremendous grand day, more like spring than winter. The saying is true - If the sun shines through the apple trees before dinner time on Christmas day, it is going to be a fine harvest.' The month ended up with very windy days on 27th, 28th and 30th and 31st.

Here are some 1983 prices:

500 Suffolk Hoggs bought in, we paid an average of £31.20 each

Milk in November 15.523 a litre

Newly calved cows in York, December, £570

Fat Hoggs 28 Kg £53.

7th April sold mangles in spring £16 per ton.

1984

1984 was the beginning of a new era in the life of New Leys. In 1983 we had decided that we would call it a day with showing our Masham and mule sheep. Dad had been showing for 30 years. In October 1983 we had bought six pedigree Suffolk ewes for our Newsley flock. Three came from Alan White's flock at Bartindale near Filey, and three from Roecliffe Farm near Boroughbridge. It was with some excitement on llth January that our first lamb appeared. We did very well the first season, rearing 11 lambs off 6 ewes.

The first fortnight in **January** was open and mild with a lot of wind on the 7th, llth, 13th and 14th. We had snow on the 15th and 16th blowing our road in. We had some nice winter days up to the 21st. We had the keenest frost of the winter on 21st. The 22nd had been a rough night and we had to lead the milk to the road. This is what I wrote in my diary on 23rd January: "Started to snow and blow first thing and snowed and blew all day, still snowing at 9 o'clock. Very bad reports about weather on TV in Scotland and North East. David Cussons came and opened road out but he might as well have been in bed, it blew it in again. Got milk tanker in." We had some more nice winters days. January ended up with a real grand dry winters day.

February greeted us with a foggy frosty morning, came onto snow and turned off with rain with a very wet afternoon. The first fourteen days were quite mild and the rest of the month was a combination of fog and frost with some snow on the 21st. **March** was a combination of damp and dull days with not much wind. We started sowing corn on 23rd and finished on 9th April. On the 24th, 25th and 26th we had a lot of rain. The last day it was white over with snow, as were 1st and 2nd of **April**. We had a very keen frost on the 3rd. **April** on the whole was a good grow month. Not a lot of rain. From 20th - 28th we had some very fine warm days, some more like summer. The month ended up dry but a lot colder.

May was a contrast of real warm days against some real cold days. We had keenish frosts for the time of year from the llth - 14th. What a contrast to last year. We only had two rains this month on 22nd and 27th against the wet May of 1983. **June** started off with a dull morning and came on a wet afternoon. Most rain since 10th April. In fact the next six days were ideal for our farm, dull and cloudy with good rains on 3rd and 5th. We started silaging on 7th and

150

finished on 8th. We had good crops, so much so we had to leave seven acre for hay as we couldn't get it in the clamp. We had a good rain on the 13th, otherwise the rest of the month was dry. June was a bit like May. A contrast of dry warm days against cold days.

We were quite forward with our work, and I said to Mam and Dad, 'Let's go up to Scotland, have a day at the Royal Highland Show, and spend a few days touring'. We took uncle Harry Wass with us. We had a good laugh and viewed some wonderful scenery. **July** started off with some very hot days. This is what I wrote in my diary: "7th July very hot day, I have looked over Old Byland and I think it is burning more than it did in 1976. Me, Mam, Dad and David had a ride up Skiplam. The dry weather isn't half getting into things." On 12th July we had a freak rain, only localised to this area. We had the most rain since 26th March. Our root crop got a mighty boost and pastures started to green. A lot of winter barley was harvested early July onwards. The rest of July was mostly hot days although we had about three hours rain on 27th.

I had really got the Suffolk sheep bug and travelled down to the National Show and sale at Stoneleigh then up to the great event at Edinburgh, where I saw a ram from the Muiresk flock make £14,000. The dry weather was very evident in Scotland. Things were really burnt up and there was a poor show of roots. I wrote in my diary; "Bentleys of Old Byland and Dunns of Helmsley have the best roots between here and Edinburgh!"

August started off with a very hot day, but on the 2nd we had a wet day, just what everything needed. We had some heavy thundery rain on 3rd and some more rain on 7th and 8th. It was tremendous grow weather for roots. The rest of August we had some good hot days. We started combining on 10th August and finished on 24th with exceptionally good yields. Again all our second crop grass was made into hay. We had now done this for four years running. **September** started off with rain, the most we'd had since 2nd August. On the 4th it had been a lot of rain during night, still raining when we got up. Been most rain since 24th March. September was a very good grow month for roots and grasses. Showers and some fine days, ending up with quite a lot of rain on the 29th and 30th.

October was a grand open month. Rains came at the right time with some nice autumn days. **November** started off dry but on the 3rd and 4th we had a lot of rain, the most since the end of March. November was another grand open month with very little frost. **December** was almost a repeat of November, very open, some real grand days and very little frost.

Milk quotas came in from 1st April and with it being a dry summer, the second driest I would think since 1959 and 1976, it began to look as though we as a country wouldn't meet quota. Dairy cows became a good trade. We sold one for £700 on 15th November in York. We had a freak trade with some fat hoggs on 10th April, graded at 28 Kg and making £69.50 in Stokesley. I think we made the most ever of some grinding barley at £122 per ton in April. We sold our first Suffolk Tup lamb in Northallerton for £280 guineas.

Fishing on Galilee

Fancy feeding a banana to a cow

Wonderful flowers and atmosphere in the garden, Israel

Author and nephew Simon outside garden tomb, Israel

I still like cows, even when I am on holiday! Israel 1981

Nothing new about grain silos. Israel 1981

Regional winners in the Golden Fleece competition. From left to right, Dad and Mam, Mr and Mrs A White and Mr and Mrs Mick Bulmer with Manager, Wool Growers

Chapter 17
1985 - 1987
Love, Courtship And Marriage

At the end of my 1984 diary I wrote these words: "This year I have learned to be considerate and compassionate to single people" as I was in that situation myself. People can be cruel by teasing you. Here I was, 39, and to many people a confirmed bachelor. I was a very shy person among the ladies. Some men are always fancying and flirting, but I wasn't like that. That wasn't to say I hadn't my fancies but nothing seemed to materialise. Life was very full for me, what with my work and all my friends, but there were times when I felt lonely and in my 1984 diary I say: "I am trusting you Lord, to lead me to a Christian wife". In Genesis we read: "It isn't good for a man to be alone. I will make a companion for him, a helper suited to his needs". It is important who we marry. Behind every man is a good woman.

They say a man's hardest problem is to find a woman attractive enough to please him, and dumb enough to marry him!

I didn't think my prayer would be answered quite so quickly, because God had Dorothy lined up for me. Dorothy had spent six years doing missionary work in the Philippines and in December 1984 had come home believing that her time on the mission field had come to an end. Dorothy had a lot of friends in her age group and they had all got married. She was the only one still single. Again we are only human and Dorothy tells me she began to ask God for a Christian husband. I remember meeting up with Dorothy at the Easter Convention 1985, at Northallerton. She looked attractive - would she be dumb enough to be interested in me? I kept putting off and being faint-hearted. They say a faint heart never won fair lady. However, early in June I wrote to her and two weeks later took her out for a meal. It was love at first sight, things blossomed and we got engaged six months later. This is what we received written on an engagement card from my best-man-to-be's wife, Carol Cornall.

Dear Mr. Dunn, what a pleasure it is
to wish you a happy engagement.
Bill seemed very calm on the phone on Thursday night,
but later collapsed with amazement.

You've studied the ladies as each has passed by,
But you've waited for Dorothy's hand.

155

We've all stood and waited and watched with delight
And by, we all do think it's grand.

We feel its our duty as old trusted friends
To give you some measured advice
For soon to fair Dorothy you would be wed
The days will fly past in a trice.

So what can we tell you that you do not know
A man of your wisdom and balance
A man of experience, travel and wealth
As you gallop headlong into romance.

We'd say, trust the Lord, and keep pressing on,
Together seek Him for His counsel,
And then, as you serve Him and set up your home
You'll say "Praise the Lord. He is faithful."

At the end of 1984 I'd asked the Lord, now it was about thanking Him. This is what I wrote in my 1985 December diary: "The Lord has been really good to me in answering my prayer regarding a help-mate, in bringing me into contact with Dorothy. She is a great girl and the Lord couldn't have given me anyone better. It is great when the Lord gives you someone who you can share and pray with. Both of us have shared that being single can be lonely. I would ask, dear Lord, in 1986, that my walk would be close with you, and that you will provide a home for Mam and Dad (and grace for me and Dorothy if we have to "live in".)

We fixed a date for the wedding - May 10th 1986. Our romance caused quite a talk. One man said, "What does this attractive young lady (actually she was 32!) see in old Paul Dunn?" My reply was "There is plenty of shelter under an old bush".

The next months were a time of planning and preparing for our wedding and looking for a home for Dad and Mother. I knew it wouldn't be easy for my parents as they had lived at New Leys all their married life and I think they thought I was a confirmed bachelor. But God was good to them and provided a house just right for them, not too modern, and in a nice position in Helmsley.

May 10th arrived and things went off well, despite Dorothy being half an hour late. I'd waited this long - I thought she was worth waiting another half hour for!! When you appear to be a confirmed bachelor, people can make big

156

claims against you. Like a friend in Scotland who said, "If Paul ever gets married, I will give him a free honeymoon". We took her at her word and honeymooned in Peebles, Scotland. Brother Christopher said he would give me a colour TV. Well, people were all good to us. We were provided for, even Dorothy being given her wedding dress by a friend. Just the style and fitting she needed. My uncle Albert wrote a poem which he read at the wedding:

We thought it would never happen:

This is the day we thought would never ever be
When Paul would get married,
But he's proved us wrong
And his bride is Dorothy.

We thought it would never happen Paul
For you to get a wife
A bachelor we thought you would be
Aye, a bachelor for life.

We thought it would never happen Paul
We never really did, I'll be bound
In fact, if I'd been a gambling man
I might have risked a hundred pound.

Because we thought it would never happen Paul
For you've travelled far and wide,
We thought you would never find a lass either black or white
That you could call your bride.

We thought it would never happen Paul
In fact we wondered how you would cope.
When one day someone said to you about a wife
Paul said:"Aye why now then, where there's life there's hope"

We thought it would never happen Paul
Until one day, just by chance,
A lady said to me, "What about Paul?
He's got caught up in this thing called romance".

We thought it would never happen Paul
But what women will do to catch us men
But of course they say that
Life begins at 30 plus 10

We thought it would never happen Paul
But such news you cannot smother
And then we heard a race was on
Twixt daughter and her mother.

And now a word for Dorothy,
Be prepared to lose some sleep.
For all Paul's got a wife,
His second love could be his sheep.

Now Paul's always been known as Paul
And it's never sounded bad.
But you never know in future years
He might be known as "Dad".

And now it's really happened Paul
How pleased I am to be a guest
To wish you both good health and happiness
And all the very best.

We came back from the honeymoon and it was all about getting your nose to the grindstone. Marriage is a wonderful institution, but you have to work at it. There will be differences of opinion, hard times, difficult situations, especially when you bring a wife into the old home. People expect, and sometimes demand, what has happened before. But love and straight talking overcome all things. One man gave me some good advice: "Don't both get vexed at the same time". We made up our minds that we would try to keep our lines of communication open, to have no secrets, to talk, share and be honest and open with one another. The institution of marriage is under attack. We see this in the alarming rise in divorce. Television and money could have a lot to answer for. The good gift of sex is abused and misused. Marriage is all about love and if we love one another we will have a healthy physical relationship. Here are some quotes about wives and their husbands:

A woman's work is never done
- especially if she asks her husband to do it.

You should never criticise your wife's judgement
- look who she decided to marry.

A good woman interests a man. A beautiful woman fascinates a man,
but it's the sympathetic woman who gets him.

Things don't always go well for the farmer. Where you get livestock you get deadstock, and we seemed to have a run of bad luck with our Suffolk sheep. In July 1984 Nicholas sent me down to The National Show and Sale at Stoneleigh and said "Try and get one from the Bentley flock from Hardings in Warwickshire. You can go to £400". Hardings had a good do, as we say, winning the supreme champion. Their bloodlines were sought after. Their females made 600 guineas, more than our pockets could afford. After the sale I happened to be talking to Mr. Tom Harding and he said they were taking some more females to Peterborough. Nicholas went down and bought one. I think it was 350 guineas and the Hardings would take it back home to mate it with one of their top rams. Unfortunately one day the Hardings found it rigged (laid on its back) and dead. Neither of us had it insured. The Hardings were helpful and let us have its twin sister at half its price. She produced 13 lambs for us in six lambings. When we dispersed our flock in 2000, over a quarter of our flock were descended from this ewe. They were good mothers and good milkers. We had made the other additional purchases in Autumn 1984 from Mick Bulmer's Salton flock and Bert Harper's Skiplam flock, plus some more gimmer shearlings from Alan White's Bartindale flock. We now had 12 ewes. This lambing time two ewes died and one or two good lambs, all round Christmas. This is farming! The farmer who never loses any stock is either a clever fellow or a big liar. There are more liars than clever fellows!

1985

January started off with a terrible stormy day, it rained, snowed, sleeted and blew all day. Out of the first fifteen days we had snow showers on twelve of them. On 16th it snowed most of the day, but was calm with it. Bad reports about weather in the south east and west. On the 19th we had a ride up Bransdale. Snow was piled up on the road sides above the Landrover. The snow hung about with quite keen frosts towards the end of the month.

February started off with a windy day. The first week was mild weather,

159

melting the snow, and after that twelve days of keen frosts, ending up with mild weather. **March** was a combination of white frosts, some keen, and there was some snow from 16th - 20th. We started sowing on 12th March and finished on 18th April. **April** was very wet until 22nd and ended up with some very cold windy days. **May** continued with these very cold days until the 14th when we had a violent thunderstorm, then we had some good grow days. The last five days in May were tremendous grand warm days. **June** started off with a continuation of the five warm days that we had at the end of May. The rest of June was a combination of cold, wet and windy days with a good day now and again. We started silaging on 11th June and finished on 17th making the wettest silage we had ever made. We started haytime on 28th June and finished on 5th July.

The first 10 days of **July** were very good hay days. The rest of the month was very muggy and wet - ideal for root crops. **August** was a repeat of the latter part of July, with a lot of wet and not many good harvest days. We started harvest on the 22nd August and finished on the 12th October. **September** was a very catchy wet month with not many harvest days. **October** greeted us with a very hot day. The next few days were catchy, then from 9th to 29th we had some very good weather. In fact, on 24th I have it recorded in my diary: "Tremendous grand day, sunny, just like summer." **November** started off frosty, in fact on the 3rd we had the keenest frost I have known for the time of year. Our mangle pie wasn't covered up and a lot got frozen and eventually went rotten. We had keenish frosts again from the 10th - 13th and from the 26th - 29th a spell of snowy weather. **December** by and large was a mild wet month with quite a lot of wind. We had some keen frosts from 27th - 29th.

1985

In many ways 1985 was an eventful year for us. We had a dispersal sale of 52 cattle, all bred and reared on the farm. Among these were seven Belgian Blue crosses. We were the first in the Ryedale area to use a Belgian Blue bull. A lot of people came to see what they were like. One bullock went to the Smithfield show but unfortunately was too heavy for its class and couldn't be shown. The weather was a big talking point - the last four summers had been good ones. It wasn't too bad in our area, but up the north, north-west, and Scotland it was a disastrous summer, wet and more wet. A lot of farmers up Lancaster, Penrith and Middleton-in-Teesdale didn't get any hay till September and October. Some dairy farmers round Lancaster area had kept their cows in since August. Last year, 1984, because of the dry summer the nationl milk quota wasn't met, and this year, 1985, it wasn't met because of the wet weather. What a contrast in the British climate!

I have always liked travelling about to different auction marts and meeting people. In September 1985 my nephew Timothy had a bad trade with some of his mule lambs locally, so he withdrew 30 of them. I received a telephone call - would I take him to Bellingham, Northumberland, with these lambs ? I said I was game, "But think on - we are going to a different place amongst different people." The first person I met when I got there was Mr. Iveson the auctioneer and I said "These sheep have got to make a good price. I have brought them eighty miles. They belong to Walter Bainbridge's grandson". Walter did, and still does, a lot of trade with Iveson's via Hexham auction mart. Mr. Iveson said "I will do what I can". The next man I met was a friend called Jack White from Riding Mill. We knew Jack well, having shown Mule sheep against him. I explained to Jack what my mission was. I showed him Timothy's lambs. Jack did a bit of trading and said "I have an order for a packet like them". They went through the ring and made £14 a head more than Timothy had withdrawn them at. Jack bought them; a friend in need is a friend indeed. It was obvious as we travelled into Northumberland what an effect this wet summer had had. This was around 20th September and there was hay laid out in flat eight bales as black as coal, and grass grown up around them. I remember going to the Lancaster Friesian Bull Sale on October 3rd and talking to one farmer who hadn't got any hay. The day before, he had started to big bale some grass and bogged to the axles first time round the field.

1986

January started off with a mild day, then it came a spell of frost and snow on 3rd - 9th. The rest of the month we had a lot of frost, wind and heavy snow on 29th. The next few days were damp with a strong north-easterly wind blowing from 5th **February** to the end of the month. We had wintry weather with keen frosts and drifting snow. **March** started off with a grand winter's day, but it was blowing snow about and was very bad on Hambleton and up Bransdale. On the 3rd we had one of the keenest March frosts on record. Then onwards to 23rd we had a lot of fog, rain and wind. On 24th we had the worst day of the winter. It snowed and blew most of the day, falling about eight inches on the level. March ended up with two wet days with a mixture of snow, sleet and rain. **April** started off with a dry day followed by two keenish frosts and snow on 6th and 7th. We started sowing on 10th and finished on 30th. April, by and large, was a wet month. On the 17th my diary reads: 'Been a terrible night, thunder and lightning and heavy rain, which persisted all day. I have never seen so much water about on our farm. This is the wettest I have ever known for this time of the year. Bad reports about flooding in the North East'. However, the month ended up with a welcome five days of drying weather.

This weather continued for the first four days in **May**, then by and large May was a wet growy month. On 20th we had a violent storm with a cloud burst and water everywhere. It even flooded into our back toilet. Down our main road newly planted potatoes were washed out on to the road and you could hardly travel because of the soil. In Kirkbymoorside some of the tarmac in the road was washed up, but at Lastingham, four miles away, they hardly had any rain. On 27th it was a terrible windy day - the windiest I have known in summer. The last four days of the month were dry and growy. **June** started off with a warm day. The next ten days were showery with a lot of wind and a very wet day on the 10th. The weather took up and for the rest of the month it was dry with some very hot days. We started silaging on 17th and finished next day - a record for us.

July was a continuation of this dry hot June weather until 23rd when we had some rain. We had another good rain on the 29th, the most rain since 10th June. **August** was a wet month with a terrible storm on 25th and 26th. This is what I have recorded on 26th in my diary: 'Terrible first thing, wind and rain. They call this storm Hurricane Charlie. It is the worst I have known for this time of the year. Bad reports of floods at Reeth in Swaledale'.

As I watched the news, caravans were floating about like little ducks on water. **September** started off with a good drying day. On the 3rd it was very wet. The rest of the month was characterised by some very keen white frosts followed by some very hot days. We started harvest on the 15th and finished on the 2nd **October**. For some reason we hadn't sown any winter barley last autumn and as a result a lot of neighbours had finished harvest before we started - quite frustrating. The first 17 days of October were dry with some grand days.

On the 18th, I note, came some rain, most rain since 3rd September; helped with sale for the late Billy Bell in Helmsley; vintage motorbike made £1,240; The rest of the month was quite wet and windy.

November was a very wet mild month with odd very sunny days, especially the 27th - 29th; On the 29th I note: another really marvellous day more like spring than winter, everything looks so green.

December was very much like November, wet and mild; But with the keenest frost of the autumn on the 14th and snow on the 21st and 22nd.

Tradition dies hard in every walk of life and if traditional ways are best I say stick to them, but sometimes you have to question tradition. As a new Suffolk sheep breeder I said; "Why has everybody got to trim their sheep up?" Commercial buyers, especially the further north you sold, were saying they ought to be in their natural state, because trimmed sheep are more prone to

162

pneumonia. I remember taking six tup lambs to Malton Michaelmas fair, all untrimmed. Nobody would look at them, everyone else's sheep were trimmed. I remember turning our best lamb out of the ring unsold at 140 guineas. I sold the same sheep the following Friday in Darlington at £230. Today over 70% of the Suffolks sold in Malton are untrimmed and as I write this in 2002, some of the established breeders are showing them untrimmed at the national sales. Here are some 1986 prices:

25 Suffolk Tups this year averaged £210

Friesian Bull Calves averaged £100 each

Geld cow could make £500

26.5kg Fat hoggs made £67.20 in April

1987

1st **January**, this is what I recorded in my diary: "Rained all day, terrible and wet. It is the wettest New Year's Day I have experienced." From the 8th to the 10th we had fairly keen frosts, and a spell of wintry snowy weather till the 19th. Here are some extracts from my diary: 12th, been a very very keen frost according to the TV, the keenest for 100 years. It certainly is the keenest since 1963. Messing about thawing off taps all day. On the nine o'clock news it said most of the roads are blocked into Scotland, the A66 Scotch Corner to Penrith, and Pickering to Whitby. 14th has been a very rough night. Blown snow about a lot and blowing all today. Very bad reports of weather all over Britain, especially up the east side of England, Kent and the North east. For the next 11 days it was very mild and the month ended up with three nights of keen frosts.

Over the years I have tried to do a bit of sick visiting and this month I visited Percy Sherwin in hospital. The cold weather must have got into the hospitals because Percy was sat up in bed with his cloth cap on. Percy was a real show ring character. He always had the best sheep until he got beaten by us, and we would pull his leg. Percy once told George Coverdale, Dad's friend - "Willie Dunn was a grand fellow but he couldn't stick the lads, especially Paul" Percy was capped as Punch to see me and remarked to his sister who was sat by his bedside, "This is one of Mr. Dunn's sons. They are all good lads are Dunns". It's surprising how quickly people can change their tune!

February started off with the keenest bare frosts of the winter. You couldn't get the electric fence posts into the ground. The next fortnight was relatively mild, then we had a spell of wintry weather from the 16th - 25th. Dorothy was beginning to have kittens, as we say, as our first baby was due. She said "You will look if you have to get a helicopter out to get me into hospital". That wasn't necessary. I was able to take Dorothy in by car and on the 20th Feburary a new chapter was born. Miriam came onto the scene and life has

163

never been the same since!

March started off wet and then we had another spell of wintry weather from 6th - 11th. This was quite localised and it blew snow about a lot. This is what I have recorded in my diary: 7th had been a very rough night, blown snow about a lot. A very cold Southeasterly wind. Fairburns opened road out but it blew it in. No postman. Had to take milk to the road with emergency tank. March 9th, Jonathan Fairburn opened our road out and I don't think I have seen as much snow in it. The rest of March was a combination of wet days and keen frosts at times. The first fortnight in **April** was very wet. We started sowing on the 16th and finished on the 23rd. The last eight days in April were very hot for the time of year. On the 28th it was the hottest April day since records began.

May started off with four very cold days with snow showers on the 2nd. For the rest of May we had a lot of dull, dry, cold days with draughty winds. It came a very good rain on the 30th. **June** was a very wet and humid month, the wettest I have known. We cut some grass on the 1st to make into big bale silage. Out of the first seventeen days it rained every day, all but two. This grass went very yellow and we didn't bale it but put it into the bottom of the silage clamp. There was a bit of respite in the weather. It was fine from the 17th - 21st when we got our silage in. It started raining again on the 22nd and was wet for the next seven days. It got out a grand day on the 30th and the next ten days were fine and hot. This was the only spell of hay weather we had this year. We started hay time on the 4th **July** and finished on the 8th. We had a lot of rain from the 10th - 30th, and July ended up with a very windy day.

The first ten days in **August** were quite reasonable. The rest of the month was wet with some real humid days. On the 26th it was a terrible wet, windy and stormy day, almost a repeat of Hurricane Charlie a year since. There were awful pictures on the TV of floods. Egton show was a washout. We started harvest on the 31st August and finished combining on 28th September. There used to be a saying that **September** was the harvest month. This year it was very wet and catchy with very few good harvest days. **October** was also a very wet month with a keen frost on the 29th. We grumbled quite a lot about the wet weather, but decided on 16th October to count our blessings as we looked at the television. There had been a very bad storm down south with hurricane winds uprooting trees and damaging property, the worst for 300 years.

November started off with two grand mild days, more like spring than backend. We had a lot of dull, foggy damp days but on the 20th I recorded a tremendous grand day, sun and wind, best drying day since 3rd October. **December** greeted us with a dry, mild windy day and most days were mild except for the 8th and 9th when we had two keen frosts. I noted that it was the wettest and muckiest on the sheep fold that I have ever known.

Hats were always a funny point in our family, Mam's 80th birthday 1985

Family group, Mams 80th birthday, 1985

Special friends, who have always meant a lot to me and Dorothy: George and Gladys Breckon

Dorothy with two of her Philipino friends

From left to right Dad, Rachael Donaldson,
Dorothy, Nicholas and Brenda Moules. I
tease Dorothy because even at this time she
said she had a shine for me

Our engagement, Christmas 1985

Friends who were at our wedding, mentioned in the book, from left to right:
Esther Dennis, Lorne and Mary Wilkinson

George and Mary Ford, at our wedding *Dad and Mam on our wedding day*

Wedding day, Dunn family group photo

Weddings are a time of bringing family togther, here we are with the Dunn and Wass clans

A bigger family - students and their wives, from Cliff College days, along with Ron and Mary Abbott

Chapter 18
1988 - 1990
Famous Farndale And Its Characters, Family And Marriage Responsibilities

1988

Over the years we, as a family, have been blessed with quite good health. It was this year that we came face to face with illness. Dad had started to feel unwell in late November last year and was admitted into hospital just before Christmas. In all he spent thirteen weeks in hospital. As a family we rallied round and with our close friends and relatives we took Mother to see him most days. He always kept his interest in the farm and, like every farmer, he would ask about the weather. My reply was: "You aren't missing much good weather".

January was a very wet month. On the 6th there was a tremendous amount of rain with terrible floods in the North east, Durham and Northumberland. There was very little snow and frost except for the 23rd. It snowed most of that day and then turned off with rain. This weather seemed the worst for sheep folded on roots. On the 30th we had a ride out and remarked that we had never seen sheep on roots so mucked up. It was so wet for some of ours that one morning four hoggs were stuck fast in the soil. This was the first time it had happened since the January of 1961. We had to put quite a few through the dipper to clean them up. Down Thirsk way some farmers were told by the RSPCA to bring their sheep off roots on to grassland. The first eighteen days of **February** were a continuation of the wet weather we had experienced in January. However, it came a real contrast on the 19th - a really grand drying day. You wouldn't believe how things could dry up and we had some good drying days right to the end of the month. **March** started off with snow with some grand days till the 9th, then we had a lot of wet. I don't think I've known it so wet for the time of year. Nature never lets us down it began to dry up on the 29th we started sowing on the 31st, and finished on the 9th April. In **April** we had a lot of springlike growing days until the 24th when we had some keen frosts. We turned our cows onto grazing rye on the 11th - one of our earliest turn outs. **May** started off with quite a lot of rain, then we had some really good growing weather. This was the first time we had made silage in May, cutting it on the 28th and big baling and wrapping it on the 30th. **June** was a dry month with some really hot days, but on the 8th and 9th we had a terrible wind, worst for the time of year. We started the main crop silage on the 4th and finished on the 9th. We started hay time on the 25th and got some baled on the 30th then came thunder and lightning with torrential rain. **July** was a very wet catchy month. The hay that was left was turned on the 9th. This hay was later baled up into big bales on the 18th. It was just like muck and we led it into a heap to rot and burn. The first nine days of **August** were dry with some really hot days. Then we had quite a lot of wet with odd good days but very catchy for hay time and harvest. **September** started off with a terribly wet day - thunder and lightning. Bad weather for the time of year but as the month progressed it wasn't a bad harvest month after all. We started harvest on the 5th and finished on the 17th. On the 29th I wrote in my diary, 'Grand fine day for Michaelmas'. There is a saying that "If the buck rises with a dry horn on Michaelmas morn, we are in for a Michaelmas summer," meaning an Indian summer. **October** was more like summer than the previous months, although we had nine days with fog. The first 16 days of **November** were good for the time of year but winter came early. We had snow showers on the 20th, about six inches on the 21st, and a keen frost on the 22nd. **December** was a very mild month, so mild that they were still picking potatoes on the 23rd on Hambleton. Christmas Eve was more like spring than anything else. On 30th it was a very mild day, sunny just like spring. There were several reports on the TV about spring flowers coming out. Even though we were enjoying spring-like weather in winter we were overshadowed by the terrible air disaster in Lockerbie when 250 people were killed on the 20th. I end my 1988 diary with some comments that Lady Feversham made when we went carol singing. She said that I ought to start writing a book about Yorkshire dialect and I would make a fortune. Well, here I am in December 2002 writing down my memories and dreaming big dreams about my book!

Here are some 1988 prices:

Our Friesian Bull Calves averaged £144

Our best geld cow weighed 735 kg and made 92.80p per kg totalling £682

November milk 18.50p per litre

34 tup lambs averaged £272 each (top price £390)

Fat sheep were only a moderate trade. At the highest subsidy level, 121.7 pence per kilo was being paid, which could amount to more than the market price.

Stock numbers at 31st December, 56 cows, 45 followers, 506 fattening hoggs 36 Suffolk ewes and 9 gimmer hoggs

I once remember seeing an advert in a furniture store saying, "It's the furniture that makes a home". I would disagree. To me a home is about love, understanding and comfort. Mother was a homely person, never happier than when she was making a fire up or gathering sticks. To a certain degree I was in the same mould but changes began to take place. Dorothy was away in hospital having our second baby and I was left to do the housework which included stoking up three fires, putting coke in the Aga, fetching coal and wood for the water heater and an open fire on a fire plate in the room. Fetching coal and sticks in was a mammoth task in itself. Most of the heat seemed to be going up the chimney and even with three fires burning we were starved. Big farm houses take some heating. Farming was prospering and I felt we needed some changes for Dorothy and the childrens' sake. So over the next eighteen months the Aga was converted to oil and we installed an oil-fired water and central heating system, with radiators in every room. We replaced the open fire in the living room with a multi-fuel stove. Previously Dad could sit over the open fire with his top coat on and still be starved, now he had his coat to take off! He remarked that the house was the warmest he had ever known it to be. The systems were a great asset to us all, especially our young children, Miriam and Philip - and myself when I had to sit up with ewes in lambing time. With the old system I would wake up many a time starved, which didn't encourage you to get out among the sheep. It's no use making heat if you can't keep it in the house. Our windows were draughty and rotten so we replaced them with plastic double glazing. It's a good job we did it then - farming wouldn't stand it today!

1989

January started off with a real grand day, more like spring than anything else. This mild weather continued making it the mildest and driest January I have experienced, very similar to 1975. I predicted in my diary that we could get a dry summer, as flowers were coming into bud that January just like in spring. **February** was relatively mild with a bit more rain. **March** was similar but not very drying. We started sowing on the 30th and finished on the 26th April. On the 3rd and 4th of **April** we had the most snow of the winter, followed by some wet days. On the 11th I note: "Land is the wettest it has been all year. It seems a shame when you have a bite of rye and it is too wet to turn cows out." We did turn them out on the 18th but on the 24th they couldn't go out. You couldn't see the rye for snow, we had about three inches. The first eleven days of **May** were dry with some good grow days. We had rain on the 12th and from the 16th - 29th we had some really hot days. We cut some grass on the 27th and baled it on the 29th, our earliest yet. On 30th there was a big change in the weather. It was so cold it was fit to starve you to death. **June** greeted us with a cold day. On the television it showed one inch of snow in Weardale. The first nine days were a bit mixed with damp mornings and bright afternoons. We started silaging the main crop on 6th and finished on 9th. From 10th to 26th we had some real hot days. We started hay time on 20th and finished on 26th. On 27th we had a lot of rain, the most we have had for two months. This rain was quite localised to our area. They had nothing at Pickering and Northallerton. We had some very hot days in **July**. This was the first time we had cut corn in July. We started on the 20th. This land was cleared, the stubble burned, cultivated and sown with rye grass by 31st. The first eight days of **August** were grand and dry, in fact very droughty. You could see grass burning off on thin land. On the 9th and 10th we had some rain which gave everything a drink. The next thirteen days we had some tremendous grand weather. The month ended up with some dull days and some rain on the 30th. **September** came in with a good harvest day. We finished combining on the 2nd. It was a real grand harvest month. You could have harvested time and time again. **October** was dry again with rains coming at the right time to help roots and backend grass. On the 6th we had a good rain, the most since the 26th August. **November** was a relatively dry and mild month with the keenest frost on the 26th. **December** started off with a grand mild day, more like summer than winter. Again December was relatively mild and dry, although we had wet days on the 13th, 14th and 16th. It was an almost frost free month.

Well, here we are at the end of 1989. Within four years I'd acquired a wife and two children. A friend once warned us that when you get two children, it's like lambing time all the year round. I think she is right and it's also more expensive. I am reminded of a little quotation: "Two love birds get together - and then come the little bills."

This year had a rather sad note for me and a lot of others. I have mentioned George Ford in previous chapters, and this year he died at quite an early age of 66. I note in my review of 1989 that he was a great man and I feel in many ways I have to step into his shoes regarding relationships. He knew how to reconcile differences.

As I write this in December 2002, farming isn't easy for us. We have had a cut in milk prices; cows are not milking like they should be and grain prices are the lowest for years. It makes you wonder where it will all lead us. It is my Christian faith that keeps me going, along with a good wife. I keep saying to myself and other farmers when they have a moan "Watch your marriage and family life". Marriage is a great institution but it has to be worked at. Somebody said to me, "You and Dorothy seem to have a wonderful marriage. You seem to worship one another". They don't know the other side of the story ! We have had our problems and trials. George Ford once said to me that men have to understand women as they are complex creatures. I remember reading a book about marriage called "Loving against the Odds" by Rob Parsons. I would recommend it to anyone. This is how Roy and Fiona Castle review it:

"Here is a book for all couples - those with strong marriages who want to protect their relationship - those going through difficult times and those considering marriage. With humour and honesty it deals with issues that are relevant to every marriage, including communicating more effectively, overcoming financial pressure, why interest in sex sometimes dies, the affair, and dealing with conflict. This is not just an honest book, it is a book filled with hope and compassion; with understanding and down to earth advice bursting out of every chapter". Reproduced by permission of Hodder and Stoughton Limited

Well, we have to face facts that we are in a battle. Marriages are falling apart all over. I once heard an auctioneer and valuer say that a lot of his time was spent in valuing for divorce. You can only learn about marriage by being married and I have had a lot to learn. Marriage is a bit like travelling on a journey. Sometimes it is uphill; sometimes round corners; sometimes in the valley; other times on the hilltop when everything is o.k. Sometimes you can get lost and you don't know where you are going. It is at times like these that you need to get out the map, (for me it's the Bible), or to take a closer look at the signposts. Sometimes both of these can confuse us and then we need to ask the way. For me, this means asking others who have travelled that way before. Human nature hasn't changed. The problems we face today have had to be faced by couples who have gone before. We all need to be more honest and open with one another as a lot of couples who are struggling think they are the only ones with problems.

It is never easy fetching a wife into the old home. People can still think Mother is there and so did I for a long time. When you are the last to leave home your parents can be a bit possessive of you and I had to learn that my wife must have the first love. It is true what the Bible says, that a man should leave his father and mother and be forever united to his wife (though that isn't to say you should forget the needs of your parents.) There has never been a time when we husbands have needed to be more loyal and faithful. I like this quotation that one man said and to which I subscribe: "When I got married 1 closed the door to every other woman in the world and since then I haven't even peeped through the keyhole".

Sometimes I think I haven't succeeded materially like some others, but I am reminded of some words from Ecclesiastes, Chapter 9 verse 9: "Live happily with the woman you love through the fleeting days of life, for the wife God gives you is your best reward down here for all your earthly toil".

Family life is also a challenge today. Again there seems to be a lot of emphasis on material things, when really children need to be given the things that money can't buy. The chief things to me are love, time and encouragement. I read a quotation that said the best inheritance parents can give their children is a few minutes of their time each day. As well I thought it important that we had family holidays, and that didn't mean we had to spend a lot of money. We have never been abroad but have tried to take Miriam and Philip to interesting places in Britain. With the best will in the world they can still tell us they are bored!

1990

January was quite dry and mild until the end of the month when we had some wet windy days with little snow and frost. We can all have trying and disappointing days. This is what happened on 9th January: calf laid out with septicaemia. We had to get the vet to it. The cow that calved on Saturday had a twisted stomach. Pure Suffolk gimmer dead up fields with a lamb hanging from her. To crown it all we have e-coli scour among the lambs. **February** was milder and drier than normal. There was a keenish frost on the 16th. Wensleydale had torrential rain on the 20th - four and a half inches fell in 24 hours, causing floods. On the 22nd it was an exceptionally mild sunny day - according to the TV the mildest February day for years. **March** arrived with snow showers followed by the keenest frost of the winter on the 2nd. The next few days were mild and windy. We started sowing corn on the 7th and finished on the 18th. This was only the second time that we had finished sowing in March - the first time was in 1961. We had some exceptionally warm, sunny, springlike days on the 12th, 17th, 18th, 30th and 31st. **April** began with a foggy morning but got out a fine day. We had snow on the 3rd and a keen frost on the 4th. We turned our cows out on the 9th - our earliest turn-out yet. April was a dry month with a lot of wind and white frost. We had a damp day on the 26th, the most rain since 13th March. The month ended up with a really hot day with temperatures up into the seventies - one of the hottest April days on record. The first five days in **May** were very hot. In fact the 3rd was the hottest May day since 1775. Hot days can affect the meat trade. Fat hoggs were down £20 a head in a fortnight. From the 6th to the 10th we had showery rain with good rains on the 10th and 15th. The rest of the month we had a lot of sunny dry weather, in fact, very droughty. We cut some grass for big bale silage on the 26th and baled it on the 30th. The first ten days of **June** were dull, cool and showery. It came the most rain since

174

13th March. We started the main crop of silage on the llth and finished on the 14th. From the 15th to the 21st we had really humid growing weather. On the 22nd we had a lot of rain, the most since winter. The rest of the month was very humid with odd heavy showers. The first nine days of **July** were showery with quite a good rain on the 4th and 5th. The rest of the month was dry with ten very hot days. In fact, on the 31st it was the Ryedale show and we were all plagued with black thunder bugs. It was quite an early harvest. Corn was cut in Ryedale from the middle of July onwards. As you travelled around you could see this drought had really got into things. We were fortunate, we had more rain than many people and the further south you went, the worse the drought became. The first four days in **August** were very hot, followed by some showery days. On the 18th we had a wet morning - the most rain since July the 7th. We started harvest on the 21st and finished on the 31st - all spring barley which yielded very well. **September** was a decent month. You could have harvested most of the month although there were odd bits of rain that refreshed everything. **October** was a good month until the 26th and from then onwards it was very wet. The first seven days in **November** were quite wet, otherwise it was fairly dry and mild with a keen frost on the 20th. The first six days in **December** were grand, mild sunny days. There was a real change on the afternoon of the 7th, it came on to rain then turned to sleet, and later snow. It became very windy and stormy. This is the entry in my diary for the 8th: "What a day. Wind and wet snow, drifting a lot. No electric - went off at 1 o'clock this morning. Cut off from the outside world. Very bad reports on the wireless. Milk tanker didn't come. Stephen and I went to sheep in Wilks field. All electric fences laid flat." We had no electric for five days. Electric poles were broken off all over the place, as were the telephone poles. A lot of trees were brought down especially in young plantations. There were quite a few sheep blown over and suffocated on Hambleton. The snow storm was pretty general. I remember talking to Mr. Tom Harding at Newark show, and he said it was one of the fiercest storms they had ever faced in Warwickshire. December ended with a lot of mild, damp days.

This was quite a sad year for us. At Easter, my Uncle Harry (Wass) died. Uncle Harry used to visit us quite a lot and would travel with us to the shows, always watching the heavy horses being judged. Uncle Harry and Mother were very close and I don't think she got over his death. It came as a shock to her and she died in the following August.

I want to dedicate the next part of this chapter to Mother, and to tell you a bit about her life and the characters in Farndale. For Mother there was no place like

175

Farndale. If ever she wanted a ride out it was always "Take me up Farndale", and there she would look at Hon End, the place where she was born and brought up, and remember days gone by up Wass Ghyll and Hon Nab, the hill above the farm.

She would tell us about Christmas in the past and how she felt it had got out of hand now. For her it was all about plucking and dressing poultry and preparing for the carol singers who always had their dinners at Hon End on Christmas day. Evidently in years gone by it was quite a tradition in the Dales and some villages for carol singers to go out on Christmas Day itself. As far as I know, Farndale was the last place to have Christmas Day carol singers - this tradition being kept up until the early eighties.

In years gone by the Love Feast was quite an event for the Methodists in the dale. What is a Love Feast? It is a meeting where Christians share their conversion experience and how they are getting on in their Christian life. Depending on the district, participants partook of biscuits or currant cake and drank water out of a big mug, called a loving cup. This celebration in Farndale was held on the second Monday in June and in its heyday the men who worked on farms had a holiday on that day. I remember attending such meetings in Farndale which latterly were held on a Sunday. I have happy memories of conducting these meetings at Wilsill near Pately Bridge and West Scrafton near Leyburn.

Mother would tell us that funerals were quite an occasion in the Dale. They used a term in Farndale, and I would imagine in other Dales, called 'bidding to the funeral'. A relation of the deceased would go round the dale telling people where and when the funeral was to be held and inviting them along. Before the public funeral there would be a service at the home of the deceased, usually taken by a local preacher. After the service for general mourners, all would meet up for the funeral tea, which was always a big spread

Mother loved to tell us about some of the old characters in Farndale and how young people would have a bit of fun with them.

There used to be a tale that there was a ghost in Farndale called Sarkless Kitty and the young teenage lads, who met in the cobbler's shop, were teasing an old man called Bob Breckon about it. Bob said "I don't believe there is such a thing - and if there is, I ain't frightened !" One night one of the lads put a sheet over his head and hid behind the hedge waiting for Bob to come home. When Bob saw this figure in the hedge he took fright and had a week in bed over it! Another time the lads played a prank on the gamekeeper called Mawson. They stuck a fox's head in the slide of a poultry house and told Mawson that there was a fox among some poultry. Mawson went and shot at the fox's head. There won't be many keepers who have blown a fox's head off !

Next door to Mother's old home lived a man called Jont Maw. He married a 'townie' and she didn't take too well to the Dales people asking her business. One day she went into the shop at Low Mill and the shopkeeper, Mrs. Middleton, asked her what she was on with. She replied "Minding my own business, and that's more than most people in Farndale can do these days!"

Jack Frank was another character. He was what we call 'under petticoat government' which means his wife used to order him about. The Franks used to show blackface sheep and he would take it badly if he got beaten. One season, another exhibitor borrowed a very good tup lamb and was beating them. Jack's wife said to him "Next show, Jack, you have to object or else I'll bray tha". The next show this tup lamb came out but Jack hadn't the courage to object and he got beaten again. Somebody asked him afterwards how he had got on. Jack replied, "Not over weel. 'Ave gotten beat wi' a borrowed tup lamb. Missus said I had to object, and I hevn't. I hev worst to come on; I hev Missus to meet when I git yam".

Jack Harland was another character and I can remember him. They nick-named him Bumblebee Jack because when he talked his voice buzzed like a bee. There used to be some races at Farndale Show and Jack in his younger days used to be a very good runner. One year Jack took his trousers off, and in those days men wore shirts with long flaps. Jack tied his two flaps together like a nappy and he won the race. Next year they put on the schedule that competitors must wear suitable clothing! Jack liked a bit of poaching and he was a dab hand with a catapult. Jack also liked to drink and he was in the pub one day when the gamekeeper, Mawson,went in and said to Jack "I have a real bonny pheasant that perches up in a tree up Mill Lane. Whatever you do, don't touch him". Eventually Mawson went out and Jack began to talk and said, "Mawson's ower leat wi' 'is warning, looks tha. I 'ev pheasant in mi pocket!" and he showed the rest of the pub crowd this lovely bird! I remember going up to Farndale in daffodil time before the National Park officialdom. Jack would be leaning over the gate outside his cottage and saying to passers by who had picked a lot of daffodils. "You are tacking ower monny. Missus, leave some for somebody else". In those days there weren't many public toilets and Jack was often asked where the nearest one was. Jack would reply, "You can use mine Missus - just up top of path". Jack's toilet was a primitive affair - a wooden top with a hole and a bucket underneath. Jack was so busy being an unofficial daffodil warden that there were times when he neglected emptying the bucket and there were days when it trickled down the garden path on to the main road! I don't know what public health officials would have thought about that today.

I remember an old local preacher called Frank Potter. He was a lovely man and he had a good way of communicating with children. He always had a word for them. He used to tell a story about a lion and he once asked the children if they had ever seen a lion. One bright lad shouted out that there was one in his garden this morning. Frank said "Never!" The lad replied "Oh yes there was and he was a Dande-lion". Another time Frank was asking the children "What does the Bible say you have to do to your neighbour ?" A little lad shouted out, "Me Dad says 'watch him, 'es a rum youth is our neighbour'".

Music played an important part in Farndale, what with the band, different choirs and musical families. I have mentioned the Farndale Quartet in a previous chapter but now I want to mention the Dobsons who were a gifted family. They sang together as a family from 1951 - 1973. When they visited most chapels and circuits in North Yorkshire. Bertha was the contralto and was married to my uncle Harry Wass; Herbert was the bass; Harold the tenor; Alf the lead; Gilbert; bass; Gladys was their accompanist and was married to George Breckon. All the Dobson men were Methodist Local Preachers. I started off with Gilbert in a Mission Band and then went on note with Harold. Gilbert was a very gifted accordion player; a talent which I thought wasn't used in the circuit as much as it should be. I always made sure when I was preaching where Gilbert was that he gave us a solo, accompanied by his accordion. There was another brother, Eric, whom I never really knew. He went to Cliff College and then into the Methodist ministry. He held important ministries at Methodist Central Halls in Bradford, Blackburn and London. I want to mention another musical family, the Breckons: George was a very good bass singer; Hilda was a contralto. Both were members of the Farndale Quartet. Lena was a gifted pianist and I can still hear her and Hilda playing duets on our piano at home. Herbert was also a gifted musician, playing in the Stape band.

Both the Dobsons and Breckons had handy hands on them. In 1933 Herbert Breckon made his own electricity by rigging up a car dynamo and a bike wheel using water in the beck at Farndale. In 1938 Ernest Dobson, and his son Harold, fixed a generator up from the mill race and wired their own electricity into their own home, the band room, and eventually into the chapel. Harold was only telling me recently that he must have had the cheapest electricity ever from 1938 until the late fifties. It cost him seven shillings and sixpence for a brush in his generator! Lena Breckon went as a young teenager to train as a nurse and eventually became matron at St Thomas's hospital, Scarborough. All this is remarkable because they wouldn't have the education that there is today.

They would be self-taught people. Fred Handley, who was born in Farndale, used to say "You can't beat the people from Farndale". Mentioning the Handleys - Fred was a master builder. Mother would talk a lot about Fred and Mrs. Handley for when they first got married they lived in the cottage next to Hon End. Fred was quite a remarkable man, carrying on his building business till he was 85. He was quite a humorous character, and liked to tell you all about his past experiences. He used to say that he began his career in building as a lad of eleven years when, with his father and brother, he helped to build the Moorland Hotel at Castleton. They used to walk across the moors from Farndale to Castleton every Monday morning. They stayed on the job throughout the week. They had the benefits of central heating even in those days as they all slept in the one bed, with Fred in the middle. Fred said it was the best form of central heating you could think of! Later Fred came to live at Helmsley and built a lot of properties in the town. Fred felt it was an honour when his firm was awarded a gold medal by the Ministry of Housing and Local Government for the Elmslac Road Estate in Helmsley. It was judged to be the best of its kind in the North of England. Fred's brother, Frank, was a blacksmith and eventually started an ironmonger's shop in Helmsley. Both Fred and Frank were Methodist Local Preachers. Another brother, Robert, emigrated to Canada and became a Methodist Minister. He is remembered by a commemorative plaque in High Farndale Chapel.

It is fitting that in the middle and late eighties, Mother and others organised a Farndale reunion. I was disappointed I couldn't go, but I have watched it on video. It brought back memories of the families and characters of the Dale.

Grandad Dunn and Dad often talked about Jack Wheldons Bus
photo by kind permission of Mrs M Maw

This bus carried the groceries round in Farndale. Owned by Middletons of Low Mill

Death cards were the means of informing people - above card refers to my great Grandmother

The last man to work with horses in Farndale, Norman Duck. Photo taken 1963

Norman Duck Harrowing 1963

Another group of Farndale Singers at Mam's 80th Birthday, 1985
Left to right: Fred Wass, Harold Dobson, Harry Wass, Norman Duck,
Joe Teasdale and Alf Dobson

*3 of the Dobson Brothers, Singing with Christopher at
Dad & Mam's Golden Wedding, 1989*

Bath time, Miriam & Philip

Miriam and Philip with Dorothy's mum

*Philip acting as Grandad Dunn with
his hat and stick*

Teach them when they are young - Miriam

Teach them when they are young - Philip

Having a ride, Author with Miriam and Philip

Quad Suffolk lambs with Miriam and Philip

Family holidays are important. Here we are at the Shire Horse Farm in Devon, 1993

At a family wedding, 1992

Miriam as Joseph in the school play, 1998

185

Farndale show is a big day in the life of the Dale. Left nephew Timothy with champion Swaledale. Below right his wife Sarah receiving their trophies, 2005
photographs by Joyce Starkey

Three sheep men left to right, Len Fawbert, Harold Agar and W.H. Dunn

Hon End farm where mother was brought up, taken 1977

Chapter 19
1991 - 1993
Battling With B.S.E. And B.V.D.

1991

With the best will in the world, any farmer will have times when stock dies or crops fail. We were beginning to see on television a lot of publicity about B.S.E. (Bovine Spongiform Encephalopathy - more commonly known as mad cow disease). We hoped we would keep clear, but like most farmers we were seeing the odd case. I think we had four over the years and thankfully we were compensated for the loss. Perhaps the greatest problem we ever had to face or the biggest set back or run of bad luck, as we say in farming terms, was Bovine Virus - diarrhoea, for which there is no cure. Out of a batch of eighteen bulling heifers, two died. Our vet advised us to have the rest blood tested and nine had to go for slaughter - quite a blow. We had sold ten heifer calves of the same batch to a fellow Suffolk sheep breeder from Skipton and I felt it only right to ring him up and ask him how his had done. He had had the same trouble, four had died out of his ten - a major blow for him, a relatively new starter. Both Dad and I said we should try and help him. We let him have two heifer calves and paid him £400 compensation. 'Always do what is right' was Dad's motto and 'Help people all you can'. David Calvert appreciated this and we have done business with him since, buying Suffolk stock rams, from him.

Good can always come out of bad. Our local vet, Mark Howells, was very helpful and told us the good news that our herd would now be almost immune from this virus. As a result of our bad time with the cattle, our profit was the lowest for 13 years. "When the going is tough, the tough need to get going" as they say. We had spent a lot of money on milk quota. Our faith was being tried, but I was reassured by the words of a hymn:

> All you may need he will provide
> God will take care of you.
> Trust Him and you will be satisfied
> God will take care of you
>
> No matter what may be the test
> God will take care of you.
> Lean weary one upon His breast
> God will take care of you.

God has been, and will be faithful. **January** 1991 was quite a dry month with a lot of frost but very little snow. **February** was a different story. From the 5th to the 13th we had snow showers and longer periods of snow, ending up with 14 inches on the level. This snow was pretty general, even on low lying ground in the York and Harrogate areas. Farmers would tell me that it was the most snow they had seen on the level. Snow causes a lot of work. We had the milk to take to the tanker at a collection point for four days. With all the snow our roots were completely buried. We had the sheep to bring off and feed on fodder beet in a grass field. The weather is a ruling factor. Winspears of Helmsley were supposed to have their farm sale on the 9th. It had to be postponed and was held a fortnight later on the 23rd. It came a very good windy thaw on this day and February ended up a proper fill-dyke - meaning there was a lot of water about. **March** started off with a springlike day. I had a welcome break on this day, attending BOCM Agriculture Ltd awards presentation and meal at Ripon Spa Hotel where we were told we had won the North Eastern big bale silage competition - an award we have been in the running for several years since. Surprises are very nice when you get a cheque for £200. Firms are no longer running competitions like this. They are tightening their belts just like the rest of the farming community. We had a lot of dry days in March with less wind than usual. We started sowing on the 28th and finished on 1st April. **April** began with a very windy day and the first ten days were characterised by wind which we would normally have in March. Our English weather can be very changeable. This is how I described the 15th: A real grand warm day - real grow day. The next day - Cold as winter and very windy. Some snow showers at night. It was followed by another four cold days with two inches of snow on the 20th. The next days were very cold with some white frosts. **May** started off with seven days of cold weather. The rest of the month was mainly dry with some warm days, except for the last four days which were very cold. **June** began with a warm day followed by a wet one. The rest of the month was wet and catchy except for the last days which were fine, warm and humid. We started silaging the main crop on the 8th and finished on the 13th - our biggest struggle yet. The first week in **July** was warm and humid with a bad thunderstorm on the 8th. A lot of hay was baled early in July that was never fit. It was annoying as the weather forecast kept mentioning rain which never came. From the 11th - 17th we had some good hay weather. Several farmers remarked that if they had known this fine weather was coming they would never have baled their hay so "near the way" i.e. not quite ready From the 18th onward we had 6 days of really humid weather. The month ended up with some real hot days. This fine weather continued into

August, followed by some showery days. We then had a lot of good harvest days. We started harvest on the 26th **August** and finished combining on the 30th. The first ten days of **September** were very fine. It came a good rain on the 15th which gave things a drink. Grass was burning up on thin land. The rest of the month was made up of some good days. **October** began with a lot of wind and some good days interspersed with three stormy days in the middle of the month, ending up with a very stormy day. **November**, like October, was very windy. We had above average weather for November. We had a keen frost on the 17th followed by three inches of snow on the 18th. The month closed with some mild dry days. This weather continued into **December** with quite a lot of fog. From the 8th - 12th we had some keen frosts - in fact, on the 12th we had the keenest bare frost since 1981. The month ended with some very mild days.

Although we had bad luck with our cattle this year, we prided ourselves on selling, surplus to requirements, nine newly calved cows in York with prices from £485 - £780 - several weeks topping the market.

The weather plays an important part in farming affecting every aspect. Here are a few sayings with predictions about the weather:

"If the wind is in the east, it is neither fit for man nor beast.
If the wind is in the west, then it is in the best"

'Small snowflakes make the biggest heaps'.

If Candlemas Day (February 2nd) be bright and fair, there's half
of winter to come or mare'.

'March winds and April showers bring forth May flowers'.

A speck of dust in March is worth a King's ransom' This means that if it was an early seedtime you have a better chance of a good corn yield.

'If there is snow in April, chances are that it will be a dry summer'.

'A wet May for long-tailed hay' - meaning that rain in May would enable the grass to grow into a good hay crop.

'A droppy June suits our tune'. This especially applies to farmers on limestone land.

'When grass cutters start to clatter pigs come down like rattle'.
i.e. pork is not popular in the summer months
Pork to me always tastes better in winter months. In the pig-killing and
home-curing days, it was always said 'Never kill a pig in a month
where there is no 'r' in it'.

If the buck rises with a dry horn on Michaelmas morn, the
weather will be fine and warm'. (Michaelmas Day is 29th September:)

'In October muck your field and your land its wealth will yield'.

'A white frost and a bright morning in Autumn often bring rain by mid-day,
but if you get three white frosts together and no rain then the weather will
stay fine'.

'If Autumn mists on a morning roll up on the hill top, it will come back
down as rain, but if they roll into the valley it is sure to stay fine'.

'Mist in the hollow, fine weather to follow'.

'If ice will hold a duck before Martinmas Day, the white cow has cast her
calf - This means winter has aborted and the risk of much frost and snow
is less.
(Martinmas Day is the 23rd November - a big event in the farm
workers' calendar of bygone days)

'If the hills look near, rain isn't far away'.

'Rain before seven, fair before eleven'.

'Red sky at night, shepherd's delight; red sky in the morning shepherd's
warning'.

'When swallows fly low, it is a sign of rain'.

'If crows fly through the belfry or play football (fly at one another)
it is a sign of rain'.

'If frogs turn yellow on their backs it is a sign of a good summer'.

'If sheep, not lambs 6-12 months old, are playing, it is a sign of wind'.

'If hoggs (sheep) on a turnip fold are standing on their hind legs, it is a sign of snow'.

'If cattle in a fold yard are restless and running about, it is a sign of some bad weather'.

'If sheep are coming in off the moor, it is a sign of snow'.
'A rainy thow'll nivver deea'. This means a rainy thaw isn't a good thaw.

'If the moon is laid on her back she is holding water but if she's tipped up, she's tipping it out'.

'If blackbirds are singing in cheer before 14th February they will be shedding tears before the end of February'.

1992

This I felt was a forward year. In fact the most forward in my farming experience. It was the first time we put fertilizer on the grass in February, the first time we sowed spring corn in February, the first time we made our main crop silage in May; the first time we made second crop silage in June, and harvest was very forward.

The first three days of **January** were very windy, followed by a lot of mild dry days, till the 22nd when we had eight keen frosts in a row. This was one of the driest Januarys we had experienced. **February** began with a keen frost followed by a lot of mild drying days. We started sowing corn on the 26th. **March** 1st was a wet morning to be followed by six days of springlike drying days. We had the most snow of the winter on the 15th. We finished sowing corn on the 18th. From then on there were a lot of wet nights to the end of the month. On the 31st I wrote in my diary: "Things are the wettest since spring 1989. According to the television there were terrible floods in the Rothbury area, Northumberland, and snow in Cumbria." On the 2nd **April** - "Been a lot of rain during the night and a wet day till late afternoon. There were snow and blizzard conditions in Weardale, Teesdale and Cumbria." From the 3rd - 13th we had some good growing springlike days. From the 14th - 17th we had a lot of rain and then some decent days. **May** began with a really grand fine day and we had a lot of sunny days - very hot at times. We cut some grass for big bale silage on the 15th - our earliest yet. We started the main crop on the 26th and finished on the 28th. May was abnormally dry. On the 27th I wrote: "A very droughty day. This dry weather isn't half getting into things". However on the last day it thundered and rained heavily, the most rain since the 30th April. The first three days in **June** were very humid and it came a grand rain on the 4th which saved things. The month seemed to be characterised by four or five days of cold, dry weather, then four or five really hot days. We made some second crop silage on the 27th. At the end of June I record that this is the hottest and driest June since 1976. We are now suffering from the effect of drought. **July** began with a wet morning and on the 3rd we had the most rain since the 29th April, followed by another good rain on the 4th. Harvest was early, especially for those with winter barley. Our neighbour, Fred Fairburn, started combining on the 15th- This is the earliest I have known. We had helpful rains on the 17th, 19th and 21st, otherwise it was a dry month ending up with some very hot days. **August** was quite a dry month although we had a good rain on the 9th. We started harvest on the 14th and finished on the 25th, our earliest yet apart from 1959 and 1976. **September** was decent weather until the 20th. You could have harvested on most days. The last ten days were really muggy, growing weather with odd wet days - just the ticket for roots and autumn grass. **October** was an average month. We had some snow showers on the 15th - the earliest I have known snow - and a very keen frost on the 19th and 31st. **November** was a very wet mild month. On the 30th I observed " Been a lot of rain during the night and more or less a wet day. Weather experts tell us it's the wettest November we have had for a long time". **December** started off very wet with bad reports of flooding down in the South West and Wales. This wet weather continued until the middle of the month when we had frost - two very keen ones on the 20th and 21st. The month ended with three foggy raw days.

Life has its surprises, and this year we won a national competition. This is how the Darlington and Stockton Times reported it:

"Brothers Nicholas and Paul Dunn have won £1000 after coming top in the toughest part of a competition to reduce mastitis cell count rates.

The pair, who run a 50 cow herd at New Leys Farm, Helmsley, immediately gave one tenth of their prize to Christian work.

The remaining £900 went a long way towards the 1150 guineas they paid for the freshly calved heifer, Grincle Belle 5th which was one of the lots in a dispersal sale.

"It's the most we have ever paid for a heifer. She'd calved just four weeks earlier, but we felt we were spending the money on something good", said Mr. Paul Dunn.

The brothers took part in the Orbedin extra dry cow cell count challenge run by Smith Kline Beecham Animal Health.

The condition of entry was that the product had to be used on all quarters of at least 75% of cows dried off between the start of the challenge launched in spring 1991 and the end of April 1992. Monthly records for each cow, showing the date dried off and the product used were submitted to the organisation. The herd's rolling mean cell count was also made available by the Milk Marketing Board. The competitors were split into four categories according to their cell count at the beginning of the challenge. The winners were judged on the largest percentage decrease in cell count over the competition period.

The brothers were competing in the most difficult section of the competition - their opening figure stood at 199,000. However, during the twelve months period of the contest, they achieved a 42% improvement to finish at an enviable figure of 115,000".

I wish that figure could be ours today. We, and other dairy farmers nationally, are fighting against high cell count problems. If it is high you get a reduction on the price of your milk.

My granddad Dunn used to have a saying, 'Sell when selling is in fashion' which means if people are keen to buy and the price is right, then sell. But you don't always know in farming. For example, this spring, fat sheep went down £10-£12 within a week, when normally they go up. Sometimes, with the best will in the world, it can be more good luck than good management with buying and selling.

1993

The last four years were quite dry by English standards but this year, 1993, was a different story - wet and more wet. It has been termed the wettest in living memory. A lot of wheat up the east coast was never combined. From 13th-15th September I never saw such stormy weather and how it got into things! For example, any big bales of straw that were still outside in the fields and facing east, wet penetrated in 18 inches from the ends. Our silage shed which faces east had small bales of straw stacked in it. The wind blew the rain half-way across the shed. The bales on the top were nearly as wet as if they had been outside.

We did two things on our farm that year that we had never done before. My brother, Nicholas, had always wanted to under-sow winter barley. People said it wouldn't work and I was quite dubious. However, last year, Dad and I had been visiting our friend John Metcalfe of Barningham, Barnard Castle, and he showed us round his farm.

"You have a very good grass ley here, Mr. John" I said to him.

"Yes" he said, "it was under-sown on winter barley".

As we say, I cocked my ears up. John continued that if you wanted to under-sow winter barley and make it work you must harrow it well, knock the guts out of it. So this is what we did with ours. We harrowed it over twice in the spring, when it was 9 inches high. When Dad saw it he said we had ruined it. To cut a long story short, we got a good take of seeds and our crop of winter barley was the only one standing in the district. With harrowing the crop we had strengthened it.

Another thing we did this year was to big bale and wrap the straw that had been under-sown. We would never have got it dry enough to put into ordinary bales. It turned out to be good stuff. Our heifers loved it.

Here is my account of the wet year of 1993. The first three days of **January** were foggy and frosty. We had some snow on the 4th and 12th, otherwise it was wet, windy and stormy. **February** was a mild month with a lot of dull, foggy days from the 9th - 15th and then it was windy and very drying. We started sowing corn on the 22nd, our earliest yet. The month ended with snow on the 17th and 28th and our field road was blown in. **March** brought a bit of snow. On the 5th and 6th we had two very springlike days. My journal records: "Tremendous grand day, more like summer than spring. Crocuses are coming out in the garden. On the 15th it was a real grand warm day, the warmest March day this century."

We finished sowing on 25th March. On the whole March was quite a dry month but the last day was the wettest since 23rd January. **April** was a combination of cold and wet days. I wrote on the 8th April: "If my legs are anything to go by, we are in for some wet, stormy weather". My legs always ache when there is going to be some bad weather. They were right! On the 9th it was a terrible wet day which got heavier as the day wore on. I can't ever remember such a wet Good Friday. We also had a lot of rain on the 25th - things were the wettest since April 1989. The month finished with a really grand day - very growy and one of the warmest April days I have known. **May** was characterised by several white frosts and there seemed to be an icy wind blowing all month. It was fairly dry early on, and then in the middle we had a lot of wet. My entry on the 14th said "Very wet cold morning. A lot of snow in Weardale. Where cows are strip grazing it is just like a ploughed field. Dad and I went to Joe Joel's funeral at Bentham. What a funeral ! Note of victory !"

June commenced warm and growy. From the 5th to the 9th we had some good hot days when we got all our silage in. The following days up to the 26th were quite catchy and wet at times. From the 27th June - 4th **July** we had some decent dry, warm days. From the 5th - 7th we had a lot of wind, which laid a lot of winter barley. The rest of the month was catchy with very little hay weather. We didn't seem to have a lot of rain - more bothering than anything else. Up the west side of the country they had a tremendous amount of rain. The first four days in **August** were reasonably dry, when quite a lot of winter barley was cut.

My entry for the 5th August - "What a day. Rain and wind. Started last night at 10 o'clock and rained until 4 o'clock in the afternoon. A lot of small bales that weren't stacked up were soaked through".

The 9th was also a wet day. The rest of the month was catchy and slow. We started harvest on the 21st August and finished combining on the 25th September. On the 31st August, I record: "Quite a warm day, in fact the television says second warmest this year"

September 1st was a tremendously hot day - according to the weatherman it was the hottest September day since 1959. The next six days were dry but dull and slow for harvest. From the 8th - 18th we had a lot of wet, stormy weather - "The 13th has been a rough night. Rain and wind and what a day! It blew and rained all day. Bad reports of flooding up Wensleydale. The 14th has been a rough night and a rough day. It rained most of the night with a strong north-easterly wind. The 15th was a bit better day but still quite a lot of rain. It has now rained for 60 hours non-stop, with a biting northeasterly wind"

From the 19th - 25th September we had a spell of better weather. On the 26th we had a lot of rain. On the 27th I record the coldest September day for forty years. **October** started off wet and was very wet for the first fourteen days. From the 15th - 19th we had some very keen frosts. I say on the 18th 'Been a very hard frost, the hardest I have known for the time of year'.

A lot of potatoes were frozen in the ground. The month ended with eight dull, mild days. That was the first time in my experience that we had never seen the sun in mangling time. The first nineteen days of **November** were typical for the time of year - dull, damp and foggy with a very wet day on the 14th. We had frost and snow from the 21st - 24th ending up with mild days and another covering of snow on the 30th. The first six days of **December** were mild and dry. We had snow on the 8th and on the 9th - 'Been a very wild night. A lot of storm damage in different parts of the country.' We had odd periods of snow which always ended up with rain and it was very wet towards the end of the month.

Things were peaking for the dairyman. Our Friesian bull calves averaged £155.50. Geld cows were at their highest. We sold one that weighed 715 kg which made 113.50 pence per kilo and came to £811. We were paid our highest yet for milk, over 25p per litre. These factors made dairy cattle a good trade. I remember going to the Tambrook Friesian sale, near Lancaster, when we bought a cow for 1380 guineas, the highest price we have yet paid. I think this was the first time that official Friesian auctioneers, Norton and Brooksbank, had experienced a home sale where there wasn't a cow under 1000 guineas. The sale averaged 1720 guineas.

Presentation of Silage Awards. Author fifth from left

Bradshaws Stand at the Ryedale Show, 1991.
They got 1st Prize for their Tradesman Stand.
Author with Miriam and Philip.

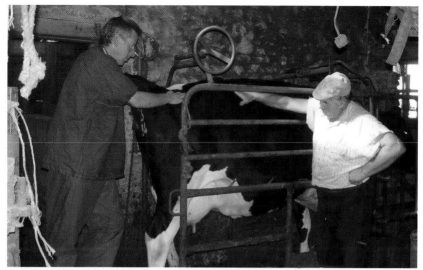

Vet Mark Howell's examining cow

Taking temperature of calf

Vets are an important and expensive item for the farmer. Here we are discussing his charges!

Chapter 20
1994 -1996
Auctioneering And
The Prosperous Years Of Farming

At the beginning of 1994 we decided that, except in exceptional circumstances, we would say no to any auctioneering. Some people were surprised at this as they enjoyed coming to our sales. However, for the bit of commission we received and the time and effort we put in, it wasn't worth it. You have to make things pay and as the old saying goes - you might as well play for nowt as work for nowt! Dad always said that if he had had a choice he would have been an auctioneer. I am told that right from being a child, in the playground at school, he would have a go at selling. As a young man, after carol singing, while they were eating their suppers, people would say "Come on, Willie, let's have a bit of auctioneering and see how tha's shaping". Dad would have a go, selling ornaments off the mantlepiece. He would also sell at harvest festivals. Dad had his first proper sale in 1945 up at Hawnby. It was all furniture and the proceeds came to £100. He had his first farm sale in 1947 at Sutton, near Thirsk, the proceeds being £1000. Dad was trusted by all people and he took advantage of no-one. I reckon an auctioneer must have a good strong voice, be able to communicate, and have a good, clean, sense of humour. Some of the best auctioneers I have known had these qualities. Every auctioneer has his pet sayings. One of Dad's was, "Look to me! You're bound to get it!"

In the late sixties, Dad would let me have a go selling at harvest festivals, and people would say that I had the gift. In March 1971 I made my first public appearance, selling at Len Bennison's sale up in Bilsdale. I felt quite chuffed, as they say. One old farmer remarked, "Tha shapes weel and if tha keeps going, tha'll mak a better auctioneer than thi faither!" From then on I did most of the selling at our sales, ably assisted at times by Paul and Stephen Dennis, sons of a well-known auctioneer, David Dennis of Malton.

Over the years we would have the occasional farm sale and furniture sales, held on the vendor's premises. These small sales created a lot of interest, especially if the vendor had lived in that village or area all their lives. Local people would buy things and give above their worth, because they had belonged to someone they knew. Things have changed now. You seldom find a furniture sale held on the vendor's premises. Instead it is taken to a local or national saleroom. When furniture goes to a saleroom, it loses its sentimental and personal value. For several years we would have collective furniture sales in summer in our big shed at New Leys, but we found out that if you hadn't one total house clearance with some good antiques included, you couldn't make them pay. Auctioneers get all sorts of tricks played on them. For example, buyers can give false names or addresses, and sometimes you would get people who would never pay, or the cheque would bounce. However, we didn't fare too badly as all our vendors were fully paid, and the amounts we were owed would neither make nor break us. A big asset to any business is having pleasant, honest clerks and I am indebted to Audrey Windress and Sheila Foster who always did a good job.

In the early seventies, things seemed a bit uncertain on the farm. Dad had tried several times to make Nicholas and I joint tenants, without success. In view of this I felt that I needed some more "strings to my bow" so in August 1971 I started working 2 days a week at Malton livestock market, employed by Cundalls, the auctioneers, where I was clerking in the pig section. I gave this up in March 1973 when I was offered the permanent tenancy of New Leys. Sadly, Nicholas could not technically be included as the Feversham estate no longer offered joint tenancies, but he was as ever a vital part of the business and we contined to trade as W.H. Dunn and Sons.

In some ways I miss the auctioneering - not the preparation - but still keep my hand in doing the odd charity auction. In 1994 I did an auction of promises for the Kevin Ellis Appeal Fund and we raised over £9000.

1994.

January began with a keen frost and a grand day. We had a covering of snow on the 2nd. Then we had a lot of wet weather, terrible for sheep and roots. On the 14th we had to bring all our hoggs off the roots. Some were stuck to the ground. The month ended with three dry, windy days. **February** was a continuation of January's weather, very wet. Whatever snow came it always turned off with rain, but we had more frost than January. The keenest frost of the winter was on the 22nd. **March** was a dry, windy month. We started sowing on the 11th and finished on the 25th. We sowed some kale on the 29th - our soonest yet. The beginning of **April** was wet - the most rain since the 3rd March The month was a combination of white frosts and wet days - not a very good growing month. We turned our cows out on the 28th April - the latest we have known. **May** was a dry month with really grand sunny days but it was very cold from the 17th - 20th. We made some big bale silage on the 20th. **June** was a dry month, contrasted with cold and hot days. We started our main crop silage on the 8th and finished on the 10th. **July** was a hot dry month. On the 12th it was the hottest July day for a long time. Several people were affected with sunstroke at the Yorkshire Show and one man died. When I came home I had a head like a ton of bricks and was as sick as a dog. I vowed that it would be a long time before I went to the Yorkshire Show again. There was a thunderstorm on the 24th and there were three hours of rain - the most since 16th June. There was more rain on the 27th July which helped the roots and grass a lot. They had had it a lot drier and hotter down in the Midlands I noticed as I travelled down to the National Suffolk Sale at Stoneleigh. Even hedges had been scorched by the hot sun. **August** was a dry month with a helpful rain on the 17th and 24th. We started harvest on the 16th and finished combining on the 22nd. We had all the straw in by the 30th. **September** was dry until the 5th, then very wet and catchy. The first four days of **October** were wet. On the 3rd it was very icy in the air and there was a shower of snow. It was white over on Hambleton. On the 4th we had a keen frost. From the 4th to the 19th we had a spell of dry weather. From the 20th to the end of the month it was quite wet. **November** was wet and mild, with some odd grand days. My journal, on the 24th, says "Tremendous grand day, sunny and mild, more like spring than backend. 26th: Tremendous grand day, just like spring. I would have liked a photo of our cows. They were all laid down basking in the sun." **December** by and large was wet, mild and windy. On the 11th:"Very windy mild day. According to the weathermen it has been the warmest December night on record." From the 20th - 23rd: "Been hardest frost of winter. Too hard to plough".

For our farm, prices for stock reached their peak. This was the first time we sold a 4th calf milk cow for £1000. Our Friesian bull calves averaged £140. We had 51 kg hoggs which made £77 in April; 41 Suffolk tup lambs averaged £278; barley was over £100 a ton. Towards the end of the year, things for the dairyman began to slide. Milk cows were down £200 - £250 each, owing to the country being over quota with milk production. Quota prices went through the roof! It was making up to £1 per litre to buy and 20 pence to lease. What a different story today, January 2003, when we are under quota. Milk quotas can be bought for 12 pence per litre and be leased for a penny. Such is the instability of farming.

The law is a funny thing and I have always been a believer in keeping on the right side of it. In early 1994 for some reason I couldn't find my driving licence and applied for a duplicate. The powers that be wrote back and told me they had no trace of me having a driving licence and if I wanted a duplicate I would have to pass a driving test. Despite the fact that I produced an old licence stating I was a fully licensed driver; despite having references from my insurance company and a local JP; despite the fact that I informed my local MP who wrote to the Ministry of Transport; they still insisted that to obtain a new licence I needed to take a driving test. I was quite humiliated. Many people said, "Say nowt and just carry on as normal!" What would have happened if I had been stopped by the police and couldn't produce an up-to-date licence, I don't know. I decided that I would have to take another test and that I needed some lessons to brush up on my driving as I first passed my test in October 1962! This was an expensive business but well worth it as, much to my relief, I passed first time again. Talk about red tape.

1995

January began with two very keen frosts. Otherwise it was a very wet month. On the 31st I wrote: "Been a lot of rain during the night and rained most of the day. Terrible reports about floods on the continent and North of England. Wettest January for 50 years. Went to a farming conference at Newton Rigg, Penrith. I have never seen so much land under flood, especially around Appleby and Penrith." The first seven days in **February** were dry and mild. The rest of the month was very wet. **March** started off mild but we had coverings of snow on the 2nd, 3rd, 5th and 7th and the most snow of the winter on the 28th. The rest of the month was a combination of wet and good drying days. We started sowing on the 20th and finished on the 6th of April. The first seventeen days of **April** were decent with four really warm days. On the 14th: "A really grand warm day, shirt sleeve day" It was a different story on the 18th, when it was white over with snow, with snow showers during the day. The 22nd was a wet stormy day and very cold - just like backend. The month ended up with a really warm day. We turned our cows out on the 1st **May**, our latest yet. The first six days of May were very hot. My journal records on May 5th "A very hot day, in fact as hot as I have known it for early May." 10th May: "A very cold day, fit to starve you to death. Stephen had gloves and coat on scruffling. What a contrast to last week." On the whole May was a dry month but on the 25th there was a good growing rain with showers the next few days. Early **June** was growy with good rains. On the 3rd: 'Wet sort of a day until about 4 o'clock. I don't think I have ever seen grass and corn grow like it has done'.

We big baled some silage on the 6th June and got the main crop in by the 15th. From the 18th - 30th we had some very hot dry days. The 28th was a really hot day, the hottest this summer. It was 90 degrees in places. **July** started off cool and dry. We had helpful rain on the 14th and 15th, otherwise we had some really hot days. On the 31st: 'Very hot day. This drought isn't half getting into things, grass is burning off." The first three days of **August** were very hot and then we had some cool days. On the 12th we had good growing rain. The rest of August was a mixture of hot and cool, dry days. We started harvest on the 7th and finished combining on the 22nd. The first six days in **September** were dry. Then from the 7th - 12th we had a lot of rain. From then until the end of the month, we had a lot of showers with some real grow days. Within a month the countryside was transformed from a desert to lovely green pastures. **October** was a really grand, mild, dry month. This is the driest, warmest and most growy October I have known. **November** was mainly a dry, mild month. We had a keen frost on the 4th and a wet day on the 11th. There was the most rain since 11th September and we had snow on the 17th. **December** was a mixture of mild days with a covering of snow on the 5th, 6th and 7th. We had a spell of very frosty wintry weather from the 24th - 30th. I wrote on the 28th: "Been, I would think, keenest frost of winter. Bad reports of snow and blizzards in Shetlands, Whitby, Scarborough and East coast. I have been talking to the Colemans from Burton Fleming, near Driffield, and they have 11 inches on the level." 29th: "This has definitely been the keenest frost of the winter. Keenest since 1981. It really stiffened things up in the milking parlour- A lot of reports of rivers frozen over".

This year would be when our milk price averaged the most - from 22 pence per litre in summer to 26 pence per litre in winter. Prices of our geld cows were beginning to slide, due to public pressure about BSE. Corn was a good price. We sold all our barley for £116 per ton. As I write this in 2003 that same barley is making £57 per ton. 2002's summer milk price was as low as 13.783 pence per litre and winter price 18 pence per litre.

One of the biggest assets to the dairy farmer is the bulk milk collection. Our old tank had served us well for 24 years. We now had to consider alternate day collection which meant that in December we bought a new bigger bulk tank. I can tell you some funny stories about past milk collection. In the hot summer of 1976 our ice bank went off but we kept the agitator going and we got butter! I skimmed a small bucketful off. We got the ice bank going and it was sent off later in the day. It would be healthy semi-skimmed!! In the bad storm of December 1990 we barrowed a lot of snow and shovelled it into the ice part of the tank which did the trick. I think we were the only one of the farmers around here who hadn't sent off any warm milk.

In 1995 I celebrated my 50th birthday. Dorothy and the children gave me a surprise party. Brother Christopher officiated and organised a kind of "This is your Life" programme. We all had a good time. As one guest remarked, "It's right what you Wesleyans say - you can enjoy yourselves without having a drink". One of the highlights of the evening was when Trudie Sanderson read out a poem about me, written by her in dialect;

AH'S NOBBUT FIFTY
A DAY IN THE LIFE OF PAUL DUNN

Ah gits mesen up about six o'clock
An gits ready for today
After all this farmin' larks 'ard work
And there isn't much time to play.

Ah tiptoes quietly down t'stairs
An rubs me sleepy eyes
Ah knows its nobut early
But it's time ti go outside

Fost ah puts me coat on
An me boiler suit an wellies
Ah leave 'em in t'back entrance
Cos me wife complains they're smelly

When ah started ti go thin on top
Ah got in quite a flap
But decided t'best solution
Were ti get me sen a cap

It disn't blow aboot like hair
An it keps me 'ead sa warm
Its grandest thing invented
For weering on a farm

Fost job is to git all cows in
Riddy for milking time
Then Nicholas and me 'ave a bit o prayer
Ti 'elp ti start day off fine

After ah've 'elped wi milking
Ah've sheep ti feed and see
Ah likes a bit o company
So ah teks me dog wi me.

Ah likes me dog 'Is name is Skip
But 'e isn't ower bright
Instead of rounding sheep up
'E likes to nip and bite.

Come back ti me, thou stupid dog
Deen't be s' downright thick
An if tha disn't behave theesen
Ah'll hit tha wi me stick

At seven ah goes back ti house
Ah's riddy for a feed
An efter shouting at me dog
A drink is what I need

Ah likes ti see me missus
An see me two bairns too
It's nice to spend some time wi 'em
Before they go ti school

There's allus 'phonecalls to be med
An t'paperwork pile just grows
Ah've got to git me sen ready
Cos it's off to mart ah goes

We'll load fat hoggs int trailer
It shouldn't be ower hard
But someyans left gate open
An they've galloped off down yard

Off Skip chases 'em for ages
An then sits down and pants
Hogg gives him a great big grin
An starts to eat mi plants

What a pantin' an' a shoutin'
Ti try and move yan hogg
We'll never be on telly
On "yan man an 'is dog"

At last I es 'im int trailer
An breathless wiv a pounding heart
A climms in ti Diahatsu
An goes off down ti mart.

Ah gits sheep weighed an' sorted
An' puts 'em in a pen
But ah reckon nowt ti auctioneer
Ah could dee a better job me sen

Ah knows this might seem strange to thou
As there could iver be
Someyans else warse harder
Ti understand than me

Ah can't understand a word he says
He talks se quick an' fast
But he walks alang on top of pens
An' sells me sheep at last

Ah finds out frev a friend o' mine
They've made a canny price
Ah'll treat me sen ti dinner
Cos a big cheque's allus nice

When ah gits back 'ome late efterneen
There's sheep ti feed again
This time ah'll leave me dog at 'ome
Me voice can't tek the strain

An when works ower for ti day
Ah goes inte house for tea
Good wife allus es a lovely spread
Waiting there for me

After tea, ah 'elps ti wesh up
An then ah ev a wosh
Clean clothes on ah's gam oot
An ah likes ti leek quite posh

At neet ah goes ti chapel
But if preacher's rather slow
Ah's sure e weern't notice
If ah es forty winks or so

It 'elps ti hev a little snooze
If t'sermon's rather dim
Tha knows ah allus wakens up
For t'collection an' t'final hymn

An as ah drive back 'ome at night
Ah've 'ad a busy day
Serving the Lord an doing me work
Ah'd ave it nee other way.

Ah's tired as ah climbs upstairs
Ah's not so young and nifty
But folks tha ain't seen nothing yet
After all ah's only fifty!

1992-1996 were to me the peak years in farm prices and not surprisingly, according to our accounts, they were the years when we showed the most profit. But we were beginning to see on television and in our newspapers a lot of publicity about BSE. This was having an effect on the beef sector. It finally came to a head on 20th March 1996 when the politicians announced that there was a connection between BSE and CJD (Creutzfeldt-Jakob disease, a human form of BSE.) There needed to be a full enquiry. All cattle over 30 months were not allowed into the food chain. The price of beef collapsed and within a week there were virtually no fat cattle on offer in the markets. The public were scared by what the politicians and scientists told them. Butchers couldn't sell their beef. As a result the price of calves and store cattle collapsed. For a while the price of pork and lamb went crazy - through the roof as we say. I believe it was at this point that the farming industry lost control of its own destiny. We were now subject to rules and regulations - paper work and more paper work. From the 1st July, all calves born had to be registered and were put on a computer at the British Cattle Movement Service in Workington, Cumberland. Traceability was now the key word. Before long we could see all sheep and goats and pigs with some kind of passport system.

1996 saw my first involvement with the Yorkshire Dialect Society and I feel honoured and privileged to be on its council. I well remember a member asking me what I thought about Mad Cow disease. I said that I was more concerned with mad people who had over-reacted. We have to face it that people with brains don't always have common sense and that means, at times, our politicians. This is only my theory but I believe that some of the animal protein put into our feeding stuffs was never cooked properly and we are not teaching our young people how to cook. Our daughter, Miriam, is now nearly sixteen and in school has never been taught to cook a dinner or roast a joint. They now call it Food Technology. Today it is all about fast and instant food. Could it be that we are going too fast?. The pace of life seems to get faster. We seem to have a lot of time-saving inventions but where has the time gone?

1996

January was the dullest month on record. It started off with six foggy days. It was very mild until the 23rd. Then we had a spell of cold, frosty and snowy conditions. On the 26th in my journal: "Been a covering of snow and some heavy snow showers during the day, blowing and very cold. Bairns came home from school early." On the 27th: "Been a pig of a night, snowing and blowing. Damp sort of snow, when you paddle it it turns to ice. Snowed and blew most of the day until about three o'clock, then it came a bit warmer. Nicholas didn't come until it was light. Stephen didn't come at all. I got up at 5 o'clock and had a good start. I was a bit concerned about ewes and lambs but they were OK. Bad reports of weather on TV. It's a bit since I've seen it blow so much". 28th:" Much better day. You can work among this. Snow seems to have settled. A strong northeasterly wind blowing. Simon came and opened the road out. Both services at chapel put off. Dorothy, Philip and I went for a ride round Hambleton. It has blown the snow about here as much as anywhere. I don't think I have seen as much snow blown into Sidney Bowes's farm road."

As I write this, early February 2003, there has been a lot of publicity about wintry weather and how it has brought the country to a stand still in places. This recent snow is nothing compared to the snowstorm I have written about above in 1996. The councils are not giving us the service we should be getting and in my opinion are spending too much money on widening and improving roads and not budgeting enough for wintry weather.

The first days in **February** were nice winter days. On the 5th I say: "Been a keen frost and a bitterly cold day. My bones aren't half aching". 6th February: "Much to my surprise no more snow. Very bad reports of snow in Cumbria, Dumfries and Galloway. Most snow in that area for 30 years, 17 inches on the level". 9th February: "Started to snow and blow first thing - quite a blizzard, then it turned off with wet stuff. Fair in the afternoon- Reports of bad weather in Scotland and Cumbria". 12th February: "Snowing and blowing first thing. Turned off with rain. Bad reports of snow in Durham".

We then had six mildish days, followed by days that were cold with a northeasterly wind and keen frosts. **March** was a dull, dry month. One of the dullest on record. We started sowing on the 8th and finished on 1st **April**. On this day we had the keenest frost I have ever known for April. So much so that the ground was too hard to power harrow before midday. The following four days we had keen frosts followed by four spring-like growy days. Then the rest of April was a mixture of cold wet days with the odd good, fine grow day. **May** came in wet and cold and turned out to be one of the coldest Mays this century - the coldest since 1979. We turned our cows out on the 1st. The first sixteen days in **June** were a big improvement with some warm days. The 17th-23rd were back to being very cold. Then, two very hot scorching days, finishing the month off with some growy showery days. We big baled some silage on the 7th and 8th and got the main crop in on the 13th and 14th. The first nine days of **July** were growy and showery and the rest of July was very hot. **August** began by being warm and droughty. We had good rains on the 7th and 10th and then some hot days. From the 23rd - 25th we had quite a lot of rain. The month ended with some decent days. The first fourteen days of **September** were dry, but dull and slow. We started harvest on the 6th, finished combining on the 10th, and finished leading bales on the 18th. From the 14th - 27th we had some decent weather. **October** was a decent grow month. There was a keen frost on the 10th and some wet days towards the end of the month. **November** was fairly mild and wet until the 18th, then from the 19th - 24th we had keen frosts with snow on the 21st and 24th. The month ended up wet and windy. For the first seventeen days in **December** it was mild with a lot of fog. On the 18th I recorded: "Dull, damp and foggy, came on very wet at night, as wet as I have known it for carol singing". 19th; "I would think it has been one of the wettest nights for a while, a lot of water about and flooding in places" From the 22nd - 26th we had frost with coverings of snow on the 27th and 31st. On the 28th - "Been quite a drop of rain during the night. A slight frost. Talk about ice - it is everywhere. I don't think I have ever known so much ice on our road".

Although there had been a collapse in the beef sector and grain prices had slid £20 per ton, our milk price was the best yet. From July - September our milk price was over 26p per litre. We had our best year yet with our Suffolk sheep. 55 tup lambs averaged £330. We sold four gimmer lambs for breeding which averaged £220. Cull ewes were making £89.50. Fat sheep had never been dearer. We had 53 kg hoggs which made £84.50 on the 21st March. A month later hoggs and fat lambs were making over £100 - absolutely crackers!

Collective sale at New Leys early 1990's

Collective furniture sale early 1990's

*Author appealing for bids at
George Moules's sale, 1975*

*A scene at George Moules's sale,
Hawnby 1975 at Shaken Bridge Farm*

*Dad selling sheep at Uncle Freds sale,
1976*

*Uncle Fred Wass's sale at Farndale.
Christopher clerking, Nicholas holding
items up, Author selling*

*A farm sale draws a crowd. Uncle Fred's
sale, Farndale 1976*

Dad selling at High Leys farm 1963. In aid of Rievaulx Sunday school extension, Dad did quite a lot of selling at harvest festivals and charity sales

Harrison Weighell, mother's cousin and one of the last men to operate solely as an agricultural valuer (taken late 1960's)

Chapter 21
1997 - 1999
Dad's Book Launch,
Floods, And Farming In Crisis

Dad kept saying he would like to write his life story. Some of us thought it was a dream, but the dream became a reality. On his 87th birthday he had a party, all organised by himself, when he launched his book "Down Memory Lane", at which he sold 300 copies. It was a great reunion of relations and friends from near and far. One of the guests was Tom Midgely from Kirkby Underdale, Malton. We had got to know Tom through his Suffolk sheep breeding. Tom, like Dad, was in his late 80's, a man with a wealth of experience who had also written a book, called "The Changing Years". This, coupled with Dad's book, gave me inspiration to write my own memoirs. I got to know Tom quite closely and he kept saying, "I want to write another book. Would the chap who helped your Dad be interested in mine?" He declined but I put him in touch with a friend and well-known journalist, Edward Hart, and they published the book, "All in a Lifetime". Latterly there is a larger book which has been written about Tom Midgely entitled, "Reflections of the Changing Years", which gives a much more detailed account of the Midgely family and the locality where they lived.

Writing one's life story is quite some task. Here I am plodding my way along in my third year and haven't got there yet, and there are times when you get despondent. It was the same with Dad. Quite often he would say to me "I don't know whether it will come off".

Dad was good at telling tales and recalling past events. He had nothing written down. All his memoirs were on tape, recorded by Harold Dobson and typed up by Rebecca, Nicholas's daughter. The book was then put together by Gary Hobbs from Kirkbymoorside. Dad always said, "I don't want it to be a money making job", and it wasn't. I think he lost money, but wasn't really bothered about that as he had the satisfaction of having published it. He often said that some people would have spent their money on a world cruise but his was going into his book.

We were beginning to see from early in 1997 a gradual slide in farm prices. Sheep kept fairly good until early November and we had our best year yet with our Suffolk sheep. 46 tup lambs averaged £340 each. Somtimes things turn out different from what you expect. I had what I thought was a good tup lamb which I took to Darlington tup sale, fully expecting thtat it would win a prize.

It didn't -and neither did it reach its reserve price. When I was loading it up at night the judge was looking on and said, "Was that tup lamb in for the judging?" I said, "Of course it was". The judge said, "He has a mucky backside - get him cleaned up. You should have known better than to fetch a mucky one. Presentation is half the game." He gave me some helpful advice on how to clean it up. When I got home I set about it, got it cleaned up and took it to Stokesley Show next day. Guess what? It got first prize. A fortnight later I took the same tup lamb to the Michaelmas sale at Malton, got first prize and the top price of 510 guineas. I was capped as Punch as the saying goes, because the same tup only got to 380 guineas in Darlington. My mucky back-sided lamb hadn't turned out so bad after all! Further success came our way when we went to the tup sale at Ruswarp. We got the Sufflok championship and the top price of £380. I think some of the established breeders were more surprised than pleased!

At the end of the year prices of everything collapsed, and this was the start of the real farming recession, which we thought would be short-lived but which has lasted six years (until 2003). Prices were the worst since the short-lived recession of 1974. Normally, when one commodity is bad, another is good, but nothing was a good price in farming. We were beginning to see that this country could import food cheaper than we could produce it, but I feel that the food we import has not been produced to the same standards as ours. My motto is "Buy British". It is still the best!

In early 1997 a possibility of expansion came our way when a neighbouring farm was to become vacant and we, like the other tenants on the estate, were given a chance to tender for it. We gave it much thought and prayer. We never tendered for it. I was given some words from Psalm 119 verse 36, "Help me to prefer obedience to making money. Turn me away from wanting any other plan than yours, revive my heart towards you". If we had got this farm, things would have been extremely difficult for us as a lot of money would have had to be borrowed to finance the project.

I have always maintained that children brought up on a farm are privileged when they have open air and animals around them. Both our children, Miriam and Philip are animal lovers. So, at Christmas 1997 I bought Miriam a large black gilt (pig) and Philip a British Saanen goatling. It was good for them both to get into the discipline of feeding these animals before and after school. Miriam's pig enterprise was short lived due to her pig going lame after its first litter, but Philip's goat herd has increased to five. I think there could be a future for goat farmers. It is interesting to note that in the year 2002, the main NFU Enterprise award was given to a goat farmer near York.

1997

According to weather records this has been the driest **January** for 200 years. The 14th was a tremendous grand warm day, more like spring than winter. **February** was a wet mild month, quite windy at times. **March** was one of the driest on record. We started sowing corn on the 6th and finished on the 19th. The 11th was a grand springlike day, the warmest March day for years. **April** was a very growy month with some hot days. The 9th was a grand day, very warm and growy. I would think it was the warmest April day we have had for a long time. The 30th was another grand warm day, just like the middle of summer. **May** started off with two very hot days then on the 5th it was a terrible wet cold day with the most rain since 21st February. On the 6th we had a covering of snow. The rest of the month consisted of good grow days with some thunderstorms. We baled some silage on the 26th and finished the main crop on the 29th. **June** began with some very hot days but from the 10th we had a lot of rain. On the 30th I wrote in my diary - "Rained all day. Things aren't half wet. Where heifers are grazing it is just like a ploughed field round headlands".

The first three days of **July** were a continuation of the June weather, then we had a real contrast with ten days of very hot weather. On the 11th I record - "Very hot day again. Almost too hot to work". From then on we had odd days of wet, with some more hot days. **August** was very much like July with some very hot days. We started harvest on the 18th and finished combining on the 22nd. The month ended up with a wet day, thunder and lightning in the early evening with a cloud burst. Most water about I have ever seen. We were all shocked when we turned on the TV to learn that Princess Diana had been killed in a road accident. **September** was above average with some good harvest days, and it was drier than average. We got all our straw baled and led by the 6th. The first 10 days in **October** were similar to the good September weather. On the 26th - "A dull day, but mild. Wonderful weather for the time of the year". The first 17 days of **November** were relatively mild and open but towards the end of the month it came very wet. On the 24th - "Wet first thing and I would think it has been a lot of rain during the night". Things are the wettest now since the end of June. **December** started off with a keen frost and we had a lot of wet from the middle to the end of the month. On the 24th - "Came on a very wet day. It got up terrible and windy". We saw on the TV the next day that a lot of villages were without electricity. NO Christmas dinners! There was quite a lot of damage done to farm buildings locally. Farm building tops were blown off and a near neighbour found his fold yard roof blown on to the top of his Dutch barn.

1997 had been quite a kind year weather-wise. We had a relatively early spring, grass had never stopped growing all summer, almost a dairy farmer's dream, and there was decent weather to conserve and gather the crops. 1998 was a different story

1998

We had a wet spring, a wet summer and a wet backend. Quite a bit of wheat was never combined in places, and a lot of winter corn was never sown. The decline in prices and the overall depressed picture of farming was described as the worst since the slump in the 1930's. Only two things were reasonably good, the price of potatoes and the price of straw.

We were beginning to see that due to the financial crisis in farming, farmers were cutting down in labour where they could, and bringing in specialised contractors to do the job. We had had the help of a self-employed man, Stephen Watson, since March 1987 on a part-time basis. At the end of 1997 he reached pension age, which was a blessing in disguise as we couldn't afford to pay him any longer because of the recession. At the beginning of 1998 my nephew David, Nicholas's elder son, started working for us 2 days a week and continued until May 2000. We were beginning to see that the government wasn't a lot interested in what British farmers could produce, as they could get cheaper food from abroad. There was also emerging a body of opinion against country sports and pursuits. On the 1st March, country people took to the streets of London to show their support for country pursuits in general, and fox hunting in particular.

Here is a more detailed account of the weather in 1998. **January** was terribly wet for the first few days and the 3rd was a very mild day with some very heavy showers. I have recorded - "Talk about rain and hail stones. I don't think I have ever known the land so saturated for the time of year, with water running off the fields. The beck in Helmsley was orange in colour." Then we had a lot of mild dampish weather. On the 9th - "Tremendous mild day. According to the TV it has been one of the warmest January days on record." **February** was mostly mild and dry but the last two days were very cold and wintry. We started sowing corn on the 18th March and finished on 1st April. On the 13th February - "Tremendous grand warm day, more like the middle of summer than February. It was the warmest February day on record, registering 68 degrees fahrenheit at Worcester". The first 13 days of **March** were a combination of snow, frost and rain. Then, from the 14th - 23rd we had some good drying days. The rest of the month was mild and wet. It rained every day for the first eleven days of **April** with a covering of snow on the 11th. I say on the 10th: "A strong northeasterly wind with some rain through the night changing to heavy rain mixed with sleet and snow. Terrible floods in Worcestershire and Warwickshire". We had frosts from 11th - 16th with dustings of snow, and the rest of the month was wet and mucky, very difficult for lambing time. **May** began with three dry very cold days with a strong northeasterly wind. We had rain and more rain for the next ten days. It was a backward spring, so we only turned our cows out on the 4th May. From 13th - 19th we had some real hot sunny days. Then back to wet thundery catchy weather for the rest of the month. We cut some grass for big bale silage on 26th and baled it on 1st **June**. I wrote on 2nd June - "Dry and windy first thing then it came on to rain". And didn't it rain! It was stormy and cold with it. The rest of the month was very catchy and wet. We got our main crop silage in on the 12th, all in one day. It was the first time that a self-propelled forage harvester had been used on our land.

July was a catchy month with not too many good hay days, and was very wet towards the end of the month. On the 27th - "Been some rain during the night and came odd showers during the day with a terrible downpour about 5 o'clock". 28th -"The Ryedale Show field is in a terrible mess. It took a long time to get on to the ground. We have been very fortunate with the weather in the past". On 31st - "Been a downpour up Bilsdale, stone and soil worked out from farm roads and fields into the road". I don't think land has ever been so wet for the time of year. **August**, like the previous months, was catchy with not many harvest days. We started harvest on the 19th August and finished on 18th September. Again **September** was very catchy until 18th and from then on until the end of the month it was dry but slow. There tended to be foggy mornings and bright afternoons. **October** was quite wet, the best days being at the end of the month. **November** was near average with wet and foggy days. The keenest frost of the backend was on 2nd. **December** was relatively mild and mucky with bad storm damage on 26th. We had quite a lot of tiles blown off. Just to remind ourselves of the wet year I record on Dec 31st - "Wet mucky morning blew out in afternoon - I don't think I have ever known things as wet and mucky. The Landrover wouldn't travel up cow pasture".

1999

Several people have asked the question - "How did I come to be involved in the television programme 'The Dying Breed.'" It happened like this - One Sunday, early in June 1999, I happened to be in High Farndale chapel at a circuit united service and I noticed a stranger in the congregation. I got into conversation with him. He told me he was a cameraman for Channel 4 television, which was hoping to produce a documentary on farming in crisis. He said "I am filming a sheep farmer in the dale, a pig man down York way, I would very much like to film a dairy farmer. Do you know of one?" I began to tell him that my brother and I were in dairying and that I had kept a day-to-day diary over the years with records of prices. He said to me, "I think you are just the right man for the job". Could he come and see me the next day? He came, and from 13th June 1999 to February 2000 the camera crew were on the farm filming from time to time. I wanted to show the general public what was happening to the farming industry. Farming has always been subject to short term fluctuations in prices but we were now in our fourth year of a total collapse in the prices we were receiving. Over the years we have run, for the size of the farm, a large bank overdraft, paying our bills at the month end, but we were finding that our bank overdraft was going up and up. What could we do about it ? Surprisingly the bank never put any pressure on us but in January of 1999 we were over our limit. Fortunately, Nicholas had a Life Insurance Policy which matured at this point and he decided to put some of this money into the farm to keep us going. Even with this help, eight months later we again went over our limit. I happened to be talking to Dad one day and he said, "I have had Frank Flintoft in today and he paints a depressing picture of farming. Is it as bad as he makes out ?" I said, "Yes it is, and it is worst for the pig and dairy men". I proceeded to say, "If things don't improve I will have to go to the bank and ask them to increase our overdraft facility". You didn't mind going to the bank if it was for expansion but this was to keep ourselves afloat. Dad said, "If I can be of any help I will lend you some money, providing you pay me the same interest that I am receiving". We accepted his offer and paid him interest each month above what he had been receiving. I am glad to say that this money was paid back and our overdraft brought down to a satisfactory level within 3 years.

The farming crisis became a local and national talking point, in our newspapers, on radio and television. This is what our local Methodist minister, Sue Greenwood, wrote in her December 1998 newsletter. 'Living as we do in a farming community, we cannot fail to appreciate what a difficult year this has been for farmers, with prices so low and costs remaining so high. Farming families, including my own and those affected by agriculture have had some hard thinking to do and some serious decisions to make about their future. At times like these people can easily feel hopeless and abandoned'.

Well, we had some serious thinking to do. We decided to cut down on our root acreage and grow more corn, thus receiving more subsidy. Our dairying would have to change. We abandoned strip grazing our cows and instead gave them free access one week in three to different fields. This way we produced a lot more milk from grass and forage. We planned to go more for all year round calving as we were also finding that from August onwards our dairy bull calves were almost worthless. Some farmers, as shown on TV, were shooting their calves at birth. This was very demoralising. We decided to rear ours, selling them as store stirks.

Financially we were struggling and trying to tighten our belts. Dorothy, like a lot of farmer's wives, was subsidising our income by doing home help work four mornings a week. I remember talking to a Christian friend one day, who said, "How are you coping financially Paul?" I replied that it seemed to be a struggle at times and she went on to ask if we had thought of applying for Family Credit. I had never heard of such a thing and she proceeded to tell me that her two sons who owned their own farm were drawing this benefit. I got the shock of my life. Neither Nicholas nor I had drawn any state assistance in our lives.

To cut a long story short, I rang up my accountant and asked if he thought I qualified for this assistance. I was a little bit angry with him and said that if I did, he ought to have been advising me about it before. My accountant applied for it and since August 1999 we have had its help, the amount depending on the profitability and income of the farm. When I declared this publicly through the newspapers and television, a lot of other farmers who, like me, didn't know it existed, applied for it. Some months later in the Farmers Weekly, an article was written about Family Credit and there were over 17,000 farmers and farm workers being subsidised by it. Do I feel guilty about receiving Family Credit? No - in the past we had paid a lot of tax and we were now getting something back from the system.

In August 1999 I happened to be at York Livestock Centre selling a cow. Ben Gill the President of the NFU was there that week and Channel 4 filmed me sharing with him the following prices and how costs had gone up:

INCOME					EXPENSE	
YEAR	MILK	FRIESIAN CALVES	CULL COWS	BARLEY	WATER	DERV
	Per litre	Per Head	Per Head	Per Tonne	Per cubic litre	Per litre
1993	24.87	155.00	642	100	51.90	36.65
1994	22.86	140.00	601	100	54.10	37.65
1995	26.00	42.00	489	116	58.10	40.75
1996	24.70	85.00	471	90	64.20	45.95
1997	20.47	79.00	399	70	67.60	48.55
1998	18.69	74.00	267	74	69.80	51.00
1999	16.72	35.00	280	70	80.90	60.15

Our local paper, the Malton Gazette and Herald, got hold of the figures and produced them the next week. This set our telephone ringing from other papers wanting to come and interview me. I said "no" to all of them except the Daily Telegraph, as sometimes you can over-publicise a thing even if it is true and I didn't want people to think that I was pleading poverty, just stating facts. In the event the Daily Telegraph went on to produce a decent article about the plight of farmers.

In contrast to 1998, the weather in 1999 was ideal for our farm. We needed something to be cheerful about when prices were so depressing. It was a good year. It was a year when we did well in the local NFU crop competition, winning firsts with spring barley, roots and grass, and second with winter barley, making us the overall winner on points. Our neighbour, George Hawkins, said to me at the NFU dinner, "I'm proud of you winning, it is a great achievement for a high side farm". We were competing with farmers who had a lot better land in the vale of Kirkbymoorside and Pickering. I knew our root crop was quite outstanding as we had never had bigger mangel-wurzels, and were never beaten at the local shows. We took some to the Northern Counties Show at York Livestock Centre weighing over 40 Ibs each.

Here is a detailed account of the 1999 weather. **January** was a combination of mild days, a lot of wet with a period of frost from 10th - 14th. On the 2nd - "Mild warm day, warmest January day in London since 1841". On the 6th - "Been a lot of rain, I don't think I have ever known land as wet and saturated". On the 31st - "Went to sheep on roots. I have never known them so mucked up".

The first eight days of **February** were a real contrast. Things dried up tremendously. We had snow on the 9th and 10th. On the 9th - "Been a rough night snowing and blowing. A while since I have seen as much snow blown into milk parlour and fold yard. Blowing most of day. Miriam and Philip didn't go to school. No school bus running". We had quite a lot of wet and some snow from 10th - 22nd. Then it dried up in a remarkable way and we started sowing corn on the 24th with a really good drying windy day on the 27th. Dust was flying everywhere - what a contrast. The next few days, **March** 1st - 9th, it rained most days with heavy wet snow on the 5th and 6th. This rain was mainly up the North-east coast region. On the 7th - "Rained most of the day. I have never ever seen anything like it for water - river out at Rievaulx, Malton and Norton in flood". On 8th March - "Rained most of day, bad reports about flooding at Norton, Stamford Bridge and Malton area. A lot of farm land around Salton, Brawby and Malton under flood". From 13th March to the end of the month it dried up nicely, with the occasional wet day.

The first thirteen days in **April** were reasonably dry and we finished sowing corn on 3rd. There came another spell of wet from 13th - 20th and the rest of the month was reasonably dry. **May** was a combination of good growing days, odd wet ones, and a typical May variation of cold and hot days. We got our main crop silage in on the 27th.

June began with a real warm day and it was a good growing month with rains coming at the right time. **July** was dryer than normal with some very hot days. The first three days of **August** were very hot with some good rain on the 9th - the most rain of the month. The remainder were good growy days with rains coming at the right time interspersed with some good harvest days. We started harvest on the 23rd and finished combining on 28th. The good summer weather continued during **September**, almost a repeat of August with everything coming at the right time. Almost a farmer's dream. **October** was above average. On the 20th - "Windy day. Very dry for time of year". From 26th - 30th we had some exceptional days. Again, **November** was a good month with the odd stormy day, with some real grand mild days towards the end of the month. On the 27th - "Decent sort of mild day, things look tremendous and green". **December** was very windy with very little snow and keen frosts from 18th - 20th.

Gazette and Herald, October 1999

GROWING WELL: Nicholas Dunn (left) with Paul Dunn and the giant worzels. *Picture by Andy Bulmer*

Are these big enough for you?

ARE these mangel-wurzels a record ask Helmsley farmers the Dunn brothers?

Weighing in with two other mangels at the Northern Counties Fatstock show at York Livestock Centre last Saturday, they swept the board with first and second prizes with mangels averaging over 40lb each.

At the show, Paul Dunn ran a guessing game with another mangel-wurzel raising £11 for multiple sclerosis. Peter Rowson of North Lincolnshire guessed correctly the mangel weight of 33lb.

Mr Dunn is a lay Methodist preacher. "I often use the mangel crop in sermon illustrations," he said. "There was a time when we felt like ploughing the crop out and giving the crop up."

Paul Dunn added this was what it was like in farming at the moment. "We feel some-times like that in the Christian life. But we have to realise we learn the most from our hard times and we have a lot to be thankful for. God has given us a wonderful summer."

Paul and Nicholas Dunn have also won first prize at the local NFU root competition and first prize at the Farndale and Stokesley shows.

In the past, they have grown mangels of 44 and 45 pounds.

Dad and Tom Midgeley at Ryedale Show around late 1990's

Champion Suffolk Tup at Ruswarp, 1997

Champion Roots at Northern Livestock Show 2000

Photo of Author and family for Millennium, 2000

Miriam with her large black pig 'Beccah'

Philip with his favourite goat 'Silver' and her kids

*Skip our dog is a favourite
with Miriam and Philip*

Chapter 22
2000 - 2001
TV Fame, More Floods, Foot And Mouth

2000

We were beginning to realise by our latest accounts that 1998/1999 was the lowest profit we had ever made. Things seemed quite depressing. A lot of sheep in 1999 and 2000 were being sold at give-away prices. A lot of dairy bred bull calves were being shot at birth. Also our milk price was the lowest for years. When bills come through the post you can't say to the people who sent them "I'm taking a lot less for what I'm selling. Will you take a cut ?" No, you either pay or do without.

We could see through the farming and national press that some landlords were voluntarily giving their tenants reductions or rebates. This was the first time this had ever happened in my farming experience. The rent of our farm has always gone up. Rents are to do with the earning capacity of a farm.

Our income and profit had fallen dramatically. Our rent was due to be reviewed in March so I went to see our agent, and asked him what he was doing about rents this year. He said, "We are keeping them the same". I showed him my last accounts. He admitted they made dismal reading. I said to him, "In the light of my accounts we should either have a reduction or rebate. Have any other tenants been to ask for a reduction or rebate?" His answer was "No".

I was quite surprised and proceeded to put my case before him. Our farm is the only farm in dairying on the estate and the least subsidised of any farm in the area. But ever since milk quotas came in we have been faced with what feels like a second rent because of having to purchase or lease milk quota. In the last ten years we had spent over £50,000 on milk quota. If you milk cows you must have milk quota.

In December 1999 we leased quota at 8.5p per litre. In May 2000 we thought we would do our job better and leased it at 4.5p. As it turned out we needn't have leased any. The country ended up under quota and the price came down to under 1p per litre. It shows we can all make our plans but the market place and the weather have the last word.

What was the outcome of my visit about the rent? That is between me, the agent and my valuer. Suffice to say that I felt they were helpful in my situation. Any tenant who in the last three years hasn't talked with his landlord about the financial situation in farming has missed an opportunity.

It was as well we asked for help. When our accounts came back for

1999/2000 they showed a loss of £3,500. This was the first time in the whole of my farming experience that we had ever made a loss.

Since the recession in farming a lot of farmers, and especially farmers' sons, have done some serious thinking. They have asked themselves the question, "Is there a future for me in the industry, especially running small units?" People outside farming can earn a lot more money. You find this out when you get a bill from a builder, joiner, plumber or any tradesman outside of farming. No wonder farmers' sons are leaving the industry and taking on building and gardening jobs, for example my Nephew, David, decided that there was no future for him on a farm this size. He got a job fork lift driving. It made me and Nicholas think - within 3 years our work force had gone. It was as well as we were finding it difficult to pay them. One of the points made when our agent looked through our accounts was that our labour and contract bill was high for the size of the farm.

There is an old saying, "Plan your work then work your plan". Our plan in the past was to try and breed as good stock as you could, and sell when prices were at their peak. We tried to calve the main of our dairy herd from May to July. Dairy bred calves were the best price during these months. In July and August the milk price was at a premium and when you sold your fat cows between January to May, they were normally the best price. But everything had changed.

Within 5 years our calves that had been making £100 - £150 weren't making £20, and in some cases were being shot at birth. July and August milk wasn't yielding as big a premium and our fat cows were worth half as much, none going for human consumption. It was back to that painful word called "change". We couldn't carry on as we had always done.

Our Suffolk sheep had served us well, but their needs were beginning to clash with our dairy enterprise. With rearing our dairy bull calves, our winter lambing accommodation was being squeezed and in summer the sheep were taking grass from the dairy herd. So we decided to make the hard decision of culling the sheep via a complete dispersal sale on the farm in November 2000. I felt we had a disappointing sale as prices were at rock bottom at the time. We consoled ourselves with the thought that the Suffolks had started off as just a hobby.

Several people have asked me whether I miss the sheep and of course I do, especially going to shows and sales, where you meet old friends and make new ones, but I have to say that it has been much easier since the sheep went. In particular it would have been difficult getting to Sunday morning worship if we still had the sheep.

A wise old Christian once said to me, "Don't cut your soul in two for money". He meant that if you were too busy to get to worship you were too busy trying to make money.

At the end of July 2000 the TV programme 'The Dying Breed' was shown on Channel 4. It was quite embarassing at the Ryedale show as I heard some people saying "That is the man who was on TV". It was good to hear thoughts of other people's reactions to the programme via letters and phone calls. I felt that I had tried to make a good case for the farming industry, and for my Christian faith. I tried to make it plain in all the filming that there were three things important to me: my faith, my family and my farm, and in that order.

Those of us who were filmed had no control over what was screened. I felt they ought to have shown me selling a cow at York Livestock Centre when I was also interviewed with Ben Gill, President of NFU, giving him my list of prices. I also felt that the title for the programme could have been better. Originally it was to have been called "Under the Hammer" as quite a lot that was shown was at York Livestock Centre and Blakey Sheep Sale. Farmers are not a dying breed, but as an industry we are being hammered right, left and centre, whether it be our prices or rules and regulations.

It is interesting to note what was reported in the national and local papers about the situation in farming. Let me quote the following statistics about tenant farmers:

'Sixty per cent have been forced to lay off staff, eighty per cent have stopped or reduced investment in their business. Fifty-one per cent are having difficulty finding their rent. The average age of Britain's tenant farmers is 58. In the twelve months to June 2000, 23,800 farmers and farm workers in England left the industry.'

This is how I reviewed the weather in 2000. Weather-wise the Millennium year will go down in history. From May onwards, rain and more rain. Poor silage and harvest time. A lot of straw has never been baled. Good straw is dearer than corn. A lot of potatoes are still in the ground and a lot of winter corn has never been sown.

Here is a more detailed account of the weather in 2000.

January was a mild month with fourteen mild days. The 17th and 20th were both like spring days. We had very little frost and no snow but two windy days on 29th and 30th. The first seven days of **February** were mild again. Like January there was very little frost and no snow. According to the weather forecasters this is the sunniest winter we have had for years.

March was fairly dry, above average. We started sowing corn on the 6th and finished on 29th. **April** made up for the three previous dry months with a lot of rain. The 3rd was a real stormy day with rain, sleet and snow. Castleton Rigg was blocked and there were six inches of snow up Bransdale.

We had a spell of decent springlike weather from 5th - 10th and then we had a lot of wet days and nights. On the 17th it came a lot of wet and my diary reads, "The land is the wettest it has been this year." We turned the cows out on the 28th. Although April had been a wet month it ended up with a fine day. 30th was a real grand day. I record "It isn't often you get weather like this".

The first 16 days of **May** were dry with some hot and cold days. On the 14th - "It was a real grand hot day. It isn't often you find it as warm as this in May." But what a contrast two days later when - "What a difference from yesterday and the day before when you needed your coats off. Today you needed them on. It was fit to skin you to death". We then had some wet showery growy days. We started silaging on the 25th and finished on 26th. We were extremely fortunate as the next fourteen days were wet and catchy, with very little silaging done.

I wrote on 4th **June** -"A lot of rain during the night and a damp sort of day. I don't think I have known it as wet for the time of year. There were bad floods in Todmorden and Bishop Auckland areas." From 13th - 20th we had a spell of dry weather with two very hot days on 17th and 18th. On the 18th - "A very hot day. According to the weather forecasters it was the hottest June day for 25 years". The rest of the month was a combination of hot and cold days, but it was mainly dry.

The first 10 days of **July** were catchy and not much hay weather. On the 10th - "A terrible wet, windy, stormy day. It was more like backend than summer." The rest of the month was quite an improvement and on the 29th - "It was a very humid day with thunder showers falling very oddly. In fact, in the Summer field, where our gimmer lambs were, half of the troughs were wet and the other half dry".

August was quite catchy, showers and rain falling very oddly. There were some good harvest days, 4th - 8th and 23rd and 25th. We started combining on 18th and finished on 30th. We finished baling straw on 4th September. **September** was a very wet month and there were hardly two dry days together.

October was the wettest I have ever known. On 30th - "Rained and stormed all day. I have never seen as much water about for the time of year. Water was flowing down Oscar Park potato rows, through our hedge, just like a beck. It was only the second time I have known snow in October".

November started off with a very wet day. There were bad reports of flooding in York and Malton. Within 18 months some people in Norton and Malton had their properties flooded twice. This weather continued most of the month, but we had some dry days from 26th onwards.

December was a wet foggy month with keen frosts from 26th - 31st. The year ended up with quite a snowstorm, blocking our farm road.

2001

It was good to turn our backs on the past year. What with the appalling weather and low prices I felt in many ways 2001 was a year of New Beginnings. It was the first time we hadn't had a lambing time. Lambing pedigree Suffolks is hard work, as they are different from cross breeds. A lot of births are not straightforward. Some lambs have their legs back, some don't come head first and when they arrive they generally need suckling. So, if you are going to do your job well you have to be there when they are born, which means night duty as well. For three weeks in the peak of lambing I would never go to bed, I just slept in the chair.

It was a year of new beginnings in our church life. As from 1st January we were now partners in the New Life Baptist Church at Northallerton.

I felt that from the middle of January farming was looking up a bit. Calves were a better trade, as were store cattle and sheep. But another crisis was on the horizon. This was the Foot and Mouth epidemic. On 20th February the first case of Foot and Mouth Disease was confirmed. From then on it spread like wild fire.

This had a devastating effect on farming and tourism. All auction marts were closed. No agricultural shows were held, and a lot of country sports were abandoned. The farmer's life now was all about disinfecting, licences, and a whole lot of new rules and regulations. There were some farmers who never left their holdings for months.

We didn't fare too badly. We kept up our social life, going to church. I never had any fear that we would get Foot and Mouth disease. One day we had a scare but in my Bible reading for that day from Psalm 91, verse 3 it said - "For He rescues you from every trap and protects you from the fatal plague". I have talked with several friends who were in the centre of the epidemic. They felt that those who were hardest hit were those who never got it as they suffered all the restrictions without any compensation.

For me, two things stood out. I had never seen so much cruelty to farm animals. I don't know where the RSPCA were in all this. For example, we saw sheep being hungered to death, and ewes lambing in appalling conditions.

DEFRA handled it very badly. They never consulted our local vets about what to do about moving stock. We had to talk to vets in Leeds who were looking at maps to know where we were.

Our biggest problem was that our autumn calving heifers were away at grass. This is how long it took us to get them back home.

We applied on July 10th to DEFRA for a licence to move them back home. The licence was refused. I appealed against this on 22nd July. This was also refused. I appealed again on 15th August and from that date I kept phoning them. I was promised I could move the heifers on 7th or 8th September. Then I got word to say I could not move them because I was only allowed to travel 6 miles by road. The actual distance was 7 miles. What do you do when dairy heifers are in calf to a beef bull so are more likely to need assistance, and are near to calving? They need to be at home where they can be attended to.

DEFRA's suggestion was that we should move them to another dairy farm or put a milking bail in the field. As a last resort we could send them on the Livestock Welfare Disposal Scheme which meant they would be slaughtered. The price I was offered was an insult to a pedigree breeder! How ridiculous can people get?

We were getting desperate as the heifers were beginning to calve. We were making two journeys a day to attend to them. This was a round trip of over 30 miles and we had already lost one calf.

I thought that I wouldn't be beaten and went to see my local MP, John Greenway. I then consulted my local NFU Secretary, Wendy Jefferson. They both wrote letters to DEFRA explaining that the heifers needed to be moved immediately.

On September 7th I received a phone call from Wendy to say that I shouldn't lose hope. She thought that we could get the heifers moved. Later that day I received a phone call from DEFRA saying we could move them but I had to ring the following day at 10 o'clock.

I rang the DEFRA vets at 10 o'clock the next morning to find nobody was available. I was informed by their secretary that they had had a party the night before and were all suffering a hangover. I did eventually get a vet two hours later, and they arranged that we would have the cattle moved on the following Wednesday. A Ministry vet would be at our farm at 12 o'clock.

The great day arrived. It was September 12th at 12.30. There was no vet! I rang them and they told me not to worry as a vet would be with me shortly. At 1 o'clock I received a phone call to say that a vet from Leeds was just setting off. I had to ring up my Haulage man to explain the situation. If I hadn't rung no-one would ever have turned up. Apparently the vet who was supposed to come was having his day off, and the authorities hadn't realised that. I can tell you when I heard that I was fuming. It had taken us exactly 2 months to get the heifers shifted.

Well, all in all, we didn't fare too badly. We had our monthly milk cheque, and with a lot of cows being slaughtered, milk was wanted at a decent price. There was also the bonus of not having to pay much for leased milk quota.

But for many farmers, especially those in the Dales who relied on income from store cattle, it was very bad. They never sold any for months, plus the fact that extra foodstuff had to be bought to keep those cattle and sheep which would normally have been sold months before.

It is at this point that I want to mention two people known to me. My cousin, Rosamund Dyson from Scarborough and Howard Petch from Cherry Burton. Both were involved with a Christian charity called "Farm Crisis Network" which has branches in most parts of the country.

Howard, who is a former Principal of Bishop Burton Agricultural College, talked with Bank Managers in the country, advising them not to put pressure on farmers and farm related industries as the situation was serious.

I kept in touch with Rosamund by telephone and some of the situations and people she was helping were unbelievable. I got Rosamund to write a few notes of her impressions of the Foot and Mouth epidemic. She wrote the following:

"The plight of farmers, in fact anyone and everyone connected in any way with agriculture, was indescribable. The epidemic seemed unending for almost nine months. Rural life seemed almost to come to a standstill as virtually all movement was stopped. In those areas most badly affected people were virtually prisoners in their own isolated homes for months. If it had not been for the telephone then there would probably have been no communication at all in some areas. Words seem inadequate to describe the situation and especially for farming folk and those involved in the Tourism industry which is such an important part of the rural economy these days. Scenes on the TV screens of burning animals and deserted fields had an immediate affect on potential visitors. They just stayed away.

The already horrendous situation seemed to be compounded by Government instructions, or lack of them! No one in authority seemed to be able to get a grip on the situation. Communication with MAFF and then DEFRA was virtually impossible at the grass roots level. There were, however, agencies, usually voluntary, who were trying to help people where it mattered most. One of these was the Farm Crisis Network, a

Christian Charity which has branches in most parts of the country. The Yorkshire branch had already been set up before the Foot and Mouth epidemic began, and we thank God that this was so. Our motto "Folk who know farming talking with farming folk" proved true. Not only were volunteers talking, but we were helping in many practical ways, often with financial matters which assumed massive proportions for many people. Immediately there was no animal movement, there was no income and there was no money to buy food for the family, or an increasing number of animals. Life for many was truly desperate.

Members of FCN frequently acted as agents for the two largest charities which gave away massive amounts of money to desperate farmers and others. The Addington Fund and the Royal Agricultural Benevolent Fund were a lifeline for many whose lives and livelihoods were at crisis level. Following on from the Foot and Mouth epidemic many reports have been commissioned and many questions asked about the handling of the situation. The National Audit Office asked FCN and other bodies for their views. I wrote to them as follows:

"I must have spoken to more than 100 people directly affected by Foot and Mouth Disease since the epidemic began in February of this year. I have spoken to farmers, seed merchants, hauliers and caterers, to name just a few. Many of them have been desperate, extremely worried and frightened for the future. Some have been ill with terminal illnesses, some have become ill because of the stress, some have had children who have become ill through the situation. The true cost of the epidemic will never be known, especially in terms of human suffering and misery. Much of this is indescribable.

I will never forget the disabled, distressed, housebound farmer's wife who said she had to be taken to hospital because whilst she was confined to the house all she could hear was the bang, bang, bang of her animals being shot. I will never forget the farmer who didn't think he could cope with waiting for another blood test result on his animals. Because he mentioned suicide I phoned him again the next day - fortunately the result of the blood test was negative.

I remember the farmer who told me that his 400 cattle had been culled because his neighbour's stock had the disease, only to learn that this was not so".

When you look up the DEFRA figures which were issued after the epidemic they make staggering and frightening reading. They are as follows:

There were 2,026 confirmed cases of the disease. There were another 8,446 cases where stock was either taken out or slaughtered on the Livestock Welfare Disposal Scheme. These two figures added together make a total of 582,000 cattle, 3,487,000 sheep, 146,000 pigs. 3,000 goats and 1,000 deer which were slaughtered. The county worst hit was Cumbria, where they had nearly 900 cases, resulting in 40% of the Swaledale breeding sheep being culled, and 60% of the Blue-faced Leicester breed being slaughtered.

Farming life has never been the same since the Foot and Mouth epidemic. We hardly see any Reps for farm companies nowadays. Marketing is different. A lot of prime stock is being sold dead weight. Auction marts are under pressure and in some cases have never re-opened since Foot and Mouth. I am a firm believer in both live and dead marketing. When the auction marts were closed we came to be at the mercy of buyers.

Weatherwise this was a much better year. There was good grow weather. We got some good silage and had a relatively good harvest. Straw was very scarce and dear. It was a good backend for drilling corn.

Here is a more detailed account of the weather in 2001:

January started off wet. Otherwise it was quite dry and mild. We had little frost and very little snow.

February was quite dry. We had snow on the 4th and a very cold easterly wind. From 13th - 20th we had slight frosts with bright days. We started sowing corn on 20th and finished sowing on 14th April. February ended up with a winter's day - "A real winter's morning with 4 inches of snow."

March was frosty for the first six days. On the third day we had the keenest March frost for 36 years. From 7th - 15th it was mild and drying. We started to sow corn again on 15th. The rest of the month was relatively dry, although we had a lot of rain on 27th

I mentioned that at the end of 2000 there was quite a lot of straw still to bale. I noted that some of this was baled in 2001 on 13th January, 22nd February and 15th March. Some of it was drier than at harvest.

April began with a nice springlike day. There were odd periods of dry weather, otherwise it was wetter than average. We turned our cows out on the 30th.

1st **May** was a tremendous grand day followed by some good dry days. From 10th - 13th we had good warm days. The rest of the month was quite growy, with three really hot days from 22nd - 24th.

The first five days in **June** were dry, but on the cool side. On the 3rd -"It was very cold first thing and windy - almost as cold as Christmas". The next day was a grand day. We cut all our grass and got it in on 5th. We had a lot of rain from the 6th - 18th with some cold stormy days. The rest of the month we had some good weather. It was very hot on the 25th.

The first ten days in **July** were quite good hay weather, with quite a lot of rain on 11th. From 11th - 21st we had a lot of rain. The rest of the month we had some good days. The 28th was a real hot day - "A scorcher!"

The first five days in **August** were a continuation of the late July weather then we had a lot of rain until 13th. We started harvest on 18th and finished on 29th, there being some good weather towards the end of the month.

The first 11 days in **September** were good harvest days. The rest of the month was quite wet and stormy at times.

October was quite a good month with a lot of mild days.

November was above average. On 6th - "A tremendous grand day with sun and wind. What a contrast to last year!" On 15th - "It was a tremendous grand day. I went up the fields and the 22 cattle we still had outside were laid down just as if it was summer".

December was decent weather. We kept the 22 cattle out until 20th when we had some snow and it blew our road in. The month ended up with quite a keen frost.

Our Suffolk ewes before the dispersal sale, 2000

Our Suffolk gimmer lambs before the sale, 2000

One of the best gimmer lambs sold at our sale, 2000

Nicholas and Bert Harper at our sale, 2000

Part of the crowd at our Suffolk sale, 2000

Auctioneer Peter Woodall selling at our sale, 2000

Floods, Malton area November 2000 (*Photos courtesy of Peter Smith*)

Chapter 23
2002
Prizes And Surprises,
Dialect And Past Christmas Traditions

We were beginning to see that for the farmer and tourism life was returning to normality. Auction marts were beginning to open from late February onwards, and things began to look up in the prices for livestock. Those who had been taken out with Foot and Mouth were restocking. There didn't seem to be a shortage of money. I think most farmers were well compensated, although people will never know the stress they went through in the process. Several people have said that they would still rather have their stock. You can spend a lifetime building up a pedigree herd or flock and it takes time to build your stock up again. I felt sad that most of the best sheep sold in our Suffolk sale in 2000 were taken out in the cull.

It was good to see the Agricultural Shows back again although livestock entries were down a lot. I don't think we will see record entries again, especially in cattle and pigs. Showing is becoming a very expensive hobby, and as we are seeing less labour on farms, farmers can't devote the time they would like to it. I know from experience that it is a time consuming job.

Weatherwise in 2002 we had a very good springtime. It was the first time we had turned our cows out in March, on the 28th, and it was the most forward seedtime. We finished in record time, starting on the 7th March and finishing on the 14th. It was the first time I had seen silage taken in April. Near Northallerton there was some cut by the 24th.

We had a very good harvest. I would think we had the best yields I have known. We sold the most corn off our farm but at a price we were getting 28 years ago. Our milk price dropped dramatically as well. In some of the months we were being paid less than we had been getting 15 years ago.

In August and early September we were experiencing a hygiene problem with our milk and also having problems with our bulk tank. It meant we had a deduction in our milk price and had to put four days milk supply down the drain. Well, as the saying goes, "It never rains but it pours".

Owing to a higher profit in 2001, our Family Credit was cut by four fifths. This situation got me down and I was battling against my weakness, depression. It is hard to understand depression until you have had it. I have learnt that it is best not to bottle things up but to seek help, both from family, friends and your doctor. Most of all, as a Christian, I have learnt to talk with God about it. He cares and understands, even if our feelings say He doesn't.

There is a lot in the book of Psalms about depression. The Bible is a very relevant book and I have learnt to hang onto the promises it gives us, as when we are depressed problems get blown out of all proportion.

In these past years we have seen, and are seeing, that the farming industry is being swamped by rules and regulations. We are being ruled by people who have very little practical knowledge of farming. I am reminded of a poem I read in a farming paper. It goes like this:

"When your land is office planned
And fed with streams of ink
And ploughed by men with fountain pens
What shall we eat and drink ?"

We have seen farmers demonstrating against low prices at supermarkets and ports where cheap food has been shipped in. Perhaps the biggest demonstration was on the 22nd September 2002 when Philip and I went to London on the Countryside Liberty and Livelihood march.
I wrote the following in my diary: -
"Me and Philip went to London on a coach paid for by the Estate on a march called Countryside Liberty and Livelihood. Set off at 6.30am.
Arrived about 11.30. Quite a long drawn out affair. We were two and a half hours walking before we started the march and we finished about 5 o'clock. Arrived back at 1.30 in the morning. I don't think I would do it again. I went for Philip's sake as he says I must march for my future."

My reflections are that it was too orientated towards hunting. One or two things stand out. We were given instructions not to drink any alcohol, either on the march or on the coach. Not bad for my teetotal principles. Over 400,000 people went on the march. There were thirty one specially chartered trains and a further 2,500 coaches. They all took protestors to the capital for the demonstration which ended with only four arrests of anti-hunt supporters. 1,600 police officers and 1,800 Countryside Alliance stewards supervised the event.

The demonstration was believed to be the biggest since a march in 1834 and was quite an emotional affair for me. People were waving flags, banners and placards. It was good to see the NFU President, Ben Gill, there. He said to the press, "I am here with everybody else because there are really serious concerns about the economic meltdown that is taking place in the countryside".

240

Personally, I have never been hunting in my life, and have no desire to do so. However, I wouldn't vote to ban it. Once they ban hunting, the next thing will be shooting and then fishing. I feel that farming and the countryside is being influenced by people who have little awareness of rural life.

2002

Here is a detailed account of the weather in 2002;

January started off frosty. On the 2nd there was a very keen frost, keenest of the winter. The temperature was minus 12 in Rievaulx. The rest of the month was a combination of fog and wet and mild with no snow. On the 28th it was a terrible windy day. A lot of damage was done up and down the country. Roofs were blown off and vehicles were blown over.

February was very wet and mild with hardly any frost. On the 23rd we had four inches of snow, blowing our road in.

March started off with a good drying day and this dry weather continued for 18 days. Towards the end of the month we had five springlike days

April was a relatively dry and bright month. There were a lot of white frosts and bright days but towards the end of the month we had quite a lot of rain, and it was stormy with it.

The first twelve days in **May** were dry and quite droughty. It came a much needed rain on the 13th. The weather in May can be from one extreme to the other. On the 16th I recorded it was a different day altogether from yesterday. It was dull, cold and cloudy. The rest of the month was wet and showery, ending up on the 31st with a real grand day.

June began with a very good day. We got our silage in on the 5th. We were very fortunate as in some places it had poured down. The first half of the month was wet and catchy, with thunder at times.

At the beginning of June Dorothy and I spent a few days near Kirkby Stephen in Cumbria. As we travelled round Lancaster and Cumbria it was obvious that they had had a lot wetter weather. There was very little silaging done and in some cases dairy cows had had to be brought back in after only having been turned out a week.

From the 16th to the 29th it was quite an improvement. First crops of silage were got in and some hay was baled.

The first twelve days in **July** were very mixed, we had five hot days then a lot of wet until the 24th. We then had some decent days until the end of the month.

August started off wet. On the 2nd it came a month's rain in 24 hours. There were some bad floods around the Northallerton area. That day we took 3 calves to Leyburn and there was water everywhere. We called back to try and collect a bull at Tommy Spence's but Brompton was in flood, so we had to turn back.

The weather improved and we started harvest on the 7th August. We finished combining on the 27th and baling on the 28th. It was all led in by the 2nd of September.

In the binder and sheaf days **September** was reckoned to be the harvest month. This year it was the best month of the year, with not much rain and a lot of good harvest days.

The first ten days of **October** were a continuation of the good September weather. We then had quite a lot of wet with keen frosts on the 19th and 24th.

November was mild, a wet and foggy month with no frost.

December was almost a continuation of the November weather but we had keen frosts on the 18th and 19th.

I think that at the end of 2001 and in the beginning of 2002 a lot of farmers did some reflecting on how the foot and mouth epidemic had affected their lifestyles. For me, three things which I missed the most, and which were cancelled, were our annual rounds of carol singing, not having any agricultural shows to go to, and no auction marts to attend.

It set me thinking about shows, and the characters connected with them. My mind went back to the middle and late 1950's. Dad never moved far away from the Masham and Teeswater sheep pens. As a lad at the Yorkshire Show, I would listen to the men of the breed talking to him. These were men like Tom and Joe Addison from Cotherstone, Joe Hall from Rokeby, Johnnie Denham from Langleydale, John Liddle from Otley, Victor and Herbert Verity from Pateley Bridge area. There was also John Hodgson from East Witton, Sid Watson from Penrith, Jack Ripley and Stanley Bainbridge from Richmond. At the local shows like Ryedale, Sutton, Farndale, Danby, Rosedale and Stokesley Dad would meet up with other exhibitors and reminisce about past characters and shows. The show scene at that time was dominated by Bulmers of Habton and Colemans of Speeton showing English Leicester sheep. Bulmers of Dalton Holme, Tom Midgley from Kirby Underdale, Harpers of Skiplam, Eddie Teasdale and sons of Skiplam and Farnell's of Slingsby were leading exhibitors in Oxford and Suffolk Sheep.

In the Scotch sheep section leading men were Teddy Hebden from Snainton, Arthur Hammond from Sawdon, J.R. Steel from Potto and Fred Boocock from Moorsholm. In the Swaledale section it was Garb and Harold Agar and Len Fawbert from Farndale, Ernest Metcalfe from Rosedale, Willie Wood, and Wood Brothers from Bilsdale. In our own section, which was the Mashams, leading exhibitors were Rodney Ramshay from Catterick, Percy Sherwin from Bedale, Ernie Patterson from Boroughbridge, Jack Musgrove from South Kilvington, and Bunt Lawson from Richmond. Local men were Arthur Garbutt and Digby Bowes from Hawnby.

In the cattle section dairy shorthorns were shown by S.A. Boocock from Kirkbymoorside, Cyril Pettit from East Ayton, Alf Sleightholme of York, Herbert Dickinson from Sawdon and Smith Brothers from Nawton. Round the Dales area it was John Lister from Glaisdale and Willie Garbutt from Loftus. In the beef shorthorns it was George Kirk from Sutton, Robin Turton from Upsall, George Boak from Burythorpe and Arthur Cussons from Kirkbymoorside. In the Friesian section it was F.K. Abbey and R.H. Ford from York, R. Harland and J. Todd from Whitby area. From the local area it was Willie Jeffrey from Nawton.

The heavy horse section was dominated by Harpers of Skiplam, Cumbers of Great Ayton, and Nunns from Northallerton. There was also A. Bell from Whixley and John Teasdale and Sons from Low Woods, Helmsley. I remember the Teasdales had a very good foal in 1955. It won 13 first prizes and five cups. In the Whitby area shows were dominated by horses from Norman Nellis and R.M. Pearson.

Some shows are remembered by the adverse weather on the day. In 1954 Danby Show was an example of this. It was a terrible wet stormy day and the produce tent was blown down. Dad came back soaked to the skin. I remember talking to Jack and Richard Bulmer about this day.

As the Bulmers were travelling up near Danby there was a man leading a cow and thumbing a lift! The Bulmers had a very good in pig, Large White sow that year and they took it to Danby Show. It got loose from its pen and landed up underneath the produce tent. Such are the experiences of showing!

Perhaps the best known show ring character in our area is a man called Bert Harper. Bert lives quite locally at Skiplam Grange, Nawton. He specialises in Oxford and Suffolk Down sheep. At the Yorkshire Show, between 1955 and 1992 Bert won the Champion Oxford 13 times and the Reserve Champion 13 times. He won the Suffolk Champion 3 times, the Masham twice, and the Commercial Lambs twice. Bert was also an expert at showing wool and he won the Champion Fleece several times. He also exhibited at the Royal Show winning the Oxford Champion several times. Once the Harpers went to three shows in one day - Bishop Wilton, Sutton on Forest and Wakefield. On that day they showed 62 sheep and they took the championship at all three shows.

The Ryedale Show was Bert's big show. Not only did he show horses and sheep but also cattle and pigs. There is a cup given for the most points in the livestock section, and the Harpers have won it over 30 times. It was fitting that Bert was made President of the Show in 1997.

Not only was Bert a great showman, I think he would have been a champion ice cream eater. On a hot show day Bert could devour ice creams like rattle, as we say.

At this point I want to mention Ellen Jane Harper, Bert's mother. She was a lovely woman, a real Dales person. She didn't stand on any ceremony and she treated everybody the same. Mrs. Harper was given to hospitality. She did a lot of work behind the scenes, cleaning the horse harnesses, making sure the men were sent off with clean white coats and packing up food for them all. When mother and I used to go up to see her she would tell us all about her young days and how hard she had had to work.

I remember Mrs Harper telling us that she liked milking cows (by hand) as it was the only time she got to sit down and rest! After she died it was fitting that Bert gave a cup in her memory to the Ryedale show to be awarded for the best sheep in the show.

There is an old saying "What is bred in the bone will come out in the flesh". This means that our genes are a strong influence, and for me, showing was in my blood. My maternal grandfather, James Todd Wass liked to show heavy horses and my paternal grandfather Fred Dunn, showed half bred lambs.

My grandma Wass was a Waind of Ankness, Bransdale. The Wainds were great stock breeders and show men. In my mother's press cutting book the first page carries a report of when the Wainds left Ankness in the late 1930's. Records show that it was during the lifetime of the third John Waind that the foundation of the Ankness herd of Shorthorns was laid. They started from very modest beginnings - just a pair of young heifers, secured from the herd of the Stampers of Highfield, Nunnington. Scottish blood from the best herds was secured and a bull which added lustre to the record of the Ankness herd was Sir George, a grand roan bred by Mr. John Cran.

Probably the two best heifers ever bred at Ankness were members of the Jewel family. Bright Jewel 5th and Bright Jewel 6th. These won prizes at the Royal, Royal Highland and Great Yorkshire Shows as yearling heifers. They were later sold to Mr. Haley of Malton. The same gentleman gave a big price for a promising young Ankness bull which later made £400 for export.

Most people in those days would walk their animals to the shows, but the Wainds had a special bull cart - a cattle wagon type of thing pulled with horses.

Dad started showing in 1953 with half bred Masham lambs. I was drilled at an early age to get to the sheep on time before and after I went to school.

Sheep are like humans because they do better if they get regular meals. They say that half the pedigree goes down the neck.

Over the years we have won lots of prizes. From 1978 to 1983 we seemed to do a lot more showing. I think it was because we had sold our main flock. One of my disappointments was that we never got the Championship at the Yorkshire Show. However, several times we had the pleasure of beating the Yorkshire champions at the local shows.

You can never be sure with showing. It is a very unpredictable business. I well remember being at the Yorkshire Show when we had some very good mule ewes and shearlings. On the Monday night everybody said that we would win the next day. Well, we got first with the shearlings and the ewes, but when it came to the championship, two little lambs won. One man said it was highway robbery and the last thing people expected. Showing is all about prizes and surprises!!

At the Yorkshire Show in 1982 we won the Reserve Champion Mule and Masham prizes. At Northallerton and Ryedale Shows we were awarded the Champion Masham and Mule prizes. We ended up that year winning the regional Golden Fleece Competition. The same fleece went to the Smithfield Show. It got first in the Masham class and was only three points away from being the Champion Fleece.

We decided that 1983 would be our last year showing Masham and Mule sheep. This was our 30th year and I said to Dad "Let's go out in glory, not in shame". So we pulled out all the stops to make it a good year. We went to 25 shows in four different counties. We won 11 Championships, 6 Reserve Champions, 75 first prizes, 68 seconds, 38 thirds and 8 fourths.

Later when we got our Suffolk flock built up we showed them locally on a limited scale. We won Championships at Stokesley, Burniston and Danby Shows.

Mother used to say that showing was a jiggery pokery business. You got some fakes and some judges could show favouritism. Some exhibitors are bad losers because they do not like being beaten, but when you show you have to be prepared to be beaten by worse stuff than your own.

Exhibiting livestock is a bit like a lady entering a beauty competition. They have to look nice and attractive on the day. Some exhibitors are clever show men, they know all the wrinkles, how to trim, shave, wash and dip them in the right kind of dip. Some are clever breeders, they know how to breed good stock. If you have a combination of the two then you are likely to win some prizes. You learn as you go on and you learn by your mistakes. If you do something wrong then people will criticise you.

I remember in our early days we showed some sheep that didn't look right.

An experienced man came to us and said "You have been dipping them sheep when it has been too hot. Their coats have got burnt". I well remember a lady coming to me at one show and asking me "How is it that your sheep look so curly in their coats ? Have you permed them ?" I replied "It's like this. I can't tell you in five minutes what it has taken me 30 years to learn about how to present them like that". If an animal is right to start with you have something to work on but some animals can get past their best. It's all about your animals striking twelve o'clock on the day.

I am thankful for good contacts and I want to mention one man who helped us a lot with mule sheep, Alf Dent from Weardale. We used to buy his best lambs and he would come and help us to trim and dip them. Alf was an artist and quite a pioneer of the mule and blue faced Leicester sheep in their early days.

There are all kinds of tricks played at shows. Some exhibitors will do anything to win, borrow or buy. Most shows have a list of conditions, such as that stock must be in the exhibitor's ownership at the time of entry. This rule is broken time and time again.

I remember one exhibitor showing a tup at Stokesley Show. He had bought it the week before at Kelso - and it won, also the Championship. Another exhibitor said to me that money can buy anything. I said "Can it ? Have a good look at that man's face. He looks as miserable as sin"!

I have shown different kinds of livestock - cattle, goats, pigs and mainly sheep. I can honestly say that what we have shown has always been our own property. I would rather stand at the bottom of the line with our own stock than at the top with something that wasn't ours.

I often say that it isn't only the winners that make a show. It is the losers as well. A very important person is the judge, as at the end of the day judging is one person's opinion. I once heard someone say that if every man thought the same we would all be chasing the same woman! It is a good job we don't all think alike.

I remember a sheep exhibitor flying at the judge, cursing and swearing and telling him he reckoned nowt to his judging. The judge replied "I mustn't have reckoned nowt to your sheep"!

Over the past years I have tried to be a faithful member of the Ryedale Show Committee, helping to select judges. I remember asking one man if he would like to judge. He said "No. I can make plenty of enemies without judging"!

Here are a few lines I read in a farming paper recently, describing the judges role:

"This lonely man does a job without pay
Picking out the best animal which he sees on the day.
He stands in the ring with no help from a friend
Knowing he cannot please all in the end.
Respect he deserves but rarely receives
The show can't go on without his expertise.
So let's give him credit where credit is due
You would expect some of it if it were you.
Let's make his task pleasant, not such a drudge
A very important person the judge".

Over these past few years I have become quite involved in, and am an enthusiastic member of, the Yorkshire Dialect Society. I find different dialects fascinating. If you listen carefully you can generally find out where people come from by the way they speak. Dialect and speech can vary within a matter of miles, or between hills, as we say in Yorkshire.

One of the highlights of the Yorkshire Dialect Society is the annual "Christmas Crack" held in York. Contributions of poems and stories are made from all areas of Yorkshire. In 2003, one of the contributions was made by a local lady, Eva Ward, from Helmsley. Eva read a poem from her son's book "A Shepherd goes Courtin'." This is, perhaps, one of the more recent books of local dialect poems and is worth reading.

In 1999 at the Christmas Crack I read a poem, again written by a local young person called Trudie Sanderson, from East Moors. The poem is entitled "There's a Crisis in Farming - Who Understands ?" It goes like this:

1. Now whenever you open the Yorkshire Post
    There's a farmer complaining of the brass that they've lost.
    When they take calves to the mart the price is so small
    For old ewes they're lucky to get a bid at all.
    And nobody understands, no nobody understands.
2. You switch on the radio and hear them speak
    Of pig farmers going bankrupt every week.
    But how can folks believe us when they live in a town
    And the price in the supermarket never goes down
    How can they understand ? How can they understand ?
3. Now there's form filling, paperwork, passports for cows
    Subsidy, IACS, and quotas for ewes.

We can't dip our sheep now, it's making us vexed
That's more legislation they've hung round our necks
But they don't understand, they just don't understand.

4. Joseph had a crisis, he woke up from a dream
   He realised it was an angel that he had just seen,
   Telling him that Mary was to have a little lad
   Conceived by God's spirit, what a shock he must have had.
   But Joseph understood. Aye, Joseph understood.

5. So Joseph married Mary, two thousand years ago.
   Because of Roman regulations they had many miles to go.
   From Nazareth to Bethlehem a donkey Joseph led
   The only shelter they could find was in a cattle shed
   Because nobody understood, nobody understood.

6. And so in the stable on that first Christmas mom
   Among the cows and the donkeys a tiny bairn was born-
   An army of angel voices rang through the night
   And poor humble shepherds hurried to see the light,
   Then they understood, the shepherds understood.

7. The bairn grew to be a carpenter, mending carts and ploughs.
   He was the shepherd preacher, folks followed him like ewes.
   He talked to the folks about sowing in the field,
   Gathering the harvest and how much the corn would yield.
   Jesus understood, Aye Jesus understood.

8. Two thousand years later His spirit is still here
   He knows all our problems, knows our doubts and fear.
   So whenever you've got a crisis on your hands
   Turn to the One who always understands,
   Because Jesus understands, Aye, Jesus understands.

9. So let's all cheer up and stop all our moaning
   It's a time for festivity, not grumbling and groaning.
   A time to join with our friends and families again,
   And hear the Christmas message. Peace, Goodwill to all men.
   Hear the Christmas message, Peace, Goodwill to all men.

Often at past Christmas Cracks, and it was mentioned again this year there were references to customs and traditions of Christmases years ago. This started me thinking about Christmas as I knew it as a boy.

248

It was quite a tradition that for your tea on Christmas Eve you would be given 'frumety'. What is 'frumety'? Its proper name is frumenty and it is a kind of pudding made with pearl barley. This was washed and soaked over night in water. It was then cooked rather like rice pudding, with milk added to it. To serve you added sugar and cinnamon.

As I remember it our parents and grandparents were quite superstitious. It was reckoned to be bad luck if you cut into the Christmas cake before Christmas Eve. You mustn't bring any holly into the house before Christmas Day or go Carol Singing before Christmas Eve. Perhaps this was the reason why at Rievaulx we always started Carol Singing on Christmas Eve and sang round the villages of Rievaulx, Scawton and Old Byland for the following four nights. Now we sing before Christmas, finishing up on Christmas Eve.

In mentioning carol singing, I must add that people sing different tunes to carols in different areas. For example, at Rievaulx we sing four different tunes to "While Shepherds Watched". These are Lingham, Christmas tune, Ilkla Moor, and Sweet Bells tune.

One tradition which has died out is the carol singers beggar man. This was the person who had the collecting box. The beggar man used to be asked in at certain houses for cake and wine. Especially in the days when they used to walk, it was a well-known fact that you could lose the beggar man in the process!!

There is another tradition which, as far as I know, has died out. I think I was the last boy to go round what we called "Christmas Shouting". This happened on Christmas morning and involved saying a rhyme outside peoples front doors. If you were a favourite at certain houses you were asked to be the "lucky bird". No other boy was allowed to shout until the lucky bird had been. This was the rhyme which the lucky bird said:

"Lucky bod, lucky bod, chuck, chuck, chuck,

Maister 'n Missis it is taam ti git up.

If ya deean't git up ya'll ev neea luck

Seea please will ya let the lucky bod in?"

They would let you in and give you Christmas cake, ginger wine and some money. I remember I was once given half-a-crown which was two shillings and sixpence in old money. When this happened you thought you had been given the earth !

If you were an ordinary "shouter" you would say this rhyme:

"A wish ya a Merry Christmas, a Happy New Year,

A good fat pig, a new caulven cow,

Maister and Missis, hoo dae ya doo ?

Seea please will ya give mi a copper or two ?"

Different areas had their poems and the following was passed on to me by Eva Lofthouse from Helmsley, which was 'shouted' by the boys up East Moors.

"We wish you a Merry Christmas and a Happy New Year.

We are all teetotal and don't drink beer.

A little bit of gingerbread, a little bit of cheese

A cup of cold water and a penny if you please.

If you haven't got a penny a ha'penny will do

And if you haven't got a ha'penny. God bless you".

Over the years, as lads, we got to know the best houses. A good place was where you were asked in. There you had cake and wine, were given an orange or some sweets and a two shilling bit. At an average house you got a shilling. Below average was a sixpenny piece. Those who were greedy gave us a three-penny piece. Those who were very greedy didn't answer the door at all !!

Joe Bowes, to whom I have referred in earlier chapters, was quite a character. He used to say to us "Thou mun cum tee shoot on Christmas Morn. Thy Mam and Dad are good tee me, giving me ten o'clocks (lowance). A's giving thoo two bob, rest o't lads gits a tanner" (six penny piece).

I did quite a round. I started at Ouldray farm where I was the lucky bird, and then I followed all the top farms round and down into Rievaulx village. Then all the farms out of Rievaulx, landing up at High Leys. You weren't allowed to shout after 12 o'clock midday.

On New Year's Day it was the girls' turn. They went New Year's Gifting. But again, a boy was asked to be the lucky bird as on Christmas day.

This was the poem the girls used to say:

" 'Tis very seldom I call here

To wish you Good Morning and a Happy New Year.

I mustn't stay long, but quickly pass on

So please will you give me my New Year's Gift ?"

I have often wondered about the reason for Christmas Shouting and New Year's Gifting. I think that years ago children would be a lot poorer and it would be a means of swelling their savings. Now things have altered. As I write this, I have just heard on the radio that Christmas, for many, is a time of over spending. It is a well known fact that after Christmas debt collectors are kept very busy.

In December 2001 Rievaulx Chapel members took the decision not to go carol singing. Even though the Foot and Mouth Epidemic was over several farmers had indicated that they didn't want us to go as they wanted to take all the precautions they could. I must say I missed the annual rounds of carol singing.

Well, here we are, at Christmas 2003, and back in full force. Over twenty of us are spreading the Good News and raising money for needy charities. This Christmas we raised over £700.

John Potter Waind with his prize beef shorthorn, early 1930's

Bert Harper and his Dad, Thornton Dale Show, early 50's

Albert Boocock with one of his prize dairy shorthorns, middle 1950's

John Cussons with his prize beef shorthorn bull, early to mid 1960's

George Teasdale with his prize winning decorated horse, early to mid 1950's

Bert Harper's champion Oxford, late 1950's

253

Bulmer family from Great Habton, middle 1950's. Left to right Jack, Father, David and Richard

Peter Aconley from Pickering with Newcliffe Glady 2nd Supreme champion, Royal Dairy Show, London, 1961

Group of Scotch Sheep Men, late 1960's.
Left to right: Steve Hill, Mr and Mrs Bill Todd, Wilf Milner and Herbert Pearson

John Lister and Sons from Glaisdale, best group of dairy Shorthorn cattle, Danby
Show 1977

Geoff Wood from Ryton, prize Saddleback pig, Ryedale Show late 1980's

Alf Dent from Weardale, 1979

Emma and Stephen Dodsworth in fancy dress as Prince Charles and Lady Diana, 1981

*Bert Harper, Champion Sheep
Masham Sheep Fair, early 1990's*

*A regular winner on the Swaledale Sheep
scene, Arthur Carter from Farndale*

*Richard Bulmers, winning Suffolks
Smithfield Show, 1980*

*Ernest Sherwin and Author at
North Yorkshire Show 1982*

*Nicholas with Interbreed Champion
(Danby Show, 1982)*

*George Otterburn, Champion beef animal
Ryedale Show, 1985*

Prizes won with our sheep, 1983

W.H. Dunn and sons Mule shearling and Masham ewe never beaten in their class 1983

*W.H. Dunn and sons
Group of Mule Shearlings
1983*

*Group of Masham Show
sheep belonging to W.H.
Dunn and sons (1983)*

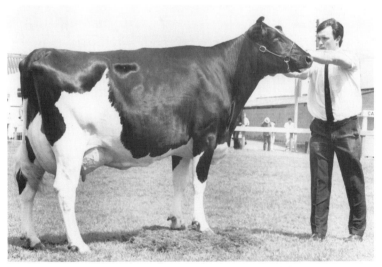

David Wilson's Champion Holstein cow, Yorkshire Show, 1991
Photo by kind permission of Farmers Guardian.

Junior Interbreed beef Champion Royal Highland, Royal show, Royal Welsh 1999. Limousin Bull shown by Peter Lang and partners Hawnby, Helmsley 1999

Christine Thompson's prize Ile-De-France Ram 1990's

Stephen Dodsworth's Jacob Ram, Champion at Royal and Great Yorkshire Show, 2004

260

Alan Myers from Rosedale Prize winning Ayrshire at the Great Yorkshire Show, 1988 belonging to Alan Myers

Stenton Family from Thornton Dale, Pickering, with their prize winning sheep, 2004

Above: Our Prize winning roots, 2004

Left: No show could carry on without judges four men who have done a lot of judging. Left to right, Willie Dunn, Tom Midgeley, Doug Ward and John Cook

Chapter 24
2003
Characters Dad Met, And His Passing On

Since farming went into recession we have often been asked whether we had ever thought of diversifying. Before Dorothy went out to do home help work we had thought seriously about developing a small caravan site.

We followed the necessary procedures of applying to the Caravan Club to see whether our farm was suitable. They told us it was, but that we would need permission from our neighbours who share the same road. We would also have to apply to the Council to see whether they thought the access was safe. The Council said it was a busy road and would be dangerous for caravans pulling out. I did not agree with this and told them that either we or our neighbours were regularly pulling out with Landrovers and trailers and there had been no accidents.

After some hassle I eventually got a councillor out to have a look and they finally agreed that the access would be safe. However, I began to seek advice from other caravan site owners and they said that to do the job properly we would need electric hook-up points, also good shower and toilet facilities. When we were given rough estimates to erect such facilities, the price frightened us and we forgot the idea of a caravan site. We decided that instead the best thing would be for Dorothy to get some employment outside the farm.

Over recent years a lot of farmers' wives, and farmers themselves, have gone out to work or have diversified. Tourism is quite an "in" word. Some recent statistics show that some farmers are earning more from tourism than from farming. We have seen farm buildings turned into holiday accommodation, farmers' wives doing bed and breakfast and catering. Some farmers have gone into contracting to subsidise their incomes, also doing school taxi work. One farmer's wife, Sally Robinson, has made a name for herself, both locally and nationally, by forming a company called Ample Bosom, which specialises in selling underwear to well endowed women.

Since January 2000 I have been diversifying by trying to write this book!

The only other minor diversification we have gone into is growing game cover for the Estate shoot. We started this in 2001 and there are ten acres altogether. It is quite difficult to grow as it has to occupy the same site year after year, near wood sides handy for the game. Flea beetle and wood pigeons are quite a problem, but it doesn't matter what crop you grow there are always some pests or diseases.

Locally, game shooting has become big business. Our Estate rears thousands of partridges and pheasants which adds a lot to the local economy, Hotels, shops, suppliers of four wheel drive vehicles and many others benefit.

This last year, 2002 - 2003, was a special year for the Dunn family. In late December 2002 we met to celebrate the wedding of my nephew, David, the elder son of my brother Nicholas. We were all especially thrilled that he bought the house Dad had occupied until he went into hospital. When we look back, it is amazing how things work out. In March 2003, my nephew Simon held a Hog Roast and open evening to celebrate 20 years of being in business as an agricultural contractor. He and his team provide an excellent service with the most up-to-date machinery and have over 350 customers on their books. Dad, though frail, was determined to attend - "no show without Punch!" and did so with the support of Beechwood Place nursing home staff. This event proved to be his swan song as he died shortly afterwards, but more of that later.

In July we met to celebrate Dorothy's 50th birthday. We had a party at church when a life-long friend gave a bit of a "This is your life" programme. Home Group members sang and gave their good wishes. My brother Christopher sang a solo and Dorothy's brother Ken gave a commentary on his sister's life. A good time was had by all.

It was a year when we did well in the local NFU Crop Competitions, winning first with grass and silage, and third with roots, making us the reserve overall points winners. It was a successful season with our silage, roots and grain at the local shows, going to eight shows and winning twenty-eight first prizes. My nephew Timothy had an outstanding season with his Swaledale, Blue faced Leicester and mule sheep. He won five Championships and over thirty first prizes. Not only had he a good 'do' with showing but he also had a good trade selling 300 Mule gimmer lambs averaging £70 each. To crown his success he sold a Blue-faced Leicester Shearling ram for 7,500 guineas.

Dad said when the farming recession began in 1996 that there would be 7 lean years. However, things have improved in most aspects except for the price of milk, which is our main source of income. There is something wrong when the farmer receives 18 pence per litre for our milk, yet the consumer pays more than double that. This is the first time in my farming experience that we have seen farmers protesting and picketing at Dairy depots, such is the serious state of the dairy industry.

Out of all my records the year 2003 will go down as the best year, weather-wise, that we have ever known. It was almost a farmer's dream. In this area rains came at the right time, with a lot of sunshine too. Our cows were turned out to graze on rye on March 24th, the earliest ever. This same land was drilled with kale on May 5th and we started grazing it on July 31st.

Here is a more detailed account of the weather in 2003:

January started off very wet. There were floods again in the Stamford Bridge and Elvington areas. We had frosts from 4th until 12th and then there were six days of windy weather with everything drying up. This was followed by a lot of wet, windy but mild weather. There was a real contrast on the 30th. I wrote that it was windy and there were some snow showers, a real blizzard at times. Miriam and Philip came home early from school. I wrote on the 31st "It had been a very rough night with a very cold strong wind. Our road was blown in, I have never seen so much snow blown into our cow shed so we had to barrow it out. Breck House men came and opened out the road. Miriam and Philip didn't go to school. There were reports of bad weather down the east side of Lincolnshire and in the Peterborough area." The first six days in **February** were grand winter days, with frost. There were snow showers on the 3rd and 4th. On the 4th it got up very windy and blew our road in. It came some mild days till the 14th and then we had frosts from the 15th to the 20th. Over the next few days things dried up and we started sowing corn on the 25th. The month ended with a wet night - the most rain for over a month.

March was above average. The rain on the 4th and the 7th was quite localised. We finished sowing corn on the 18th. On the 19th I went to a farm sale at Scackleton near Hovingham and they were taking potatoes up as there were quite a lot of them which could not be harvested in 2002.

April started off with a showery, wild cold day, then we had some tremendous warm days, with white frosts. On the 15th I recorded that it was a mild day and very warm. It was the warmest day down south for 100 years - up in the 70's. I wrote on the 16th that it was a tremendous warm and sunny day, the best April day I had experienced. It was like blazing June. Gardeners were beginning to cry out for rain. People had sprinklers on their lawns, a thing unheard of in April. Fortunately we had a good rain on the 28th and another good soaking, growy rain on May 2nd.

We experienced a good growy month in **May**. A good rain came on the 16th and then we had a lot of showery weather from the 17th to the 25th. The month ended up with three warm days.

June started off quite thundery and very humid with some rain on the 2nd. We got our main crop of silage in on the 3rd. The rest of the month was quite hot and dry, except for the 28th and the 30th when we had some good helpful rains - the most since March.

July was a good month with a lot of hot days. Our neighbours, Fairburns, Bowes and Hawkins, all started harvest on the 16th. This was very early for our part of the country. We had a very good localised rain on the 25th and again in the late afternoon of the 29th, which was the Ryedale Show. It rather spoiled things at the show.

August was a really grand month. We started harvest on the 14th and finished baling on the 16th. It was all led in by the 20th. There were some record-breaking hot days in August. I recorded that on August 6th it was a very hot day and 96.6 degrees in London. Some farmers had to stop combining because the corn was coming off the combine so hot that it couldn't be cooled down in the grain stores. I recorded on the 9th that it was a very hot day and almost too hot to work. John Medd was wet through with sweat seated in the combine cab.

When you get hot weather you can draw thunder, and, sure enough, on the 10th we were travelling to Northallerton when a massive storm brewed up. It came in very dark, with torrential rain. It was so dark that all the traffic stopped. Northallerton and Osmotherley were flooded. When we got home there had only been a light shower. Down south they had record-breaking temperatures. 101 degrees had been reached at Heathrow. There was very little rain in August - only three hours on the llth, which did a power of good. There were also light drizzly showers towards the end of the month.

September was another dry, warm month. On the 14th it was a real grand warm day with the temperatures in the eighties. It was the warmest September day for a while. On the 16th I went to Hawes Mule gimmer lamb sale. I noted in my diary that it was a tremendous sunny day. There won't be many years when it was as dry when lambs were born and still as dry when they were sold. It came a lot of rain on the 19th - the most rain since July 25th. On the 24th we had one of the keenest frosts in September for years.

October was a dry month. On the 1st it was a glorious day, more like summer than backend.

November was another good month with rain only on three days.

December started off with a wet day. On the 1st I recorded that there had been a lot of rain during the night and it came a lot during the day. Things were the wettest and muckiest since January. We had quite a lot of mild days, enabling us to keep some cattle out until the 23rd. The month ended up with three keen frosts and a snowstorm on New Year's Eve, when, for the first time in our lives we got snowed out and had to stay the night at Paul and Gillian Ashbridge's at Cold Kirby.

When Mam died in 1990 a lot of people wondered how Dad would cope on his own. We had Mam's funeral service on the Saturday and Dad judged

Masham sheep at Danby Show on the following Wednesday. The Friday of the same week he went down with me to a Friesian sale in Derbyshire. On the way back he said that he thought he would go with me to Darlington Show the next day. He said "I isn't going to give in yet, I have a lot to live for". Not bad for an eighty year old !

He managed very well on his own, with the help of family, friends and neighbours. Later on he also had good support from the home help service and district nurses. He got to the shows and sheep sales when he could. He always kept an interest in everyone. Dad was a very good customer of British Telecom, ringing people regularly, especially people who would talk about sheep.

In March 2002 his health started to deteriorate and he spent six months in hospital, followed by six months in a Nursing Home where he died in March 2003, aged 93 years. He maintained his interest in chapel and farming matters to the end. With great determination he made it from hospital to the Ryedale show via wheelchair ambulance in July 2002, when he was presented with the annual award for the person who has contributed significantly to farming and rural life in the area. It was a proud moment, and he really enjoyed his day talking with sheep friends and the show officials

Dad's funeral service was a real time of celebration and thanksgiving. Hazel read the lesson, Christopher sang a solo and I gave the address. I summed up his life by quoting two texts. The first was from Proverbs Chapter 10 and part of verse 7 where it says we all have happy memories of good men who have gone to their reward. The second was Psalm 37, verse 37 saying "But the good man, the blameless, the upright, the man of peace, he has a wonderful future ahead of him. For him there is a happy ending". I had eleven points, all beginning with the letter F. These were that Dad was a Funeral man, a Farndale man, a Family man, a Farming man, a Feversham man, a Friendly man, a Famous man, a Forthright man, a Forgiving man, a Forward-looking man and a Faithful man.

As Dad looked down from Heaven, I feel sure he would be thrilled with his funeral. A lot of people commented afterwards that it was the best funeral service that they had attended.

Dad never stopped giving orders. When we went to see him or when he rang up his first question was "What are you on with? I would be getting on. There is nowt to be gained by being last."

I want to dedicate the rest of the chapter to Dad, recalling his sayings. Grandad's sayings, and the colourful characters that we and they met.

From an early age Dad and Mam taught us to get up on a morning and get done at night. Dad would tell us that you can't both sit up and get up. One hour in the morning is worth two at night. You can't burn the candle at both ends of the day.

If we were slow in responding to his call on a morning he would quote the Christmas Carol "O come all ye faithful". Then he would say "None of you are so joyful and triumphant". Also from an early age Dad and Mam taught us to observe Sunday as a day of rest and for worship. They used to tell us that if you worked hard enough on a weekday then you would be ready for a rest on Sunday. We have never harvested, haytimed or silaged on a Sunday and we have no intention of starting now. When we advertise anything in the paper we always put "Not Sundays". I am reminded of the following verse.

"A Sabbath well spent brings a week of content. Its joys are the hope of the morrow. But a Sunday profane, whatever the gain, is the sure forerunner of sorrow."

Dad would often quote some of his father, our Grandad Dunn's sayings. For example he would say:

"Your Grandad would say that a woman can spend money faster
  than a man can earn it".
"When you get married your penny buns become twopenny ones"
"If a lad is earning a pound away, he is worth two at home".
"If your hands don't take any notice of your brains, you might
  as well cut them off'.

We would be sat over the fire at night and if it was storming and raining, Dad would say "Your Grandad used to say that houses are worth more than land on a night like this".

Cattle dealers were men that Dad would often quote. Jack and Reg Sunley were father and son and both were cattle dealers. One day Jack went to a farm to see some cattle and they were what we called poor sorts. Jack said to the farmer "You don't call them cattle, they are rubbish that grows up among them". When Jack was making a deal he would say "I am bidding you twice, my price and good day". At the end of his life Reg was in hospital and one of his friends went to see him. He said "How is tha Reg ?" Reg replied "A's sick of me job, I want ti be out of here or in a box, yan or t'other, sharp"

Jim Dixon, from Harome, was another cattle dealer. He had a real dry sense of humour. He loved to tell tales to us. He used to say "I lays in bed on a morning and I looks through the deaths column in the Yorkshire Post. If my name isn't there I decides to get up".

Jim was good at quoting sayings of auctioneers. If I was selling cows in York he would pass the stalls and, tapping me on the shoulder, he would say 'Willie Dunn would say "Look to me, you are bound to get it."

If someone had died Jim would say that everyone was enquiring about how much money the person had left. This happened when a customer of his died. He left a son who was a bit simple. The son was asked how much money his father had left and his reply was "He left the lot, he did."

Teddy and Lorne Wilkinson were father and son cattle dealers. The Wilkinsons farmed at Ankness Farm, Bransdale, for a time which is the same farm to which I have referred in an earlier chapter (Mother's relations on the Waind side came from there.) Bill Teasdale, who now lives at Fadmoor farmed at the next farm to Ankness, along with his uncle. Bill used to help the Wilkinsons to gather sheep on the moor.

Bill told me about an experience or two. He said that they were once gathering sheep and they had them all penned up in a walled circular pen. On top of the wall was a wire net leaning inwards. It was quite easy for a dog to jump in but nearly impossible for a dog to jump out. Teddy said to Bill, "I'm not a gambling man but if tha can git thi dog te jump out of t' pen ah'll double thi sheep gathering wages". Much to Teddy's surprise the dog did jump out. Teddy stuck to his promise and doubled Bill's wages.

On another occasion Teddy came to Ankness in his car. The Wilkinsons also owned and ran a cattle wagon which was at Ankness that day. Teddy wanted the wagon back to their home farm which was at Snape, near Bedale. The main driver of the cattle wagon was Carl, Teddy's son, who did most of the farming at Ankness. Carl wasn't game, as we say, for bringing it back. Teddy said to Bill, "We won't be beat lad. Let's put my car in the back of the wagon and I'll drive the wagon myself." And he did.

When petrol was rationed the Wilkinsons would often put the car in the back of the wagon whilst piling a lot of young folks in both the car and the wagon. Off they went to the theatre. It would be a luxury coach ride !

Lorne was a real character and a very good friend to the Dunn family. He loved to tell stories about his past experiences and travels, especially if he had a responsive audience.

In the late forties even animal feeding stuffs were rationed and Lorne felt he needed a larger ration to feed his pigs. It would seem, like nowadays, that the powers that be weren't understanding. So, in June 1948, along with his cousin and his sister, Esther, Lorne cycled to London to meet the Minister of Agriculture personally. When the Minister found out that Lorne had cycled to London on this mission he was so impressed that he awarded Lorne an even bigger ration than he had asked for.

Lorne loved to tell us about his trips around the world, the different people he had met and the places at which he had worked. Perhaps his most colourful story was when he met a lady aboard ship. Lorne was chatting her up nicely and felt he was getting somewhere when the lady told Lorne that he was like an icicle. Lorne thought of an icicle as cool and refreshing so he asked her what she really meant. She answered "A drip that gets no further".

In his latter years Lorne had a lot of dealings with Bert Harper who I have mentioned in a previous chapter.One day Bert was telling Lorne how many prizes he had won with his sheep and what money he had made selling his corn and cattle. Lorne turned to Bert and said "Thy trumpeter must have died long ago 'cos all tha dis is blow tha own"! Another day Bert was complaining about some cattle Lorne had bought on Bert's behalf. He said "They were far too dear and they have lost me money. You will have to knock some money off". Lorne replied "If you want me to share in your losses I want a share in your profits an all".

Lorne had quite a lot of sayings. If you asked him how he was he would say that he was right down one side and he hadn't a ticket to certify the other side. If you were shaping badly at something he would say "Tha shaped like an old hen hoeing carrots". If somebody needed straightening up he would say that they needed "bunching up backside to third lace hole." Sometimes Lorne would offer you some cheap cattle he had bought. If you didn't want to buy he would say "I puts meat in your mouth and still you won't chew it".

Lorne was a real fighter for his rights and he was often in disagreement with the National Park authorities and the officialdom of the Ministry of Agriculture. He was a regular contributor to the national and local papers, expressing his views. He was also very good at writing poetry. One poem that needs mentioning is "The humble hawthorn hedge" which goes as follows:

THE HUMBLE HAWTHORN HEDGE

Some visitors from overseas are often quite impressed
When driving through our countryside to get a well-earned rest.
They see the hawthorn hedges, in springtime, such a sight
Just when the leaves are breaking out, and sunshine is so bright.

Those close-trimmed hawthorn hedges, that grace the countryside
Are practical defences, where birds their nests can hide.
Those hedges did not happen, some men quite long ago,
They planted and they tended those saplings in a row.

Some rows are curved and twisted beside the country lanes
While others run between the fields, enclosures to maintain.

Those hedges make a shelter for new-born lambs in spring
When cold winds from the north do blow, to perish everything.

The hedgesparrow and robin, the blackbird and the thrush
Nest safer in a hedgerow than in an open bush.
Marauders cannot reach them, their young and eggs to steal
That trimmed hedge is impregnable, much safer they do feel.

While sitting musing on her eggs, the blackbird wonders how
Things are arranged so perfectly, such joyous peace to know.
She's seen the farmer working while others are asleep
She's seen him toiling on 'til dusk with cattle and with sheep.
She's seen him trim those hedges and wondered "How can he
Afford to spend time at this task, and not be paid a fee"?

So once her mate has fled her, he flies on urgent wing
Into the tree above her, where he decides to sing
That song of purest music, no greater gift can he
Give to that thoughtful farmer who gave his efforts free.

The thrush in different tempo, he sings a mellow tune,
Tis equally as joyful, to share that nesting boon.
The robin and hedgesparrow, they set to work with glee
To rid the farm of aphids and slugs and snails you see.
They too must help the farmer, who simply by tradition,
Had made it safe for them to rest without need of petition.

But "Rights to Roam" folk never ask "Who trims hedges so neat?"
Or "How much has it cost to give us such a scenic treat?"
They don't approach the farmer to say "Here's twenty pounds,
We much admire your handiwork, accomplished so profound"!

No! They expect the farmer to keep the countryside
A place of sheer tranquillity where they can walk or ride.
While Eurocrats wide ranging powers the farmers do oppress,
How long the farmers can hold on is anybody's guess.

W. Lorne Wilkinson
21st April, 1998

271

We met quite a lot of characters on the agricultural show scene. I will mention a few.

Percy Sherwin was a sheep man who married late in life. He was 57 when his twins were born. When his wife was in hospital he went to see her and he said to the first nurse he met "I have come to see Mrs. Sherwin, she's had twins". The nurse replied "I'm sorry, no grandads are allowed to visit".

Bob Bindlass from Kendal was another character. He used to say that you judge a fellow by the company he keeps. He said that "Some people are like dogs - when they are on their own they'll bite tha, and when they get among their mates they'll kill tha."

Harry Huddleston from Lancaster was another man we used to meet up with at shows. Harry was an enthusiastic sheep dog trialler. At one show Dad asked him what sort of a run he had had, Harry's reply was "Dog shaped well but t' sheep wouldn't behave themselves".

Harry had a brother called Bill, who is quite a character. I remember being sat near him at Lancaster Friesian Sale, and a cow came in with its teats cocked back. Bill remarked "She's happen been in a draught and the wind has blown them back".

One day an insurance man went to Bill's farm who was trying to sell life insurance. Bill had quite a job getting rid of the man so he started running round the yard, with his head on one side. Bill heard the man mutter that he had better go. "The man is going mental" he said, "And I don't think he is insurable".

George Kirk from Sutton near Thirsk, was another dry humoured man. He always had a funny answer for everyone. George kept a lot of cats, and one day, when a man went to see him he remarked on the number of cats. George replied "You had better have cats than rats'"

Once a car overturned near George's farm gate and a policeman went to see George. The policeman asked George if he knew what had happened and George replied "Ah santered on last neet ti hev a leek an ah thowt that he ad just tonned her upside down to grease her".

On one occasion it had been a covering of snow. George said to his neighbour "You will have more snow than we have". His neighbour said that this was not so, but George persisted "O yes you hev more 'cos you hev more akkers, you see".

Another day it had been a lot of rain and George and a friend were watching ducks swimming in a pond. George said "You would have thought that with all that rain water would have been further up 't ducks backs"!

Tommy Denham, from the Darlington area, was a chap who did a lot of judging at shows, especially he judged inter-breed champion classes and Dales

272

ponies. Tommy was known as the black bullet goody man because he always had a packet of those sweets in his pocket and he would always offer you one. One day he was in the company of Prince Charles, and he said to him, "Hev one of me black bullets lad".

We had some local people who were characters. They were known for their droll sayings and experiences, also how they would describe a situation. Bob Fenwick from Rievaulx was such a man. Bob had just gone on to the pension when Dad met him a day or two after. "How are you doing Robert?" Dad asked. Bob's reply was "I'm alright Willie. I have everything to be alright for. I works for missen on a morning and t'Government keeps me on an afternoon."

Ron Teasdale, who followed Granddad at Abbot Hagg farm, was a man who had some profound sayings. He loved an argument and discussion about politics and farming. A strong Tory supporter, Ron was once telling me about seeing the Prime Minister, Harold Wilson, on television. Ron said "He talked a lot of rubbish, and if I could, I would have broken the glass in the television and got hold of him and wrung his neck!!" He proceeded to say that it is all a matter of politics when you have finished.

I remember being at a Ryedale Show meeting and we, as a committee, were proposing that as we had had some good years financially, we should give the secretary an increase in salary. Everyone agreed, but Ron got up and said "If we have some bad years will the Secretary take less?"

James and Elic Bentley from Old Byland were characters. They were hard workers and very good farmers, as are the next generation, Brian and Doreen. I would say they are the best fodder root growers in the North of England. Elic was listening to another farmer saying that he had some big swedes, Elic replied "If they are any bigger than ours they are too big"! Elic had a saying that work never killed anyone, but it has given many a man a nasty shock.

James did all the market work and he was always interested in what you were on with or what you were selling. He had just got a new car and I asked him how he liked it. His reply, "Alright, alright, but if I could get a new one like the old one I would have one".

Jack Marsden, the gravedigger at Helmsley, was another character. One day he was digging a grave and someone said to him "How's tha coming on, Jack?" He replied "Not ower weel. It's stony. Ah nivver did reckon mich to't fellow we're putting in here. As lang as we git him covered up that'll dea me" One day Jack was digging a grave and some men came to measure up for a fence to go round the cemetery. Jack went over to them and asked them what they were on with. They said "We're measuring up for a fence." Jack replied "You must be daft! You don't need a fence! Them that's in can't git out and them that's out dean't want to be in!"

Sometimes our relatives can be characters. Mother's maternal uncle Sidney Waind, from Great Edstone, was such a man. He liked visiting his relations and having a discussion. He could argue over nothing. My uncles used to call him Mr. Contrary Man. No matter how good an idea was he liked to argue against it. Sometimes I think that my brother Nicholas inherits this from the Wainds!

Uncle Sidney did a lot of judging at agricultural shows and if any exhibitor was cocksure of winning then Uncle Sidney would put him down on purpose. He also had a habit of getting words wrong. There used to be a man called Jack Brocklebank, who was Secretary of the Farmworkers' Union. He was not a favourite of Uncle Sidney who used to call him Mr. Brockleshanks. Uncle Sidney could not pronounce the word "technical". My cousin Audrey had just started going to the Technical College at Scarborough and Uncle Sidney could not believe that the Education Authorities would pay her travelling costs. He said to my Uncle Fred, "Is it right that you get paid for taking Audrey to the Testicle College ?"

Aunty Blanche was Uncle Sidney's sister and she came to live with us for a while in her old age. We used to tease her as we thought that she was quite cantankerous and a kill joy. She used to say "All you lot mind is raking about on a night. You want to stop at home". We would reply "It's better going out than being sat at home and miserable". She said "I am not miserable". She bore an uncanny resemblance to Ena Sharples of Coronation Street.

Aunty Blanche was always a big believer in bartering, or "bantering" as she called it. She believed that when you bought apples you should always buy them in separate pounds. She once went to the market at Helmsley and bought a stone of apples, all in separate pounds. The fruiterer asked her "Are you sure you don't want the lorry to take them home luv?" Aunty Blanche was heard to mutter in reply "Cheeky beggar"!

Harrison Weighell, from Appleton-le-Moors, was mother's cousin. As well as being a farmer, Harrison was also an agricultural valuer. He had a droll way of expressing himself. If you asked him how he was he would reply "Fairly well and not so bad, or so, alright, thank you ta". Once Harrison shot out of a road in his car and nearly collided with a lorry. The driver got out and gave him a real telling off. Harrison responded with the words "Alright, thank you, ta, cheerio". The driver was fuming. The Bible is true when it says that "a soft answer turneth away wrath."!

I could go on and mention many more characters who I have met, as I like meeting up with different people. Someone remarked to me that it seems that these old characters are dying out. I think it's because of education, people being more enlightened and travelling a lot more.

Aunty Blanche

Percy Sherwin

Teddy Wilkinson

Reg Sunley

Bill and Harry Huddleston

Uncle Sidney Waind at Ankness 1962

Lorne Wilkinson at York market

Nephew Timothy's Bluefaced Leicester Ram, which made 7,500 guineas 2003

Nephew Timothy's top twenty mule gimmer lambs 2003

Jim Dixon

Chapter 25
Sayings I Have Heard
And Collected Over The Years

WORDS

If in doubt say nowt.

A good thing to remember and a better thing to do is to join the construction gang and not the wrecking crew.

Don't knock down, build up.

Great minds discuss ideas. Average minds discuss events. Small minds discuss people.

The man with the loudest voice hasn't always the strongest argument.

A man of his words and not of his deeds is like a garden full of weeds.

The trouble is when you let off steam you get into hot water.

As a man grows wiser he talks less and says more

A sharp tongue is no indication of a keen mind.

Do be careful to remember that your tongue is in a wet place and is apt to slip.

A wise old owl sat in an oak
The more he saw the less he spoke
The less he spoke the more he heard
Why can't more folk be like that bird?

Five things observe with care, of whom you speak, to whom you speak and how and when and where.

Always remember God gave us two ears and one tongue. In other words do twice as much listening as talking.

If you must speak your mind then mind how you speak.

A good liar has to have a good memory.

If it is not right don't do it. If it is not true don't say it.

Nothing is sometimes a good thing to do and always a clever thing to say.

It is good to be wise and wise to be good. A wise man thinks what he says, a fool says what he thinks.

Those who tell white lies soon become colour blind.

FRIENDS AND FRIENDSHIP
A friend in need is a friend indeed.

Keep your old friends and make new ones.

It is true that a man is known by the company he keeps. It is also true that a man is known by the company he keeps out of.

A trouble shared is a trouble halved.

The family that prays together stays together. The family that talks together clings together.

The way children turn out depends a lot on what time they turn in.

To have a friend is to be a friend.

MONEY
Some people spend money they don't have to buy things they don't need to impress people they don't like.

It's great to be able to make ends meet, but it's even better if they overlap just a little.

If you can't pay the first bill you won't be able to pay the second.

If you think education is expensive, try ignorance.

Stop spending before you run out of money.

Do your giving whilst you're living then you're knowing where it's going.

Try to be satisfied with your lot even if you don't have a lot.

If your outgoings are more than your incomings you won't last long.

It's tough to be poor but not as bad as being in debt.

Money doesn't make you happy but it does make you a bit more comfortable in your misery.

It doesn't matter how much water is in the well, it can run dry.

If it wasn't for expense I could live.

You have to speculate to accumulate.

Money can buy food but not an appetite
Money can buy education but not brains
Money can buy medicine but not health
Money can buy makeup but not beauty
Money can buy the best coffin but not a place in Heaven.

When lads have money they think they're men
When they haven't they're lads again.

MOTTOS AND ATTITUDES

What counts most is not the size of the dog in the fight. It's the size of the fight in the dog.

He who climbs the highest is he who helps another ascend.

Failures are divided into two categories - those who thought and never did and those who did and never thought.

If we could forget our troubles as easily as we forget our blessings how different things would be.

When the going gets tough the tough need to get going.

Experience is the best teacher.

The man who is too big for a small job is too small for a big job.

Bad habits are like a comfortable bed, easy to get into but hard to get out of.

Plan your work then work your plan.

Success is not attained by lying awake at night but by staying awake in the daytime.

There are many roads to success but they are all uphill.

Don't give up - grow up.

We all need that stuff that is on the back of a postage stamp - stickability.

Waste not, want not.

There is nothing more permanent than change.

Change is here to stay.

If hindsight was foresight and foresight was hindsight, we would all be clever people and know everything.

If we could all take the morning paper the night before, we would all be able to back the winning horse.

An ounce of experience is worth a ton of theory any day.

The spectator sees most of the game.

Most of us would get along well if we took the advice we give to others.

Help me to be careful of the toes I step on today as they may be connected to the feet I have to kiss tomorrow.

You can't get rid of your temper by losing it.

Our faults irritate us most when we see them in others.

The fellow who is on his toes doesn't usually have any trouble keeping people from stepping on them.

The man who continually looks down his nose at others usually has the wrong slant.

I have made many mistakes but I have never made the mistake of claiming I never made a mistake.

Many minds are like concrete, all mixed up and permanently set.

He who learns and learns and does not what he knows is like a man who ploughs and ploughs and never never sows.

Nothing is more exhausting than searching for easy ways to make a living.

Jumping to conclusions is not nearly so good a mental exercise as digging for facts.

Do all the good you can
By all the means you can
In all the ways you can
To all the people you can
At all the times you can
As long as ever you can   (John Wesley)

ACCOMPLISHMENT

The man who removes a mountain begins by carrying away small stones.

If you don't start the race you will never win it.

Nothing ventured nothing gained.

Don't watch the man behind you. Watch the man in front of you.

If you can't do anybody a good turn tomorrow don't do anybody a bad one.

If you can do a kindness today don't wait until tomorrow.
Tomorrow may never come.

It's better to fail trying something than to excel in doing nothing.

Blessed are they who expect nothing for they shall not be disappointed.

Great opportunities come to those who make the most of small ones.

You never get a second chance to make a good first impression.

It takes guts to get out of ruts.

MARRIAGE AND ROMANCE

Love in a cottage is better than Hell in a castle.

Don't both get vexed at the same time.

Don't love for money but try and love where money is.

The goal in marriage is not to think alike but to think together.

Men and women chasing each other is what produces the human race.

Nobody knows the age of the human race but all agree it is old enough to know better.

A woman's work is never done, especially it she asks her husband to do it.

You should never criticise your wife's judgement - look who she decided to marry.

A good woman inspires a man
A brilliant woman interests a man
A beautiful woman fascinates a man
But it's the sympathetic woman who gets him.

Man's problem is trying to find a woman attractive enough to please him, and dumb enough to marry him.

HEALTH AND OLD AGE
If you have health, you have wealth.

Some folks are never well unless they are badly, and never happy unless they are miserable.

Some folks are badly in bed and worse up.

When you feel dog tired at night it may be that you growled all day.

Some people are like a creaking gate, they swing a long time.

Old folks are like old cars, their parts get worn.

If we live long enough we will be old one day.

Those who live longest will see the most if they don't go blind

A good way to avoid heart trouble is not to run upstairs and not to run down people.

Some people battle to the top, others bottle to the bottom,

No doctor is a good doctor who has never been ill himself.

Idle hands are the devil's workshop

YORKSHIRE AND DALES SAYINGS
Describing a person who is busy:

As thrang as thrabs wife.

Going pell mell.

All of a lather.

Describing other people:

There's nowt so queer as folk, except me and thee, an me and thee can be queer at times

Describing self-centred people:

They have lived in a bottle and seen nothing but the cork.

People walk in the light they know.

People can't see any further than their nose ends.

Describing a farmer who is always away from home:

He's always marching when he ought to be fighting.

Describing something that is scarce:

As scarce as rocking horse muck.

General sayings:

Bairns and fools for the truth.

Fast women and slow horses have beggared many a man.

Little pigs have big ears - (meaning children can hear when you don't think they can)

He has a few monkeys up his sleeve - describing a clever man.

People are like water, they find their own level.

If there's trouble, nine times out of ten it can be traced to a woman, money, or strong drink.

Brains and commonsense don't always go together.

If you haven't brains hire them i.e. if you don't know, ask someone who does

Give a person plenty of rope and they will hang themselves.

Work never killed any man but it has given many a man a nasty shock.

He's bad to shave - describing a bad tempered man.

As nimble as a stone pig trough - describing someone slow to move.

As numb as a grindstone - describing someone or some thing that is clumsy.

He's that well off he's bow legged with brass - describing someone with plenty of money.

You can tak a man out of the Dales, but you can't tak the Dales out of a man.

If you are late for a meal, "tha'll git yat tongue off't missis, and cawd meat pie."

You might as well lie in bed and spit upwards - describing a method that you don't think will work.

It couldn't pull a clocking hen off t' nest - describing a tractor, car or horse that is a bad puller.

If tha disn't know what tha's talking aboot, say nowt and keep thy mouth shut.

His bark is worse than his bite - a person with a loud voice.

It taks three generations to mak money, and yan to spend it.

It's daft to fret over a burnt cake before you put it in't oven.

You can allus tell a Yorkshireman, but you can't tell him mich.

Measure twice, saw once.

It's the early bird that gets the worm, but the second mouse
that gets the cheese.

My lad is my lad till he gets a wife, but my lass is my lass for
all her life.

A greedy man has a deep pocket but his arms are short.

His eyes are bigger than his belly - (describing someone who takes
more food than he can eat)

Let him stew in his own broth

It's the bitter with the sweet that makes the sweet far sweeter.

Did ya ivver knaw a kitten carry t'moose t'it cat?
(One of mother's favourite sayings when we tried to tell her something).

When the cat's away the mice will play.

Thers nivver a craw si black but another'll sit besaad it
(You can usually find a mate)

Tide and time waits for no man.

When you're losing money you're gaining knowledge.
(meaning that you learn the hard way.)

What can't speak, can't lie: truths written down in black and white

What breaks one firm, makes another.

A stitch in time saves nine.

Where a man's treasure is, there will his heart be also.
(One of Dad's favourite quotes from the Bible).

One lad is a man, two lads is worth half a man and three lads
are no use at all.

If things don't alter they will stop as they are.

Young folks are like young hosses, they need to be yoked.

He was brusten out like a harvest toad - someone who had over-eaten.

Don't be a proud man when you go to buy, be a proud man
when you go to sell.

Two difficult things for a man to do are to climb a fence that is leaning
towards you and to kiss a girl that's leaning away from you.

Thoo's tied to a cow's tail and skittered to death - describing a
husband who is married not only to the daughter but to the mother
and father-in-law.

Thoo's better to keep a week than a fottnith (fortnight) - a big eater.

Four things a man needs - Two Hs and two Cs - Health and Happiness,
Cash and Courage.

Never cast a clout till May's out.

You never miss the water 'til the well runs dry.

Count your joys instead of your woes
Count your friends instead of your foes
Count your courage instead of your fears
Count your laughs instead of your tears
Count your health instead of your wealth
Count on God instead of yourself.

If you have a goal - Go Out And Learn

ABC of life - A is for attitude, B is for belief, C is for courage

Chapter 26
Reflections And Changes

When Dad was in his latter years people would often comment that he must have seen a lot of changes during his lifetime, and he had. Perhaps the biggest change for him would have been from horse power to mechanisation, and from horse travel to car and aeroplane. People are travelling a lot further and with television being in most homes we are a lot more informed about national and international news and events.

I once read this statement: "Change is the law of life. Those who choose to ignore it are sure to miss the future." Come to think of it, change is here to stay. There is nothing more permanent than change. As I have looked through my diaries and writings there have been a lot of changes, especially in farming. Some changes have been for the better and some for the worse.

Farming, like any other industry, has had the hard physical work taken out of it. Take, for example, the conserving of the grass crop. Hay has been almost replaced by silage. I would think that this has been the best change on our farm. The advantage of silage is that we are less dependent on the weather, it is better feed, there is a lot less waste and the growing of grass can be controlled a lot better.

The second biggest improvement on our farm has been how we harvest our cereal crop. There has been a complete change from the binder and thresher to the combine harvester. There is no more stooking, no more stacking. Both silaging and the cereal harvest are done from the tractor seat. Man has invented and made marvellous machines but we must never forget that they are all built for fine weather. We must remember that old harvest hymn that says of God "He sends the snow in winter, the warmth to swell the grain. The breezes and the sunshine and soft refreshing rain. All good gifts around us are sent from Heaven above. Then thank the Lord, O thank the Lord for all His love".

On our farm and on most others we have seen a swing away from mixed farming. My Granddad used to say ''Don't have all your eggs in one basket". But on our farm we have seen pigs, poultry and a breeding ewe flock completely phased out. We now specialise in producing milk and cereals and the fattening of sheep. Pigs, poultry and potatoes are, by and large, in the hands of big producers and growers. I don't particularly agree with this, but economics have forced this to be so.

On arable farms there have been big changes in crop rotations, which to me, have brought an imbalance in farming. There has been a big swing from spring sowing of the cereal crop to autumn sowing. This has meant far bigger yields and a lot more sprays and pesticides being used.

In our area we have almost seen the disappearance of fodder roots such as mangles, swedes and turnips. The folding on of sheep on crops of roots is also disappearing. But we think that it still has a part on our farm, especially as we now have the three strand electric fence system,

We have also seen the virtual disappearance of the small milk producer. In our own parish there used to be ten producers but now we are the only one left. We trust we can hang on until the price gets better, as Philip is very interested. At the present moment, October 2004, we are seeing the big producers quitting the industry as the price we are receiving is nothing compared with what retailers arc charging. It is a sad state of affairs when there are more people employed by DEFRA than there are dairy farmers.

We have also seen changes in the different breeds of livestock. For example, in the sheep industry wool is now worth a pittance. Some fleeces are not paying the shearers' wages. I once heard one farmer say that he clipped a good English Leicester hogg and the price he received for it paid a man's weekly wage. It is not so today. Wool is not wanted. We have man-made fibres and as a result we are seeing the disappearance of the long wooled types of sheep from the commercial scene. But it is good to see these breeds kept alive by a dedicated band of breeders with the help of the Rare Breed Survival Trust.

I have seen the great cross-bred ewe, the Masham, gradually taken over by the Mule. I well remember being at Richmond Mart in 1972 when the Porters from Riddings, Reeth in Swaledale were first going into Mules. On that day their Mules were making a lot more than their Mashams. Willie Porter said to the auctioneer "What have I to do?". The auctioneer replied that he should take notice of his pocket ! It is interesting to note that today Willie Porter's son, James, is one of the top breeders of Mules.

I have seen great changes in the different terminal sire breeds. Once the Oxford Down was the favourite, then the Suffolk Down, Now we are seeing a great influx of continental breeds such as the Texel, Charolais and Beltex. No one can deny that they have got a big hold, but I still believe that the Suffolk is the great all-rounder.

To a certain degree we have seen the same thing happen with beef cattle. Once the Aberdeen Angus and Hereford were the favourites but they have been taken over by the continental breeds such as the Charolais, Limousin, Blonde D'

Aquitaine, and the Belgian Blue.

On the Dairy Cattle scene we have seen a move from the good old fashioned Friesian to the Holstein. There are some types of Holstein which, in my opinion, are far too extreme and just like a bag of bones. They are hard to get in calf, bad on their feet and legs, and take a lot more managing.

Fashions of breeds come and go. We are seeing quite a revival of some of the old fashioned breeds like the beef and dairy shorthorns. Also we are seeing a new interest in the old fashioned breeds of pigs which are being sought after by organic farmers.

Marketing of our stock has also changed. More fat stock is being taken directly into the abbatoirs. I am a firm believer in the auction mart system but live auction marts are finding it difficult to survive. As farmers we need to support them. It is sad to note that the following Auction Marts where we used to sell stock are now closed:-

Seamer, Kirkbymoorside, Helmsley, Stokesley, Ripon, Boroughbridge, Wetherby, Pannall and Otley Bridge End.

Auction Marts are a good shop window for your stock and it is educational to see how other farmers feed and market their animals. The markets are also a good place for farmers to meet and to talk about things. Pannall, near Harrogate, was one of our favourite markets for fat sheep as it was here we saw a wide variety of breeds and different systems. Let me mention one or two farmers who always sold good stock there. There was J.B. Liddle from Otley. He was an expert, bringing out marvellous Masham wether lambs, not forgetting his home sales of progeny tested Teeswater sheep. Then there was the Craven family from Pocklington. They were experts at early spring lambs. One farmer used to say that Mr Dunn from Helmsley always had some good Suffolk cross fat hoggs.

Farming, like any other industry, has had to come to grips with the increasing amount of paperwork. As an industry we are being strangled with rules and regulations, some unavoidable. We are lectured to and led by people who have not the groundwork of practical experience.

The Powers That Be think that if we can meet all their rules and regulations then all will be well. It doesn't work that way. If you solve one problem then you make another, causing a lot of stress in the process. I would think that since BSE there have been more farmers killed through stress than there have been people who have died from CJD.

Just recently we had a visit from the Farm Assurance Scheme Officer when we had quite an interesting, and for me, a disturbing conversation. He was indicating which way rules will go - they are against the farmer.

The Government is out to stop pollution. I look at this subject from a different angle. The politicians and the television are polluting the minds of the general public and are biased against country peoples' sports and against the farmer.

The scientists and the politicians talk a lot about global warming- I don't think that the weather has changed much. You will always get abnormal seasons. My weather records show that to be true. The general public and the politicians will never fully appreciate the farmer until there is a shortage of food. The farming industry has done a great job in feeding our nation, even if the government has had to bear the cost of farming subsidies.

The biggest challenge which the farming industry has to face is the Government's attitude towards farming. Thirty years ago we were encouraged and supported to be more self-sufficient as a nation. This was so that the nation's import bill could be cut. Now we are being forced to take land out of production and are being told what to do by people who have no working knowledge of farming. The authorities are willing to allow cheap imported food into our country. Such food has no traceability and is not produced to the same standards as British food.

I feel that the farming community must stand up for its rights. We have a right to a fair price for what we produce. This is not the case at the present moment in time. To illustrate this, let me give you some updated facts. In August 1994 we were receiving 23.5 pence per litre for our milk. Ten years later we are receiving 17.5 pence per litre. Ten years ago water cost 58.10 pence per cubic foot, whereas now it is 86.20 pence per cubic foot. Ten years ago Derv was 37.70p per litre and now it is 74p per litre. It is no wonder that dairy farmers are leaving the industry.

Most areas of life and occupations have changed. So have shopping and eating habits. Ask any butcher or shopkeeper about this. The small shop is being squeezed out by the supermarkets. We have a lot of prepared fast food. One older housewife commenting on younger housewives, said that all a woman needs today is a tin opener, a microwave, and a pair of glasses to read the instructions.

In many ways we could say that society has progressed. On the farm, in the home, physically, life is a lot easier. But this has brought about a big problem - the problem of stress and debt. Credit is the new drug of this century. Almost every day letters come through our post offering credit and hire purchase. As one old farmer used to say, "We are all propping up one another, and when we pull out the props we shall all be flat on our faces." Abraham Lincoln had eight commandments to do with money. These are as follows:-

1. You cannot bring about prosperity by discouraging thrift.
2. You cannot strengthen the weak by weakening the strong.
3. You cannot help the wage earner by pulling down the wage payer.
4. You cannot further the brotherhood of men by encouraging class hatred.
5. You cannot help the poor by destroying the rich.
6. You cannot keep out of trouble by spending more than you earn.
7. You cannot build character and courage by taking away man's initiative and independence.
8. You cannot help men permanently by doing for them what they could and should do for themselves.

I have mentioned quite a few things that have changed, but what about the things that haven't changed? Night follows day, the seasons come round year after year. Everybody is given the same amount of time, 24 hours a day. Where does all our time go ? We have labour saving devices but nobody has time for one another.

Human nature hasn't changed. Morally and spiritually we are a sin sick society where we are seeing a breakdown in family and home life. Not only are relationships important, but so are partnerships. I am reminded of a conversation which I had with a disgruntled man. He is one of those who are so hard to get on with, I don't think he could agree with himself. Everybody seemed to be in the wrong but he himself. He told me that there are two ships which you should never sail in - partnerships and relationships. I am in both. The ship does take some sailing at times, but you have to give and take. Sometimes it is more giving than taking, but if you keep a level head then things work out.

Life isn't always easy. and I have made mistakes. There are times when I have struggled, whether it be with my faith, my family or in farming, I have learnt that there is no easy way out. The way to success is generally uphill, and there are more people waiting to give you a push down to the bottom than to give you a pull up to the top.

These past years have been very difficult and depressing for the farmer, and I have to admit that I have had long periods of depression. But I have pressed on. Persistence is based on character, and character does what is right, not what is easy. It is controlled by values, not by moods. It looks for solutions, not excuses.

Several years ago Dorothy gave me these verses and I have them hung up beside my bed. They go like this:-

DON'T QUIT

When things go wrong, as they sometimes will,
When the road you're trudging seems all uphill,
When the funds are low and the debts are high,
And you want to smile but you have to sigh,
When care is pressing you down a bit,
Rest if you must but don't you quit.

Life is queer with its twists and turns,
As every one of us sometime learns,
And many a failure turns about
When he might have won had he stuck it out;
Don't give up though the pace seems slow-
You might succeed with another blow

Success is failure turned inside out-
The silver tint of the clouds of doubt,
And you never can tell how close you are,
It may be near when it seems so far;
So stick to the fight when you're hardest hit-
It's when things seem worst that you must not quit.

As I close my memoirs I realise I have a lot to be thankful for. For being brought up in a stable Christian home. In many ways my parents had a hard life, but they did the best they could. I have a good wife and two lovely children. I have been brought into contact with many wonderful friends and other people.

To me, relationships are the key word to life. First of all is my relationship with God. I make a habit of spending time reading the Bible and praying each day. Secondly is my relationship with my family and fellow men. I have learnt that there are times when we need to say sorry. Never be afraid of doing a bit extra, the Bible describes it as going the second mile.

Last but not least, amid a changing world the Love of God never changes. His arms of Love are still reaching out to a sin sick world. It is His Love in Jesus that has kept me and our family safe. Over the years the Bible and hymns have been a great strength and comfort to me. I want to close my memoirs with one of my favourite hymns which is my testimony. The words are as follows:-

I could not do without Thee, O Saviour of the lost
Whose precious blood redeemed me at such tremendous cost
Thy righteousness, Thy pardon. Thy precious blood must be
My only hope and comfort, my glory and my plea.

I could not do without Thee, I cannot stand alone
I have no strength or goodness, no wisdom of my own
But Thou, Beloved Saviour, art all in all to me
And weakness will be power if leaning hard on Thee

I could not do without Thee, no other friend can read
The spirit's strange deep longings, interpreting its need
No human heart could enter each dim recess of mine
And soothe and hush and calm it, O Blessed Lord, but Thine.

I could not do without Thee, for years are fleeting fast
And soon in solemn loneness the river must be passed
But Thou wilt never leave me, and though the waves roll high
I know Thou wilt be near me and whisper "It is I".

Cutting corn at New Leys early to mid forties

New Leys, harvesting 1948

Stacking sheaves: Stan Wright, Rev. H Langham, Dad, Jack Webb, Ted & Mary, Emmitt, Christopher and Nicholas

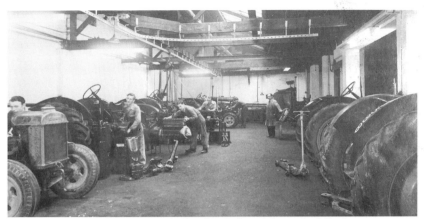

Tractors in course of repair at Bushell's of York, front left standard Fordson tractor. We used these until the late 1950's

Implement repair shop at Bushell's: turnip cleaner and cutter in front, grass cutters and binder towards back

We did a lot of business with Bushell's until the late 1950's. It is interesting to note that Brian Otterburn served his apprentiship with Bushell's, Otterburn's do our repairs now

Last people to binder in the district, Watson's of Eastmoors

Below: One of the last threshing days in the district, Lloyd Franks of Farndale, taken early 1970's

Photo by kind permission of Marie Hartley

Steve Watson combining on our farm, early 1970's

Tractors have improved a lot. One of our old Nuffields, early 1970's

296

Hay making is dependant on fine weather. Here is a tractor and baler at work, late 1960's

Silage has been a big break through. One of Breckhouse engineering tractors and trailer with Metcalfe's farms of Leyburn self propelled forage harvester, 2003

Combines are a lot bigger now, cousin John Medd's combine at work, early 2000

*Last person I know who uses a turnip hack
Doreen Bentley, Old Byland, 2005*

*I don't think we will see mangel pies
again. You can't get seed now, 1978*

A reminder of my sheep folding days, photo taken up at Bentleys Old Byland, 2005

We still scruffle our roots, early 2000

We still like to hoe, early 2000

Cows like a few roots, 2002

299

Longwooled Sheep soon get clagged up with soil

Contented cows at Lew Leys 2004

One of my favourite cows Newsley Trusting 42nd, 2004

Helmsley auction mart buyers mid to late 1950's

Good to see milk bus, better to see monthly milk cheque, early 1950's

Always smiling: Cousin Edward Atkinson with his ducks, 1995

One of the last Blacksmiths in the district, Les Wheldon from Hawnby, early 1970's

301

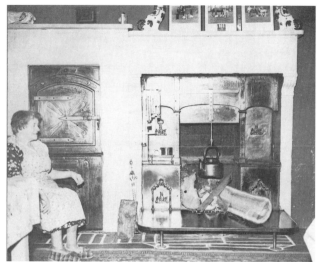

I have spent many an hour around this fire place at Skiplam Grange, Nawton, listening to Mrs Harper (in picture) and Bert, photo taken 1970's

Recent Family photo, left to right: Miriam, Philip, Dorothy and Author taken at a wedding, 2005

Landlords are important to tennant farmers. Back left, the late Lord Feversham shaking hands with Joe Bowes (back right) whom I have mentioned in previous chapters.
Foreground left, Lady Clarissa at her 21st birthday celebration, 1960 shaking hands with a tennant

Glossary

TERM:	DEFINITION:
4th calf milk cow	A cow which has had 4 calves
A big spread	Lots of food on the table
Aftermath	Grass growing after crop taken
A mucker	Disastrous prices
Backend	Autumn
Bare frost	No snow on the ground
Bothering time	Frustrating period
Bray tha	Hit you hard
BSE	Bovine Spongiform Encephalopathy (mad cow disease)
Caff hole	Place where the chaff comes out of the threshing machine
Capped as punch	Very pleased
Catchy	Unpredictable weather
CJD	Creutzfeldt-Jakob Disease (human form of BSE)
Clagged up	Muddy
Clipped	sheep shorn of their wool
Clocker	A broody hen
Cows' bags	Udders
Crosses e.g. Belgian Blue Crosses	A Belgian Blue bull siring a calf out of a dairy cow
Dab Hand	Good at something
DEFRA	Department for Environment, Food and Rural Affairs
Droppy	Showery
Drott	A loader with caterpillar tracks
Fallowed	Land cultivated but not sown with a crop
FCN	Farm Crisis Network
Fill-dyke	A lot of water about
First thing	Early in the day
Fit to skin you	Extremely cold
Flat eight	Eight bales laid flat together
Flying	Getting angry, or could mean going well
Folding on	Over-wintering sheep on root crop
Forward (Season)	Things happening earlier than usual
Gilt	Young female pig which has not had a litter
Git yam	Get home

TERM:	DEFINITION:
Give some bag	Give animals some concentrate feed such as sheep nuts
Goodies	Sweets
Growy	Ideal conditions for crops
Guineas	21 shillings (one pound one shilling)
Hack	Hand tool used for pulling up turnip roots
Handy hands	Practical people
Headland	Perimeter of field
Hogg	Sheep aged 6 to 12 months
IACS	Intergrated Administration Control System
Just the ticket	Just right
Like rattle	Quickly
Livestock Welfare Disposal Scheme:-	See page 305 for definition
Lowance	Mid morning or afternoon snack for workers
MAFF	Ministry of Agriculture, Fisheries and Food
Methodist local preacher	A layman who is trained to lead worship in the Methodist church
Migg	Smelly animal manure
Milking bail	Piece of mobile equipment used for milking cows in a field
Mission band	Small group, often of young Christians, who would help a local preacher to lead worship
Moderate	Not very good
Moor jocks	People brought up on the North York Moors
Muggy	Humid
Mule sheep	Blue faced Leicester Ram crossed onto a Swaledale or a Black faced ewe
NFU	National Farmers Union
On keep	animals sent to another farmers land
On note	First stage of becoming a Methodist local preacher, when you help a more experienced preacher
On with	Busy with
Pigged	Stack or trailer load falling over
Rank	Very close together
Reps	Travellers representing firms supplying products to farmers
Rigged	Laid on its back
Rigging up	Putting together
RSPCA	Royal Society for the Prevention of Cruelty to Animals

TERM:	DEFINITION:
Rully	A four wheeled cart
Rum	Describing a person: a real individual
	Describing things: peculiar
Sad cake	Plain pastry made into rounds, eaten spread with butter or treacle
Santered	Walked slowly
Scotch Black face	A breed of horn hill sheep
Scruffling	Cultivating between the rows of root crops using a scruffler
Shows	Local agricultural events
Shifting e.g. grass	Making it grow quickly
Silage	Green fodder, mainly grass, preserved in clamp or big bales
Skittered	Looseness of the bowel.
Starved	Cold
Stirk	Male or female calf 6 to 12 months old
Stooking	Setting ten sheaves of corn upright so that they would dry in the field
Striking 12 o'clock on the day	Peaking at the right time
Suckling	Farmer helping a young animal to get milk from its mother
Sweethearting	Courting
Taken out with (Foot and Mouth)	Culled
Terminal sire	A breed primarly for meat
Think on	Consider
To cock your ears up	To take notice
Tramlines	Space allocated with seed drill to allow later spraying and fertilizing without damaging the crop
Travellers	See Reps
Tup	Male sheep
Turn out	Outfit, or could mean letting cattle out to grass in spring
Under-sown	Grass seeds sown into a cereal crop
Welfare scheme	Minimal compensation offered to farmers whose animals did not get Foot and Mouth disease, but were adversely affected by its restrictions
Wesleyans	Short for Wesleyan Methodists
Wether lamb	Neutered male sheep, reared for meat